"Aid and Comfort"

"Aid and Comfort"

Jane Fonda in North Vietnam

HENRY MARK HOLZER *and* ERIKA HOLZER

Foreword by Col. George "Bud" Day

McFarland & Company, Inc., Publishers
Jefferson, North Carolina, and London

Excerpts from *Citizen Jane: The Turbulent Life of Jane Fonda* by
Christopher Andersen are copyright © 1990 by Christopher Andersen.
Reprinted by permission of Ellen Levine Literary Agency, Inc.

Excerpts from *The Fondas: A Hollywood Dynasty* by Peter Collier
are copyright © 1991 by Peter Collier, Inc. Used by permission
of G. P. Putnam's Sons, a division of Penguin Putnam Inc.,
and by permission of Georges Borchardt, Inc., on behalf of the author.

Excerpts from *Honor Bound: American Prisoners of War in Southeast
Asia 1961–1973* by Stuart I. Rochester and Frederick Kiley
(1999) are reprinted by permission of the Naval Institute Press.

Drawings and excerpts from *Prisoner of War: Six Years in Hanoi* by
John M. McGrath (1975) are reprinted by permission of the Naval Institute Press.

Library of Congress Cataloguing-in-Publication Data

Holzer, Henry Mark, 1933–
"Aid and comfort" : Jane Fonda in North Vietnam /
Henry Mark Holzer and Erika Holzer ; foreword by Col. George "Bud" Day.
p.   cm.
Includes bibliographical references and index.
ISBN 0-7864-1247-X (illustrated case : 50# alkaline paper) ∞
1. Vietnamese Conflict, 1961–1975 — Propaganda.   2. Vietnamese Conflict,
1961–1975 — Collaborationists — United States.   3. Fonda, Jane, 1937–
— Journeys — Vietnam (Democratic Republic) I. Holzer, Erika. II. Title.
DS559.8.P65 H65 2002   959.704'38 — dc21   2001007176

British Library cataloguing data are available

On the cover: Jane Fonda seated on an anti-aircraft gun
near Hanoi, July 1972. AP/WIDE WORLD PHOTOS.

Manufactured in the United States of America

*McFarland & Company, Inc., Publishers
Box 611, Jefferson, North Carolina 28640
www.mcfarlandpub.com*

To the gallant multi-national prisoners of the Pathet Lao,
Viet Minh, Viet Cong, and North Vietnamese, 1945–1973.
Those POWs' courage in the face of savage treatment
by their captors has not gone unrecognized;
their voices have not been unheard.
This book is an offering to their ordeal.

And to H. Ross Perot, stalwart friend to American
prisoners of war in Laos and North Vietnam.
2-2, 1-2, 4-5.

ACKNOWLEDGMENTS

Joe Kittinger, who supported this undertaking from the beginning, opened the door to Bud Day and to Mike McGrath, president of NAM-POW. Bud agreed to contribute a foreword. Mike, some of whose quotations and drawings appear in Chapter 3, in turn opened the door to many former Vietnam POWs, without whose help this book would not be nearly as accurate or compelling. Those veterans answered many difficult questions, and in doing so revisited painful decades-old memories because they understood that the Fonda story had to be told accurately. We were amazed by their strength, and by their commitment to fairness and accuracy despite the privations they had endured.

Henry Cohen, at the Library of Congress, provided historical materials without which this book could not have been written.

Stuart I. Rochester and Fred Kiley's *Honor Bound* (which we have heavily relied on) is *the* indispensable and invaluable resource for anyone wishing to know and understand the POW experience in Southeast Asia.

Honor Bound co-author Fred Kiley graciously contributed his time and expertise to improving the manuscript in important ways.

Duane Reed and Mike Kiley at the Special Collections division of the United States Air Force Academy library extended themselves in locating and making available to us material that we would have had difficulty locating.

Two veterans of the September 1972 House of Representatives Internal Security Committee Hearings, who requested anonymity, provided otherwise unobtainable information.

Cody K. Kelley, Esq., of the New Mexico Bar, greatly facilitated our legal research efforts.

John Cline, Esq., of the New Mexico Bar, contributed to our understanding of the form and content of modern federal criminal indictments.

Professor Stephen Cox of the Humanities Department, University of California, San Diego, was his usual cheerleading self, contributing subtle and useful suggestions about the manuscript.

Professor Rodney A. Smolla of the T.C. Williams School of Law at the University of Richmond, a world-class authority on the law of defamation and privacy, contributed important insights into these arcane subjects.

Phil Dragoo's Internet research was an invaluable tool in researching an important segment of the audience for this book.

During the writing of the book, friend and New York attorney Lance Gotko, was supportive in a manner well beyond the call of duty.

Bill Madison, of the New Mexico Bar, knows very well why we are indebted to him.

In their Word software, Bill Gates and his company have created a tool for writers that is truly a dream come true.

Jason Schaefer, a very talented young man, created and maintained the HANOI-JANE.NET website, which will contribute to the success of this book.

Chuck and Mary Schantag of POW Network graciously assisted us in communicating the existence of this book to many veterans whom we could not otherwise have reached.

The late Ayn Rand — friend and mentor, who helped us learn to think and to write — while never knowing the entire Fonda story, deplored her trip to Hanoi. We regret that Ayn could not have seen this case against Jane Fonda.

CONTENTS

FOREWORD

BY COL. GEORGE "BUD" DAY

Writing this foreword was a most difficult task, which took several attempts.

I was a POW in Hanoi when Jane Fonda was working against us, and for our enemy, the Vietnamese Communists. As a result, my emotions still run high.

I was also the first repatriated prisoner with a lot of torture injuries to be interviewed after the last group of prisoners had been flown out of Vietnam. I was informed that all the POWs were out, and that I could discuss our treatment freely, which I did.

My arms and hands were damaged from being hung, there were scars on my knees and Achilles tendons from torture, and my buttocks were raw from several hundred strokes of a fan belt. Some of my injuries were shown to the press. Jane immediately insisted that any POW who claimed torture was a liar.

These words are being written by a pilot and lawyer of some 50 years, with service in WWII, Korea and Vietnam. I was the camp commander of several camps and have first-hand knowledge of many, many abuses of prisoners, to include the ultimate abuse, death.

I was in Washington, D.C., shortly after our release in 1973, attending a war correspondents' function at the same time that Jane Fonda was attending a similar meeting in the same building. I agreed to publicly debate her claim that POWs were liars. She refused to debate. It was not surprising that she did not want to be confronted by facts.

This fascinating and highly readable book documents the real Hanoi Jane that the Hanoi POWs are familiar with. This book will stand for decades as the legal textbook on the ultimate infamy, aid and comfort to the enemy. Using Jane's own speeches, many of which were written by the Communists, Professor and Mrs. Holzer cleverly connect her eagerly delivered statements to the law of treason, and lead you through the thicket of law and evidence with incontrovertible logic. Follow them through this remarkable book as they prove that there was enough evidence to indict and convict Hanoi Jane of the grandfather of all crimes. Review that evidence and then cast a "guilty" ballot.

Colonel Day, USAF Ret., holds the Congressional Medal of Honor and the Air Force Cross.

Introduction:
In Pursuit of Justice

We decided to compile a list of the hundred most important women of the twentieth century... (Ladies' Home Journal)

When I began this book, I did not have an opinion about whether Jane Fonda had committed treason when she went to Hanoi, North Vietnam, in July 1972. However, my research into her pro–Communist, anti–American propaganda broadcasts and other conduct there, and into the American law of treason, have convinced me that an indictment could have been obtained in the immediate postwar years, that there would have been enough evidence to submit to a jury, that the jury could have convicted her, and that a conviction probably would have been upheld on appeal. Yet Fonda has never been charged by the United States legal system. Instead, she has made millions, been the recipient of countless awards, and has become a venerated American icon.

Many will doubtless ask: Why reopen yet another wound of the Vietnam War era some three decades after Fonda's pilgrimage to North Vietnam? It's a legitimate question, deserving of an answer. That answer has its roots in events that took place nearly a half-century ago. Let me explain.

In 1954, together with much of the world, I watched as the French poured seemingly endless numbers of soldiers into a godforsaken fortification (named Dien Bien Phu) in the northern part of Vietnam, not far south of the Chinese border. I remember vividly the nightly TV news programs showing combat-ready French paratroopers kissing their loved ones goodbye and boarding air transports in Paris, bound for drop zones in the beleaguered Indochinese fortress. The story of the fall of Dien Bien Phu is well known to those of my generation. No matter how many French troops were fed into the battle, General Vo Nyugen Giap threw more and more Vietnamese conscripts at them, until the defenders were finally overwhelmed. Thousands of prisoners were taken in this final chapter of the Franco–Viet Minh War, many of whom did not survive the Bataan Death March–like trek through hundreds of miles of dense jungle to Vietnamese prison camps, or to promised repatriation centers in coastal areas.* To this day, the French cannot report within 10,000 how many of its sons were missing in action (as opposed to killed in action) in Indochina in the 1950s.

In the summer of 1954, Vietnam was partitioned, and early the next year the United States sent a small number of advisors to train the fledgling South Vietnamese army. It wasn't long before Americans began to read about the deteriorating political and military situation in what was then being called South Vietnam: increased Communist guerrilla activity in the South; support from the North for the Viet Minh (the "Viet Cong"); increased numbers of American "advisors"; Kennedy's escalation; (alleged) attacks on U.S. destroyers in the Gulf of Tonkin; Congressional passage of the now-infamous Gulf of Tonkin Resolution; retaliatory bombing; eventual commitment of American ground forces; then more men, more bombing — and more and more American prisoners taken by the Pathet Lao in Laos, by the Viet Cong in the South, and by the North Vietnamese in their territory. Then, as Rochester and Kiley noted in *Honor Bound*, "[I]n 1970 and 1971, the Nixon administration expanded the war to Cambodia and Laos. Intended to disrupt Communist supply lines and staging areas and to underscore U.S. determination to prevent a Communist takeover of Indochina, the Cambodian and Laotian campaigns wreaked enormous destruction and dislocation without appreciably advancing American goals."[2] I watched these events with deep concern, because during my own lifetime I had seen how Asian regular soldiers, let alone guerrillas, treated subjugated civilian populations and captured military personnel.

After World War II, we learned of the Japanese Rape of Nanking, and of Nippon's attempt to build the Thailand-Burma railway (Hollywood's *Bridge on the River Kwai*) that cost tens of thousands of allied POW lives. "During World War II the Japanese handled Americans and Britons in the same brutal fashion with which they treated their own miscreants and other Asians. Thousands of Americans and English died or went mad in the POW camps. Almost all the lives of the men in the bamboo camps were shortened, even if they survived."[3]

The treatment of American and United Nations troops in Korea was no different. As Korean War historian T.R. Fehrenbach summarized it:

[T]he average Army POW would be treated much like an average Chinese felon or class enemy. No great pressures would be put on him, other than those of starvation, lack of medical care, and a certain amount of indoctrination. This was the Lenient Policy. All American POWs, however, were not subject to it. Airmen, in particular, who were bombing North Korea to rubble, rousing the hatred of both Chinese and Koreans, were criminals from the start. Later, when the typhus carried across the Yalu [River] by the CCF [Chinese Communist Forces] hordes spread to the civilian population, airmen would be accused of germ warfare, giving the CCF both an out and a chance at a propaganda coup. Airmen, and some others, would be put under acute stress to confess alleged war crimes. Some were put in solitary. Some were physically tortured. All were starved and interrogated until their nerves shrieked. They were treated in almost the identical way that political prisoners had been treated by Communists for a generation."[4]

References are to notes at the ends of chapters.

The harshness of these conditions is eloquently revealed by cold statistics: "[O]f 75,000 South Korean and United Nations prisoners taken by the North Koreans and Chinese, 60,000 never returned; and the early evidence indicated that several thousand Americans may have died or been executed in Korean PW camps."[5]

Beginning in 1945, French prisoners had fared no better (and perhaps even worse) at the hands of the Viet Minh, predecessors to those who would later be called the Viet Cong and North Vietnamese. It has been estimated that during the Franco-Viet Minh war, approximately 40,000 French and French-allied soldiers were taken prisoner. They experienced, in Rochester and Kiley's words, an "abominable captivity"[6]: forced marches through nearly impenetrable jungle; inadequate shelter; no medical attention; little food; manual labor worse than that performed by beasts of burden; exposure to poisonous insects and animals; beatings and sadistic torture.

In one of the most dreaded forms of punishment, known as the "buffalo treatment," captors confined prisoners in the manure and sewage below a hut floor with dangerous buffalos, foraging pigs, and other animals.... [G]uards routinely jammed newly arrived prisoners, already sick, starving, and exhausted, under the floors of the huts to wallow in offal, denying them medicine, soap, and adequate food for weeks.... [The guards] threw the prisoners bits of rice, often putrid and contaminated by rodent feces, and ladled out small cups of thin pumpkin broth — a meager and usually temporary relief before resumption of the abuses.[7]

Rochester and Kiley observed, "In so many ways, Viet Minh treatment of these French PWs now seems like a rehearsal for the American experience that followed."[8]

Indeed it was. As stories began to filter out of Laos and Vietnam in the early 1960s, it became apparent that the French POW experience was being visited on American prisoners, civilians and military alike. As the war intensified, with heavy bombing of the North and more and more combat and support troops committed in South Vietnam to fight the Viet Cong and North Vietnamese regulars, the number of American prisoners swelled. True to form, and just as the Chinese and North Korean Communists had done in Korea, the Vietnamese Communists embarked on a program to exploit those prisoners for propaganda purposes. However, because of the post–Korean War Code of Conduct[9] — governing the behavior of American POWs in captivity — prisoners faced a cruel dilemma: cooperate, and, depending on the circumstances, violate the Code and thus perhaps commit treason, or suffer torture and deprivation at the hands of the North Vietnamese Communists.[10]

Endeavoring to survive in Communist captivity and at the same time to maintain their mental sanity, physical health, personal integrity and unyielding loyalty to their country, the last thing the POWs needed was to be undermined by their own countrymen. Yet during the 1960s and 1970s there was a pilgrimage to North Vietnam by American anti-war activists; for example, Herbert Aptheker, historian and left-wing theoretician; Staughton Lynd, Yale history professor; author and Soviet apologist Mary McCarthy; "peace activist" Cora Weiss; son of a former attorney general of the United States and justice of the Supreme Court, and himself a former U.S.

attorney general, Ramsey Clark; Daniel Berrigan, a Jesuit priest; Howard Zinn, a Boston University professor; war protestor David Dellinger; Reverend William Sloane Coffin, pastor of Riverside Church in New York City; and still others—including Tom Hayden, perhaps the most notorious of the anti-war activists.

And, of course, Hayden's future wife, the subject of this book, Jane Fonda.

As a Korean veteran (Eighth Army military intelligence, 1955–56), I watched with anguish, along with many other Americans, while politicians threw more and more soldiers, sailors, marines and airmen into the quagmire of Vietnam, hobbling them in pursuit of unclear, unobtainable and contradictory goals, while our military forces continued selflessly to do their duty. I watched with contempt the anti-war pilgrimages just mentioned, even though the obeisant pilgrims' visits had resulted in comparatively little publicity—until actress-activist Jane Fonda went to Hanoi in 1972.

Then I was outraged, knowing that Fonda's international recognition as an actress and the daughter of actor Henry Fonda guaranteed worldwide publicity, and that her support of the Communist Vietnamese regime would, at the least, undermine our government's and military's efforts. Had I known the impact her presence in Hanoi— the bosom of our enemy—would have on our prisoners, especially those held in Hanoi, I would have been even more outraged, were that possible. At the time, all I could do was sign petitions, express my anger on radio talk shows, and support the protests of veterans' groups. Later, I boycotted Fonda's movies, took every opportunity to denounce her actions, and waited to see how the government would respond to the many patriotic cries that Fonda be indicted for treason. Nothing happened.

The war ended the next year. Hundreds of our prisoners were repatriated, and with them came stories about the impact of Fonda's trip to Hanoi. There was agitation anew that she be punished. Once again, nothing happened.

Fonda went on with her life — garnering more adulation as an actress; becoming a fitness guru; providing untold millions to her office-seeking politician husband Tom Hayden in support of an assortment of far-left causes; marrying media billionaire Ted Turner; establishing herself as a Hollywood icon; piling up award upon award; and recently pursuing other causes. But she has never been made to account for her wartime trip to North Vietnam.

Fonda's seeming apology on Barbara Walters' TV show *20/20* in 1988 was hollow and insincere—not to mention incomplete. Her pose, she told Walters, on a North Vietnamese anti-aircraft gun used to shoot down American planes was "a thoughtless and cruel thing to have done." She was sorry she had hurt the prisoners in the Hanoi Hilton. She had been "thoughtless and careless."[11] What makes Fonda's regret ring so hollow and self-serving are her revealing words in a 1989 interview, in which she stated categorically: "I did not, have not, and will not say that going to North Vietnam was a mistake ... I have apologized only for some of the things that I did there, but *I am proud that I went.*"[12] Even genuine repentance on Fonda's part would not have erased from my mind what she had done in Hanoi. But, like many Americans, including many of those who had served in Vietnam, I put the issue aside.

In 1995, I retired from teaching law. In 1999, after 42 years, I retired from the practice of law. Over those years I had represented, among others, dissidents fleeing Communism for freedom in the west; physicians choking on government regulation who couldn't well serve their patients; young men resisting conscription and the hell of Vietnam; "gold bugs" seeking to protect their assets from inflation; women trying to avoid abuse by their men and the bureaucracy; political candidates struggling against First Amendment–violating campaign finance restriction; publishers opposing censorship; refugees battling the INS; homeowners fighting destruction of their neighborhoods; students suffering from affirmative action. I represented the Ayn Rand disciples known as Objectivists, and Rand herself. I represented defendants appealing unjust verdicts. I represented "constitutionalists" who stood up to government's attempt to trash the Bill of Rights. In short, I'd spent decades fighting for rights and justice. I had started writing my memoirs when, in mid–1999, ABC-TV ran a Barbara Walters special, based on the earlier *Ladies' Home Journal* coffee-table book *100 Most Important Women of the Century*. There, profiled in the book and on Walters' TV special, was Jane Fonda. Unable to countenance this accolade, especially in the face of the unseemly soft-pedaling that Walters and the *Ladies' Home Journal* had indulged in, I made a decision. The time had come for me to investigate "Hanoi Jane." Was there a case to be made against her?

I undertook that investigation, and once I had finished, I recruited my wife, novelist Erika Holzer, as co-author. The result is this book. Its subject is Fonda's broadcasts and other conduct in Hanoi. Its argument is that she could have been indicted for the crime of treason, that there would have been enough evidence to go to a jury, that she could have been convicted, and that a conviction probably would have been upheld on appeal. I reached this conclusion based on some 40 years of practicing and some 20 years of teaching constitutional law and related courses, from a thorough examination of Fonda's propaganda broadcasts and other conduct in wartime North Vietnam, and from considerable research into the American law of treason.

It is my hope — no, my purpose — that, if the conclusion I've reached is accepted, then, in the court of public opinion, moral justice will finally be done. Benedict Arnold and Aaron Burr provide us with an historical precedent: In a *legal* sense, they were never punished as Fonda never was.

Equally important, it is my intention that this book provide closure for those American prisoners of war who suffered so much from Jane Fonda's actions in North Vietnam.—*Henry Mark Holzer, November 2001*

---

1. For this fact, and many more to be cited in this book, we are immeasurably indebted to Stuart I. Rochester and Frederick Kiley, whose book—*Honor Bound: American Prisoners of War in Southeast Asia, 1961–1973*—with its comprehensive sourcing, is not only the definitive study of the American Prisoner of War experience in Southeast Asia, but also a towering and quintes-sential scholarly achievement. (Throughout *Honor Bound* the authors use the abbreviation "PW," which is commonly used by the military services, rather than "POW," which tends to be used by civilians. Accordingly, when in this book *Honor Bound* is quoted, "PW" will be used, but otherwise we shall use the abbreviation "POW.")

2. Rochester and Kiley, *Honor Bound*, 9–10.

3. T.R. Fehrenbach, *This Kind Of War: The Classic Korean War History*, 316. This invaluable one-volume work exposes the global politics of the Korean War, examines the war at all levels from squad to theater, and manages at the same time to get inside the heads of individual riflemen and other combatants. As brilliantly described in *Ghost Soldiers* by Hampton Sides, the barbarity perpetrated on American, Filipino and Allied prisoners of war by the Japanese in the Philippines during World War II defies belief. The atrocities began with the Bataan Death March in early 1942, during which, in addition to countless other bestial acts of savagery, "350 members of the Philippine 91st Army Division were herded up, tied with telephone wire, and systematically beheaded by sword" (Sides, *Ghost Soldiers*, 90). Japanese atrocities persisted during the entire Philippine campaign, right to the end. For example, in December 1944 at the Puerto Princesa prison camp in Palawa, Philippines, the Japanese burned alive nearly 150 American POWs who were being worked to death as slaves. Early in 1945, when in a daring raid American Rangers liberated hundreds of POWs from the Cabanatuan prison camp, "[e]ven though they had prepared themselves for the worst, the Rangers were truly appalled at the grotesque condition of many of the prisoners.... It was a ghastly parade — amputees, consumptives, men with peg legs, men without hair or teeth, men with the elephantine appendages and scrotums indicative of wet beriberi.... The half-naked prisoners were dull-eyed and louse-infected, and they seemed old beyond their years. Most were barefoot, or they hobbled around on homemade sandals fashioned from string and slats of cardboard. Their hair was greasy and raggedly shorn close to the scalp with blunt knives. Lesions and battle scars marred their skin, and many had tropical ulcers as big as dinner plates.... Some of the Rangers welled with tears at the hideous procession and tried to offer comfort" (Sides, *Ghost Soldiers*, 280–81). In view of the treatment that turned POWs into the walking dead, it is not surprising that while the Allied POW death rate in Germany and Italy was four percent, 27 percent of the internees died, one out of every four in Japanese prison camps .

4. Fehrenbach, *This Kind of War*, 317–318. As to Communist captors who were not Asiatic, "More than one million World War II Soviet-held PWs were never accounted for; thousands of those who were accounted for died from inhumane treatment in captivity. In one tragic episode in the Katyn Forest in 1941, the Russians were believed to have slaughtered between 5,000 and 16,000 Polish PWs, mostly officers..." (Rochester and Kiley, *Honor Bound*, 21).

5. Rochester and Kiley, *Honor Bound*, 21.

6. Rochester and Kiley, *Honor Bound*, 15. Our summary description of what the French prisoners of the Viet Minh experienced is taken from *Honor Bound* at pages 14–25.

7. Rochester and Kiley, *Honor Bound*, 15.

8. Rochester and Kiley, *Honor Bound*, 14.

9. Promulgated as a result of what was deemed inadequate resistance by some during the Korean War, the Code required a prisoner to furnish only his name, rank, serial number, and date of birth — the so-called "big four." POW Col. Larry Guarino set forth the Code's six articles applicable to him as follows: "I. I am an American fighting man. I serve in the forces which guard my country and our way of life. I am prepared to give my life in their defense. II. I will never surrender of my own free will. If in command, I will never surrender my men while they still have the means to resist. III. If I am captured I will continue to resist by all means available. I will make every effort to escape and aid others to escape. I will accept neither parole nor special favors from the enemy. IV. If I become a prisoner of war, I will keep faith with my fellow prisoners. I will give no information or take part in any action which might be harmful to my comrades. If I am senior, I will take command. If not, I will obey the lawful orders of those appointed over me and will back them up in every way. V. When questioned, should I become a prisoner of war, I am bound to give only name, rank, service number, and date of birth. I will evade answering further questions to the utmost of my ability. I will make no oral or written statements disloyal to my country and its allies or harmful to their cause. VI. I will never forget that I am an American fighting man, responsible for my actions, and dedicated to the principles which made my country free. I will trust in my God and in the United States of America" (Larry Guarino, *A P.O.W.'s Story: 2801 Days in Hanoi*, 164–65). Since 1973, the Code has undergone minor changes. In Article I, "man. I serve" has been deleted. In Article II, "men" has been changed to "the members of my command." In Article VI, "man" has been removed and "for freedom," has been added.

The literature on Vietnam POW resistance is virtually unanimous that almost to a man, the prisoners acquitted themselves honorably and in a way consistent with the *Code's* requirements, while many suffered indescribably brutal treatment by their North Vietnamese guards (and sometimes interrogators from other Communist countries, like Cuba). In this regard, see Chapter 3.

10. Many of the early POWs in Hanoi thought the Code carried *legal* force. It did not. It was an

ethical guide, not a regulation. Under ranking POWs Jim Stockdale and Robbie Risner, the issue was clarified — which actually helped strengthen resistance and put it on a more rational basis than were the Code an *absolute* stricture.

11. *The Los Angeles Times*, June 17, 1988. During an interview in 2000, Fonda told Oprah Winfrey, "I will go to my grave regretting the photograph of me in an antiaircraft carrier [*sic*] which looks like I was trying to shoot at American planes. That had nothing to do with the context that photograph was taken in. But it hurt so many soldiers. It galvanized such hostility. It was the most horrible thing I could possibly have done. It was just thoughtless. I wasn't thinking; I was just so bowled over by the whole experience that I didn't realize what it would look like" (*The Washington Times,* July 7, 2000; commentary by Bruce Herschensohn). Fonda's limiting her "apology" to the antiaircraft gun incident is yet another example of her attempt to minimize her activities in North Vietnam. On February 9, 2001, Fonda was at it again on Walters' *20/20* show. Walters said Fonda had been "against the war," and the actress agreed, leaving the implication that being against the war justified her propagandizing for the enemy from its own soil. Yet millions of loyal Americans, who also opposed the war — including some much more prominent than Fonda — never traveled to the capital of a country that was killing our troops and torturing our prisoners. Fonda said, "It just kills me that I did things that hurt those men," apparently referring to our POWs. It's obvious she never bothered to find out how she hurt "those men" — men who were injured,

sick, debilitated and treated by their captors in a manner that in Chapter 3 of this book we could hardly bring ourselves to describe. She made no effort to learn the toll her activities took on the morale of our prisoners and men still in the field, nor the punishment some received for upholding their honor and refusing to meet with her. Worse, as we shall see in Chapter 4, after repatriation was concluded on April 1, 1973, and the details of our POWs' ordeal were revealed, Fonda called the returned POWs "liars and hypocrites" for reporting that they had been brutally tortured. Finally, Fonda told Walters and her viewers that hurting the prisoners was "not my intent." In chapters 6, 7 and 8, we spend dozens of pages discussing Fonda's intent. One wonders what Fonda's answer would have been if Walters had asked Fonda what her intent *was*. So, once more, the Jane and Barbara show allowed Fonda to offer yet another glib, superficial "apology," just like her earlier ones, aimed at convincing the gullible that Hanoi Jane is truly sorry for what she did in North Vietnam. She is not. She never was. Once the full truth is known, even the gullible will not take seriously any more Fonda "apologies."

12. April 9, 1989, interview with Daniel B. Wood, *Sun Herald*. Even Fonda's second husband, radical Tom Hayden (about whom more in later chapters), claimed to have second thoughts about his pro–Hanoi attitude and conduct: "Time has proved me overly romantic about the Vietnamese revolution" (Tom Hayden, *Reunion,* Collier Books, 243). Perhaps Hayden's awakening had something to do with his political aspirations.

"Treason against the United States, shall consist only in levying War against them, or, in adhering to their Enemies, giving them Aid and Comfort. No Person shall be convicted of Treason unless on the Testimony of two Witnesses to the same overt Act, or on Confession in open Court." (Constitution of the United States of America, Article III, Section 3, paragraph 1)

Part I

PRELUDE TO NORTH VIETNAM

THE EARLY JANE FONDA

I reached the age of thirty-two and discovered I'd wasted
thirty-two years of my life (Roger Vadim, Bardot, Deneuve, Fonda, 234)

Why did Jane Fonda travel to Hanoi during her country's war with North Vietnam? While no one can know for certain — perhaps not even Fonda herself, because of the complex psychological drives at work within her — and while motive (as distinguished from intent[1]) is not a defense to the crime of treason, still, it is useful to consider why Fonda acted as she did in Hanoi. That consideration is rooted in an examination of Fonda's background, in which much can be found to explain her radicalization and her later propaganda broadcasts and other pro–Communist, anti–American conduct. Based on that background, we offer an opinion: Jane Fonda's desperate psychological need to overcome early parental rejection, to acquire a sense of identity and self esteem, and to fill her empty value system, caused her, first, to become an anti-war militant, and then to journey to wartime North Vietnam.

Born in 1937 to one of America's esteemed actors, Henry Fonda, and socialite Frances Seymour Brokaw, Jane Seymour Fonda was not exactly the apple of her mother's eye. Frances, who already had a daughter by a previous marriage, had wanted a boy.[2] According to one of Jane's biographers, "[D]uring Jane's first two formative years, she was denied the requisite measure of unconditional maternal love. This would be a major factor in her own early emotional development. Frozen out by her mother from infancy, Jane would turn increasingly to her father for love and approval. Neither would be easily — if indeed ever — won."[3]

Jane's insecurity about her place in the Fonda family began very early. In Henry's "as-told-to" biography, the writer, Howard Teichmann, says, "Henry had filmed home movies of his wife feeding his [newborn] son [Peter] in the hospital. He took them home to show Jane.... 'I remember that movie,' Jane said [to Teichmann], her eyes narrowing. I looked at it and I burst into tears and ran from the room. I was not happy, I can tell you.'"[4] "'My mother already had a daughter, and wanted a son, but had me instead,' Jane insisted with bitterness. 'She could have only one more child. I didn't know this then, but we were three Cesareans, and at the time that was it. I had been told by my grandmother, Sophie Seymour, that mother wanted a son so badly that if she'd had a third daughter, they were going to have a baby boy at her bedside, a boy she could adopt. When she came out of the anesthetic, there would be two children. She didn't have to worry, she had a son, and that was Peter. And she preferred him, I believe.'"[5] Jane's insecurity and alienation had begun early.

Henry's movie career blossomed, with time out for World War II. While he served in the Navy, Frances began to deteriorate psychologically. After the war, Henry returned to an emotionally detached wife. Neither parent seemed very interested in Jane. "As a young girl ... most of my dreams evolved from the basic need of being loved, and being frustrated in fulfilling that need."[6] It certainly couldn't have helped Jane's sense of self when, in 1950, her mother committed suicide by cutting her throat. A more dramatic and profound example of rejection would be hard to find.[7]

Fonda then attended a private high school, Emma Willard, in upstate New York. Of that period, Fonda biographer Peter Collier writes:

Never the ugly duckling she thought herself to be, Jane was now on the verge of becoming a swan, with agate eyes that looked permanently shocked and disconcertingly ripe lips. But she continued to feel betrayed by her body—as if a different, more interesting self was imprisoned within her, as she phrased it, and unable to get out. She no longer had to worry about the pudginess or the squirrel-cheeked look she'd had as a little girl, but food—and the complex matters for which it was a metaphor—continued to be a problem. She had a recurrent dream in her first years at Willard about being in a large hall filled with mountains of food she was unable to reach. And after reading in a history class about how Romans adjourned to vomitoria after banquets, she began to binge and purge. She ate coffee ice cream by the gallon and pound cake by the pound, bagfuls of brownies, and peanut butter and bacon sandwiches. And then she retched them up. She sent for chewing gum advertised in pulp magazines that was said to contain tapeworm eggs, believing that they would hatch inside her and devour the food with which she stuffed herself.[8]

Thus, the beat went on. Insecurity, alienation, lack of self esteem, no sense of self—all continued to be the driving forces of Fonda's existence.

Five years after her mother's suicide, following her own graduation from Willard, Fonda began studies at Vassar College. It was there that the promiscuity for which she would become notorious in later years began. Collier again:

Jane decided to drop out of Vassar. It had never been clear to her why she had gone to college in the first place, especially a place like Vassar, whose main function, as one graduate said, was to prepare women for "marriage, motherhood, and menopause." She'd been there two years, and was involved less in academics than in perfecting her figure (she had added Dexedrine to bingeing and purging in her weight-loss repertory) and conquering men.

[S]he seldom attended class and she engaged in casual sex, which made her "conspicuous" and led her to be called "the Anything-Goes Girl." The realization that men liked her may not have dispelled Jane's insecurity, but it did give her a power she never had before, a power she came to flaunt. "She had a reputation for being easy," says [childhood friend] Brooke Hayward. "It was almost a joke." Novelist Michael Thomas, who eventually married Brooke, says of Jane: "She was going out with two or three guys on the same night. She was this unbelievable-looking girl.... She was promiscuous, which in those days was a way of expressing competitiveness."[9]

Fonda lasted only two years at Vassar, moving on supposedly to study painting in Paris. Instead, she partied relentlessly, adapting quickly to the pre-hippie bohemian life among dissolute Americans living in Paris. Her "art studies" lasted all of six months—until her father tumbled onto what was going on. The unloved bohemian returned home. By then, Henry was about to shed his fourth wife; still, father and daughter didn't have much of a relationship. At 20, Jane was "desperate ... for some sense of direction in her life; she had already exhausted all of the things she thought she wanted to do."[10]

Still trying to find herself, to give some meaning to her empty life, Jane dabbled some more: secretarial work, art, music. For a while, she was a successful model. Fonda studied acting with Lee Strasberg, guru of the Actors Studio, ironically trying to find out who she was in a milieu where the goal was not to be real but rather to be the character she played. "It became an acceptable cliché among her fellow students to say that Jane Fonda was looking for a father figure. She went through a number of young men in the acting community. As one of them recalls: 'She was there to be seduced by men and vice versa. Yet it was a strange feeling. Having won her, at least temporarily, you got the sense that she was hopeful you'd control her life.' Another young man who knew her during this period ... says, 'Jane was so insecure and hungry for love that she tried to swallow you whole.'"[11]

In 1959, Fonda signed a movie contract with Henry's old pal, her godfather, Josh Logan, and for the next several years Fonda made movies and acted on the stage. Then, in 1962, in what would turn out to be a supreme irony, the woman later dubbed "Hanoi Jane" was named "Miss United States Army Recruiting" by the Pentagon. Biographer Christopher Andersen has described Fonda "[d]raped in a red, white, and blue ribbon emblazoned with her new title ... [giving] an impassioned speech to officers and enlisted recruiters, praising the armed forces and defending the need for a well prepared military to discourage America's communist enemies."[12] Given Fonda's immaturity and self-admitted lack of intellectual knowledge and experience, it's likely that these patriotic sentiments were not her own, but rather scripted by the Army or even by her own publicity people.

In 1963, Fonda returned to France, this time to make a film — and to continue trying to find out who she was: "I am always Henry Fonda's daughter," she remarked, "one of Hollywood's new faces. I ended up not liking who I really was.... So I decided to escape all that and get out from under my father's shadow. Perhaps I'll be able to discover a real identity in France."[14] Fonda's European search for self began with her initiating an affair with director Roger Vladimir Plemiannikov, better known as Roger Vadim,[15] who has been characterized as "Europe's chief provider of identity to beautiful young actresses"[16] during those years. Vadim, however, was under no illusions about his new conquest: Fonda, according to the director, "was far from being as self-assured as she wanted people to believe. She asked herself many questions about her career, her father and even her emotional life. It seemed to her that she hadn't yet achieved anything, really. That didn't discourage her, but she did find it disturbing."[17] Nor was Vadim disturbed that Fonda was engaged in a "search for her true identity."[18]

In the search for the roots of Fonda's politicalization and later radicalization, it is important to note that during this period of her development, Fonda — according to Vadim, the person who probably knew her best —"had no interest yet in politics...."[19] Actually, it would have been more accurate for Vadim to have said that Fonda's political knowledge and judgment were primitive and contradictory, as evidenced by a trip the lovers made. Shortly after their affair began, Vadim took Fonda to the Soviet Union. According to Collier, "By the end of the trip, Jane was telling journalists that she had been misled in her American education about the nature of the Soviet Union and that the real evil was anticommunism."[20] Yet Vadim has written that, when in Moscow, Fonda saw a banner proclaiming that "Twenty-Seven Million Russians Died So That the Children of the World Can Live," she remarked, "In those twenty-seven million dead, do they include the Russians assassinated by Stalin?"[21] Despite Fonda's "Stalin" remark, Vadim believed that, "It was in Moscow that she began questioning, for the first time, the readymade ideas she had acquired in America and had taken for granted."[22]

After Moscow, Fonda returned to the United States for a movie, and in 1965 she married Plemiannikov-Vadim.[23] The newlyweds were soon back in France, where French "intellectuals" in the Vadim circle began Fonda's political education in earnest. These people were typical French anti–American leftists who deplored their country's colonialism, but had no trouble embracing the colonialism of post–World War II communism. They worshiped the likes of Mao and Castro and the "new" Communist revolutionary on the block, North Vietnam's Ho Chi Minh ("Uncle Ho," for short).

Henry Fonda put it this way:

Y'know, when she was married to Vadim, she got into this whole business and some of his friends sold her on the idea that America's position in the Vietnam war was wrong.

They labeled her a Communist. She did have a couple of friends who believed in that system. I know because she lived with Shirlee [Henry's wife] and me during most of this. When Jane had Angela Davis over to the house, I began to worry about her. I was not happy.[24]

Fonda biographer Christopher Andersen has written cogently about what happened to Jane Fonda in the milieu of French left-wing intellectuals:

At first, Jane was resolute in her defense of the United States. She insisted that it was unfair to compare America with the colonial powers of the past, and argued forcefully that American troops were in South Vietnam only to help that country defend itself against Communist aggression.

Predictably, this did not sit well with Vadim's left wing friends, including such leading French film notables as Jean-Luc Godard, Yves Montand, and Montand's wife, Simone Signoret. While Jane played perfect hostess at their country house ... her guests would grill her incessantly concerning what they perceived as America's culpability.

Jane was no match for them. While certainly possessed of a keen natural intelligence, she was ill-read on historical and political matters. In truth, the "facts" as stated by Vadim's sophisticated friends were nothing more than propaganda from the pages of *Pravda* embraced as gospel by the French "New Left".... In the face of such virulent and seemingly unanimous anti–Americanism, Jane stopped objecting and started listening. After months of this, her will to resist vanished.[25]

Of course "Jane was no match for them." Montand and Signoret were French communist royalty. Indeed, Montand had been "a militant communist in his youth."[26] Montand's obituary in *The Los Angeles Times* reported, "As an active communist ... Montand and fellow traveler Signoret were welcomed by Soviet leader Nikita S. Khrushchev in 1956 with ceremony normally reserved for heads of state."[27] As to "fellow traveler" Signoret, at her death, the Associated Press obituary more charitably referred to her as an "ardent leftist."[28]

It needs to be emphasized who Fonda was at that time — or, more precisely, who she was not. Given what is known about her background — and especially the emptiness of her value system — whatever patriotism she may have felt for the United States was probably as shallow as the rest of her beliefs. Add to that her desperate need to be loved, and to find (or create) an identity on which she could base even pseudo–self-esteem, and it is not difficult to understand why she succumbed to the relentless anti–Americanism of her husband's left-wing friends. Add to this the influence of two films Fonda made in 1966, and one can see, if not the beginnings of radicalization, then at least the start of politicalization.

The first film was *The Chase*, with a screenplay by Stalin apologist Lillian Hellman and starring Fonda and Marlon Brando. Characterized as "a film with impeccable liberal credentials,"[29] *The Chase* told the story of a man falsely accused of murder. In other words, the film was what has been called "an all-too-obvious indictment of social injustice...."[30] During filming, Brando would proselytize Fonda about one of his pet causes: America's mistreatment of its Indian population.[31]

The second 1966 film that influenced Fonda was *Hurry Sundown*, a contemporary story about racial intolerance and the evil of "big business." The picture was made in St. Francisville, Louisiana, with a racially mixed cast including African-Americans Robert Hooks and Diahann Carroll. There was rampant racial prejudice in the small community, threats and harassment abounded, and finally the company was virtually run out of town.

It's hard to know for sure whether these two films, and the attendant context in which they were made — that is, proximity to Brando's style of militancy, and exposure to virulent racial prejudice — were in themselves central to Fonda's politicalization, or whether they were merely additional sustenance for the seeds that had been planted by her sojourns in the Soviet Union and France. Either way, the influence of Fonda's trip to the Soviet Union, of the French left-wing intellectuals, and of the two "socially conscious" films certainly made an impact on the vacuous, impressionable and politically unsophisticated actress.

The clear turning point, however, came in 1968, through a confluence of events.

Fonda, now back in France, became pregnant in January 1968.

In Vietnam it was the time of the Tet Offensive, with its bloody scenes played out every day on international television, and the traditionally anti–American French press reveling in its "I-told-you-so" smugness.

"In Paris," said Fonda, "I also met American deserters and Vietnamese of the National Liberation Front [the Viet Cong], who knew facts that I had not been aware of. Then I saw a movie on the Washington march, boys with long hair and radicals putting flowers into the guns of the guards standing in front of the Pentagon."[32]

In Paris, Fonda became friendly with Vanessa Redgrave, a supporter of militant Palestinians and the likes of Fidel Castro. A member of the British Workers Revolutionary Party, in the mid–70s Redgrave would produce an anti–Israel documentary film supporting the PLO; in 1978, when accepting a Best Supporting Actress Oscar, she was to denounce Jewish protesters as "Zionist hoodlums" and would continue over the years to rail against "Zionist imperialism" and the "Zionist press."[33]

Fonda was also influenced by Bertrand Russell and Jean-Paul Sartre's so-called "International War Crimes Tribunal" in Stockholm, which condemned the United States for its role in Vietnam,[34] using entirely phony information that had been cranked out of Communist propaganda mills.

On television, Fonda saw hundreds of thousands of people march on the Pentagon in opposition to the war. Bobby Kennedy and Martin Luther King were assassinated. There were race riots in the streets of America.

A national strike in France turned Paris into a war zone. Fonda is quoted as saying, "In '68 ... you had to deal with it. If you were in Paris, Paris was up in arms. Most everyone I knew was in the streets. Everything was changing overnight. I didn't have any political understanding of what was going on, except that people were moving. And people were moving in Chicago.'"[35]

The Left's devil incarnate, Richard M. Nixon, was nominated for the presidency.

All of these events were being poured into the empty vessel that was Jane Fonda. The cumulative effect of the Soviet Union trip, the indoctrination by French intellectuals, the Vietnam war and its cultural fallout and the other explosive events of 1968 were to provide Fonda, for the first time in her life, a *raison d'être*.

Vadim, perhaps more than anyone who has written about Fonda's politicalization (because he was there), understood what had happened:

During that time, Jane went through a radical political metamorphosis. She, who in her mind had always refused to see any connection between the French war in Indochina and the American war in Vietnam, realized through talking to a number of committed Frenchmen of politics and literature, that it was fundamentally the same war, even though the vocabulary and the justifications used in America were different. She suddenly understood the essence of the Vietnam peace movement which was taking on new dimensions in her own country.[36]

Vadim considered himself "largely responsible" for Fonda's "newfound political conscience."[37]

On the more personal side, Vadim has called Fonda's pregnancy "a turning point for the woman in her. She had always been afraid to assume her femininity. She equated anything purely feminine with weakness. Between her mother, destroyed and propelled beyond the brink of madness by a process beyond her grasp, and the sex-object ideal generally prevalent in America, and Hollywood in particular, she could not help having a devastating image of her female identity."[38]

Apparently, motherhood didn't help Fonda's self-image either. On September 28, 1968, Fonda gave birth to her first child, a girl. She named the baby Vanessa.[39] According to Vadim, for even as long as "[a] year after the birth of her daughter, Vanessa, Fonda would say, 'I reached the age of thirty-two and discovered I'd wasted thirty-two years of my life.'"[40]

Soon, primarily because of the events of 1968, her next movie, and a pilgrimage, Fonda would begin to make up for lost time.

The movie, which began early the following year, was the grim *They Shoot Horses, Don't They?*, a metaphor for America's Depression-era desperation, told through the device of a dance marathon. The picture apparently had a powerful impact on Fonda, whose ideas were still in the formative stage. "The war we're going through now — our country has never gone through such a long, agonizing experience, except before the Depression. The Depression is the closest America ever came to national disaster. Perhaps audiences — especially kids — will be able to come away from seeing *They Shoot Horses* with the feeling that if we could pull out of the Depression, we can pull out of the mess we're in now."[41]

Back in France, she immersed herself in Indian philosophy. She traveled to India, Nepal and Sikkim, and studied transcendental meditation with the Maharishi.[42] "She still had no answer to the question, 'What do I need in my life for fulfillment?' She searched ... and searched.... She hoped she might find the answer to her identity problem there."[43] As her husband Roger Vadim put it, all Fonda got was "slightly thinner and [she] didn't seem to have found peace and wisdom."[44]

But the squalor Fonda had encountered on her pilgrimage had apparently made some kind of an impression. Again, Vadim understood what was happening: "This journey didn't provide Jane with an answer to her personal problems, but it did help her to take a great step towards social awareness. She understood that the struggle against social injustice is not waged by meditation or saving one's soul. Still troubled, she was, nevertheless, much closer to her moment of truth than she imagined."[45]

As perceptive as Vadim was, what he didn't realize was that Fonda's increasing "social awareness" was about to provide an answer to her "personal problems." She would soon use the mantra of "social awareness" to fill the vacuum that was her personal value system.

Returning to California to do publicity for *Horses*, she found the contrast between India's poverty and California's abundance to be stark, and she said so. Indeed, as biographer Christopher Andersen has quoted Fonda as saying, she now saw *Horses* to be "a very forceful condemnation of the capitalist system."[46]

Fonda's sojourns in France and India, her raised consciousness from the *Horses* experience (with the Film Critics' Best Actress Award seeming to validate her nascent political opinions), still had not filled the value void in her life. She had begun talking to New Left activists and radicals, and remarked: "I realized that I didn't believe in anything ... and I knew that people whom I might respect wouldn't respect me."[47] She cut her hair unusually close, the significance of which Collier analyzed as "a metamorphosis similar to others in her life — when she joined Actors Studio, when she fled to France — a moment when she emptied herself of a previous identity and was waiting, in a state of heightened receptivity, to be filled by a new persona. But this time the drama of rebirth was projected onto the backdrop of a radical apocalypse which gave it the added weight and resonance of a historic event. ... The Black Panthers were waging what amounted to a guerrilla war against the police forces of several major cities. There was a sense that a transcendent moment might be approaching, and Jane was desperate not to be left behind. *It was happening.*"[48]

Fonda's post–France, post–India, post–*Horses* rebirth started with dumping her husband. Vadim wrote his own epitaph: "Jane was not seeking a new love affair. She wasn't leaving me for another man, but for herself. ... She had found her way.... I turned off the stereo and walked into the bedroom, which Jane had transformed into a hippie den; Indian fabric covering the bed and walls, soft lighting, candles, red and blue light bulbs, incense burning on a low table. She put down her pencil, which she was using to underline some sentences in an article about Vietnam...."[49] It was over.

It was just beginning.

---

1. The important legal difference between "motive" and "intent," and motive not being a defense to a charge of treason, is examined in Chapter 6.

2. For the material in this chapter describing Jane Fonda's pre-radical life, we have drawn on a rich literature about all of the Fondas: Henry and his five wives, Jane and her brother Peter.

3. Andersen, *Citizen Jane: The Turbulent Life of Jane Fonda*, 28.

4. Fonda, *Fonda: My Life*, 132.

5. Fonda, *Fonda: My Life*, 167.

6. Anderson, *Citizen Jane*, 37.

7. Yet, when asked by Barbara Walters on her February 9, 2001, TV show about the effect (on Fonda) of her mother's suicide, the actress answered, "What doesn't kill you makes you stronger."

8. Peter Collier. *The Fondas: A Hollywood Dynasty*, 93. Collier's biography of the Fondas contains abundant notes, unlike other Fonda biographies, some of which borrow liberally from Collier's work without attribution. As will be seen in Chap-

ter 2, Collier, albeit incidentally, had an early role in Fonda's radicalization.

9. Collier, *The Fondas*, 106–07. Many years later, on Walters' February 9, 2001, TV show, Fonda would admit that in her Vadim–French film days she "liked being viewed as a sex-kitten.'"

10. Collier, *The Fondas*, 110.

11. Collier, *The Fondas*, 118.

12. Andersen, *Citizen Jane*, 93. Even then, in 1962, Americans were being held as prisoners by the Communists in Indochina.

13. Both as an actress and an activist, Fonda would often read words written by others, including, as we shall see in Chapter 4, by Communist propagandists.

14. Collier, *The Fondas*, 143.

15. The name "Vadim" seems drawn from the director's middle name, "Vladimir." It was with a passport giving her name as Jane Seymour Plemiannikov that Fonda would, in 1972, leave the United States and, via Paris, Moscow and Vientiane, surface in Hanoi.

16. Collier, *The Fondas*, 143.

17. Vadim, *Bardot, Deneuve, Fonda*, 214.

18. Vadim, *Bardot, Deneuve, Fonda*, 219.

19. Vadim, *Bardot, Deneuve, Fonda*, 221.

20. Collier, *The Fondas*, 146.

21. Vadim, *Bardot, Deneuve, Fonda*, 228.

22. Vadim, *Bardot, Deneuve, Fonda*, 230.

23. The intimate details of Fonda's union with Plemiannikiov-Vadim, which included drugs and group sex, are beyond the scope of this book. However, the influence on Fonda of the hedonistic and libertine Vadim (and his French friends) cannot be dismissed as causal factors in her later radicalization.

24. Fonda, *Fonda: My Life*, 301. Angela Davis was a Communist, close to the Black Panthers. To his credit, Henry Fonda, though a liberal, took this position: "I've always been for the underdog, but I personally believe that Communism is full of lies. I am definitely anti-Communist. ...I said, 'Jane, if I ever discover for a fact that you're a Communist or a true Communist sympathizer, I, your father, will be the first to turn you in. I fought for this country, and I love it.... Jane, there are less human rights in Russia than in America. Maybe we do have some inequities, but it's worse over there'" (Fonda, *Fonda: My Life*, 302).

25. Andersen, *Citizen Jane*, 145.

26. *The Los Angeles Times*, November 10, 1991.

27. *The Los Angeles Times*, November 10, 1991. Although in later years Montand turned somewhat away from the left, his antipathy seemed to be directed toward "Stalinists." He did not eschew socialism or other forms of collectivism: "Don't get me wrong," he said in 1984, nearly a decade-and-a-half after his left-wing influence on Fonda, "I have nothing against Russia, nothing at all. ... But ... we must get Stalinists out of the [French] government, and we must fight against Gulag, and we must be firm! ... But between collapsing and staying firm there is something else. Between wild capitalism and communism there is an economic system that recognizes that if some guy invests money, he can make some profit and still provide jobs and benefits for society" (*The Los Angeles Times*, May 16, 1984).

28. The Associated Press, *Release*, September 30, 1985, by Marilyn August.

29. Gary Herman and David Downing, *Jane Fonda, All American Anti-Heroine*, 60.

30. Andersen, *Citizen Jane*, 134.

31. Herman and Downing, *Jane Fonda*, 64.

32. Andersen, *Citizen Jane*, 165.

33. See, for example, *The New York Times*, November 11, 1977; an Associated Press release appearing in *The Globe and Mail* on April 4, 1978; and *The Washington Post*, September 9, 1985.

34. Andersen, *Citizen Jane*, 166.

35. Andersen, *Citizen Jane*, 167. Fonda's reference to Chicago was to the Democratic party convention that nominated Vice President Humphrey over Eugene McCarthy, where radicals rioted against Chicago police allegedly in the name of anti-war protest.

36. Vadim, *Bardot, Deneuve, Fonda*, 281.

37. Vadim, *Bardot, Deneuve, Fonda*, 281.

38. Vadim, *Bardot, Deneuve, Fonda*, 282.

39. Of the baby's name, Vadim has said, "Jane had thought of [Vanessa] because of her friendship at the time with the actress Vanessa Redgrave" (Vadim, *Bardot, Deneuve, Fonda*, 284). Actually, both of Fonda's children are named after heroes of hers. Her son with radical Tom Hayden, "Troi"—now more benignly called "Troy" —was named after Nguyen van Troi, a Viet Cong terrorist who tried to assassinate Secretary of Defense Robert McNamara in 1964 but who was himself executed for the effort. See Peter Collier, *National Review*, July 17, 2000. Nguyen van Troi "had been caught placing explosives under a bridge that U.S. Secretary of Defense Robert S. McNamara was expected to cross during a visit to Saigon" (Rochester and Kiley, *Honor Bound*, 80). It is believed that in retaliation for Troi's execution, the Viet Cong executed American POW Rocky Versace. See *Honor Bound* at 248.

40. Vadim, *Bardot, Deneuve, Fonda*, 234.

41. Andersen, *Citizen Jane*, 178. Typically, Fonda didn't specify the "mess" she was talking about.

42. Peter Collier and David Horowitz, *Destructive Generation*, 267.

43. Vadim, *Bardot, Deneuve, Fonda*, 300.

44. Vadim, *Bardot, Deneuve, Fonda*, 300.

45. Vadim, *Bardot, Deneuve, Fonda*, 301.

46. Andersen, *Citizen Jane*, 188.

47. Collier, *The Fondas*, 190.

48. Collier, *The Fondas*, 191.

49. Vadim, *Bardot, Deneuve, Fonda*, 303.

2

THE ANTI-WAR JANE FONDA

*She changed into a militant almost overnight. It was too fast for
anyone to handle (Fonda:* My Life, *as told to Howard Teichmann, 302)*

While in India, Fonda had seen a copy of the Collier-edited magazine *Ramparts*—
radical, and militantly anti-war. The cover story dealt with the occupation of Alcatraz
Island by protesting indigenous Indians. Doubtless recalling Marlon Brando's prosely-
tizing during filming of *The Chase* about the mistreatment of American Indians, and
needing to "get involved" in the "new politics," Fonda, having returned from India, had
her press agent contact Collier, asking him to open some doors for her to the New
Left.[1] Then, she called Collier directly. Would he take her to the island? "Sporting the
new short shag haircut she would wear as Bree Daniel in *Klute*, Jane explained her new-
found civic-mindedness to Collier as they stood on a fog-shrouded San Francisco pier
waiting for a boat to take them to Alcatraz. She likened her numb, apathetic, cynical
existence in Paris to a kind of limbo. She wanted to be home in America, where it's happening. When Collier cracked that maybe she was too late … a look of horror came
over her face, and she said Oh, I hope not."[2]

After hitching a ride on one of the boats that was running the Coast Guard
blockade and ferrying provisions to the island-bound Indians, Fonda reverted to
form:

After meeting with representatives of the various tribes, she realized that the Sioux, playing
on their historical identity as a warrior elite, were the most radical group, and she spent
the rest of her afternoon on the island smoking dope with them in their corner of the old
prison exercise yard and making plans to tour Indian reservations across the United States
to publicize the problems Indian people faced.[3]

Careening down this new road with unbridled zeal and the help of her Collier-
Horowitz-*Ramparts* connection, Fonda entered the world of New Left, anti-war, politics: militant Indians, radical lawyers, army deserters, federal prisoners, farm workers, aggressive feminists and, of course, Black Panthers.[4] She found the experience
gratifying: "'I was so used to being considered a sex symbol,' Fonda told *The New
York Times*, 'that I began to like it. I didn't expect people to treat me as a person who

thinks. But when I went to the Indians and I came in contact with the Panthers, the GI's my new friends, I realized that they were treating me as a person.'"[5]

The Panthers[6]— a flavor-of-the month group that was appealing to those needing to be involved with radical chic — were nothing more than drug-dealing gangsters who had wrapped themselves in the slogans and rhetoric of the race issue. But in 1970 they were in vogue, even to the extent of being entertained in the plush Manhattan home of world-famous conductor Leonard Bernstein.

Fonda jumped onto the Panther bandwagon. Extolling killer Huey Newton, Fonda characterized him as "the only man I've ever met ... who approaches sainthood."[7] She connected with communist (and later fugitive) Angela Davis. Still winging it, Fonda admitted that she "didn't have time ... to sit down with books and get a historical analysis and put it all into perspective. It was an emotional, gut kind of thing."[8] Tutored by a Marxist (Valliand), a gangster (Newton) and a communist (Davis), she made a public fool of herself. On Dick Cavett's TV show, for example, Fonda "betrayed an ignorance of history that was almost comical."[9] As Fonda herself confessed: "I was acting out of instinct and emotion. I had no structural, ideological framework in which to put what I was thinking and feeling and doing. I thought I was better equipped to handle questions than I really was. And what happens when somebody is in that kind of position? You're very defensive. And all too often I would strike back — because everyone wanted to back me into a corner and that was so easy to do."[10]

Yet, Fonda's political ignorance didn't stop her from making outrageous pro–Communist, anti–American statements. Examples abound. According to a reporter for the *Detroit Free Press*, on November 22, 1969 — during a fund raising tour for GIs in trouble with the Army, Vietnam Veterans Against the War and the Black Panther Party — she said in a Michigan State University speech:

I would think that if you understood what communism was, you would hope, you would pray on your knees that we would someday become communist.

The peace proposal of the Viet Cong is the only honorable, just, possible way to achieve peace in Vietnam.

Black Panther leader Huey P. Newton is the only man I've ever met that I would trust as the leader of this country.

[The Viet Cong] are driven by the same spirit that drove Washington and Jefferson.

[The Viet Cong] are the conscience of the world.

I think that the majority of the students are scared of the word "socialism." It's [socialism] a good message, and the more people give it, the better.[11]

On July 18, 1970, the *People's World*, a West Coast Communist newspaper, would carry a telephone interview with Fonda, reporting that she had said the following:

To make the revolution in the United States is a slow day by day job that requires patience and discipline. It is the only way to make it.

That it was the system itself which is at fault and is the problem and until something is done about the capitalist system that everything else is really superficial and meaningless.

All I know is that despite the fact that I am one of the people who benefits from a capitalist society, I find that any system which exploits other people cannot and should not exist.[12]

Journalist Karen Elliot in the December 11, 1971, *Dallas Morning News* reported a Fonda speech at the University of Texas: "We've got to establish a socialist economic structure that will limit private profit-oriented businesses," she said. "Whether the transition is peaceful depends on the way our present governmental leaders react. We must commit our lives to this transition. ...We should be very proud of our new breed of soldier. It's not organized but it's mutiny, and they have every right."[13]

Henry Fonda was not thrilled with his daughter's rhetoric: "You listen to her on the telephone, and she's like a fanatic,"[14] Collier reported. That fanaticism had seemed to jell during the summer of 1970, and Henry thought that he knew why:

He believed a good part of Jane's newfound radicalism was an attempt to confront the fact that [her brother] Peter had become a symbol of the counterculture long before her own conversion. This recalled something he had previously said to a magazine interviewer:

"My instinct is that after eight years abroad she came back to her country, America, and suddenly realized how aware Peter had become. It was almost as though she had to do it better than he. Instant causes!"[15]

But Jane Fonda's new-found radicalism had many prices, one of which was her substantial financial support of the Black Panthers. The cost was so great that she decided to do another film "[b]ecause if I don't I'll be completely broke."[16] The film, which would snare Fonda an Oscar, was *Klute*, in which she played a prostitute. "For me," Fonda said, "in a very, very deep way ... *Klute* is my internal proof that when I developed a social and political conscience, I became a better actress. I developed an ability to understand and have compassion for the character."[17]

Having refilled her coffers with her salary from *Klute*, Fonda went back to the radical wars, bringing along her *Klute* co-star and new lover, Donald Sutherland. In early 1971 they formed "FTA," popularly understood to be an acronym for "Fuck the Army," a radical anti-war, anti-American, road-show troupe that played to GIs around the country.[18] Constantly referring to The Revolution, Fonda "now freely admitted that she was out to 'change the American system through socialism. Of course I am a Socialist,'"[19] she admitted.

In March 1971, Fonda returned to France. In Paris, she had a private meeting with North Vietnam's lead peace talks negotiator, Madame Binh. Fonda told Binh that the American people opposed the war. The actress then told the French press that the U.S. Government, the Pentagon and the CIA were responsible for the My Lai massacre. "'In fact,' she said, 'these organizations are the real war criminals in Vietnam.' From Paris, [Fonda] ... moved to London, where Jane repeated allegations of U.S. atrocities: 'applying electrodes to prisoners' genitals, mass rapes, slicing off of body parts, scalping, skinning alive, and leaving "heat tablets" around which burned the insides of children who ate them.' American soldiers, she also told British reporters, were 'indoctrinated with racist thinking....'"[20]

Fonda had thus carried the anti-war movement's activities overseas. Nor were the activities of her colleagues limited to agitation within the U.S. borders. Their activities are important because they set the stage for Fonda's first pilgrimage to Hanoi, in July 1972. They, like Fonda after them, would give the North Vietnamese exactly what they needed: pro–Communist, anti–American propaganda portraying the Vietnamese as victims of post–Franco aggressive American neo-colonialism. Such propaganda sought to legitimize their attack on the South and undermine the United States' military attempt to defend South Vietnam.

These anti–American activists, many of whom were Fonda's friends, associates and fellow travelers, caught the attention of the House of Representatives' Committee on Internal Security. One of its research analysts prepared a report for the Committee and its Chief Counsel. That report is reproduced here verbatim, except for material indicated as having been omitted.[21]

MEMO RE RADIO BROADCASTS FROM NORTH VIETNAM BY U.S. CITIZENS

Congress of the United States
House of Representatives
Committee on Internal Security
Washington, D.C. 20515

September 5. 1972

TO: Donald G. Sanders
             Chief Counsel

FROM: Joseph E. Thach
             Research Analyst

SUBJECT: RADIO BROADCASTS FROM NORTH VIETNAM BY U.S.
             CITIZENS 1965–1972

This report is submitted as a succinct but comprehensive analysis of radio propaganda broadcasts by U.S. citizens from North Vietnam during the Vietnam conflict to provide additional background concerning the recent activities of June Fonda during her visit to that Communist country. It should be noted as an aside that Ms. Fonda's broadcasts now total some twelve specifically identified as addressed to U.S. military personnel. Of these, six were broadcast while she was in North Vietnam. Six others have been transmitted via *Radio Hanoi* on a delayed tape basis since her departure on July 22, with the latest sent on August 22. Eight other radio messages, which began with Ms. Fonda speaking English, were broadcast in Vietnamese and were addressed to South Vietnamese youth, students, women and the military.[22]

In general, the radio broadcasts from North Vietnam by Americans since 1965 fall into three main categories.

1. Those made by U.S. antiwar activists and black militants while visiting North Vietnam.

2. Those made by above individuals and groups made elsewhere and then broadcast on Radio Hanoi at a later date.
3. Those broadcast by captured U.S. servicemen with specific political themes.

In addition, another category which can be established (or included in #1-
3, above) based on specific message content, is that of identified U.S military personnel defectors. With respect to the period covered, that is, 1965 -1972, one Korean War defector and another of Vietnam Conflict period, have been identified
with such activities.

With respect to radio broadcasts (or English-language radio interviews) by
U.S. antiwar activists and black militants during their visits to North Vietnam, their
frequency has only become apparent in the past three years, although *Radio
Hanoi* has used direct quotes from U.S. visitors since the Hayden-Lynd-Aptheker
trip of December 1965. For example, James A. Johnson, one of the "Fort Hood
Three" defendants in 1966 and currently a member of Executive Committee of
the CPUSA [Communist Party United States of America] youth group, the Young
Workers Liberation League, traveled to Hanoi in August 1969 as part of the Ren-
nie Davis-led New Mobe group which secured the release of Navy men Lt. Robert
Frishman and seaman Douglas Hegdahl and Air Force Captain Wesley Rumble,
Johnson, then overtly representing the National Black Anti-war Anti-draft Union,
was quoted as stating:

> We consider it fitting that I, a black man and an ex-GI who spent 28 months in
> U.S. prisons for refusing to fight against the Vietnamese people, should read this.
> statement. Thousands of American GI's now feel that their fight is not with the
> people of Vietnam. Their fight is with those who make the war in this country
> ....(Quoted from *FBIS [Federal Broadcast Information Service]* Daily Report, 4 Au-
> gust 1969 in SDS Hearings, Pt. 7-A, p. 2380).

A year later, Black Panther Party Minister of Information, Eldridge Cleaver,
and Reverend Phillip Lawson, a Methodist minister closely associated with the
Panthers in Kansas City, Missouri, visited North Vietnam as part of the "American
People's Anti-imperialist Delegation." At a ceremony commemorating black solidarity with the Communist Vietnamese "struggle" in Indochina on August 27,
1970, which was broadcast two days later on *Radio* Hanoi, Cleaver stated:

> The rise of the struggle of black people inside the U.S. is a sure sign that the days
> of U.S. imperialism are numbered.... The combination of the external revolution-
> ary forces and the internal revolutionary forces is an unbeatable combination and
> together, we are going to crush U.S. Imperialism and thus usher in a new and
> happy day for mankind.

Denouncing the concurrent Asian mission of Vice President Agnew to South
Vietnam, South Korea and Nationalist China, Cleaver took his violently anti-U.S.
diatribe *ad hominem* as he characterized Mr. Agnew as "the number two fascist
pig in the Nixon clique, Spiro Agnew, Spiro pig Agnew...."

For his part, Reverend Lawson, also a New Mobe Executive Committee member, sent greetings to the North Vietnamese from that organization. While his remarks at that time were less vehement, if equally anti-American, Lawson's delayed-tape broadcast of September 20, 1970, far exceeded Cleaver's remarks in
content and aiming at a specific audience. Addressing his statement to "my black
brothers in the U.S. forces in Vietnam," Lawson declared:

For two weeks, I have been visiting with the people of Vietnam, I have seen what you have been ordered to do to these people. Very frankly, you know what you are doing is criminal, for the same action many persons were convicted of being war criminals. You must become men who will stand up and say no when you are given criminal orders.... Black brothers, do not kill women and children. You. can shoot over their heads, you can prevent the racist white soldiers from slaughtering these people: you can disobey all racist officers and their racist orders. Black brothers, the real war for independence, freedom and justice is being fought in the United States. What you do now in Vietnam will determine what you do back home. If you join the ...Vietnamese forces ... your black brothers and sisters in the United States will welcome your return as a true black man. But if you continue to be used ...your black brothers and sisters ...will surely see you as members of a black police force returning to their black community.
(September 24, 1970)

In an interview in the *Kansas City Star* in October 1970. Lawson readily admitted the accuracy of his statements as broadcast. Claiming he spoke as "a black minister talking to black soldiers," he further stated that "he did not consider the broadcast as 'giving aid or comfort to the enemy', particularly since the United States has never declared war on North Vietnam." "[I]t's a matter of defining the enemy." Lawson concluded, "In the Vietnam war, who is our enemy? I don't think the Communists are the enemy in Vietnam."

After Reverend Lawson's broadcast, a delegation from the National Student Association, which visited Hanoi to negotiate the "People's Peace Treaty" in December 1970, made six separate broadcasts from Hanoi. Such antiwar activists as Noam Chomsky, Richard Fernandez, Robert Scheer, Sidney Peck and Ann Froines also made broadcasts during their respective visits to North Vietnam in 1970. In addition, *Movement for a Democratic Military* leader Hideko "Pat" Sumi, who traveled with the Cleaver Black Panther group to Hanoi, Peking, and Pyongyang, was another individual identified as making GI broadcasts in September 1970.

On February 27, 1972, *Radio Hanoi* presented an interview with Harvard biology professor and Nobel Prize winner, George Wald. Evidently, the delayed-tape had been made a week or two before when Wald visited the DRV as a guest of the Vietnamese Committee for Solidarity with the American People, the same group which has sponsored many U.S. antiwar activists since 1965, including Jane Fonda. At that time, Professor Wald claimed that the U.S. was guilty of conducting the deliberate chemical, biological and ecological campaigns to destroy South Vietnam. Conversely, Wald claimed that the American public was being misled by the military in that the damage to Vietnamese agriculture and forests by herbicides and defoliation was "largely permanent."

Claiming that he and many other American scientists have been in the forefront of the U.S. antiwar movement, Wald added that another strong element in that coalition was the Vietnam Veterans Against the War. Recalling the April 1971 VVAW activities in Washington, D. C., Wald noted that these veterans were "now the most bitter opponents of the war," and were "ashamed of their part" in it. In addition, Wald mentioned his interview with two captured American fliers, in which he noted:

I think that from those conversations that you could find no more powerful voices against the American part in the Vietnam war than the voices of those American prisoners...they explained that they hardly knew why they were coming. They were simply following orders. But now they know, and are violently against this war and want our country to get out of it as quickly as possible. And one of the reasons for that feeling is the great consideration and kindness and care with which they were treated, immediately from their capture onwards …. (February 28, 1972)[23]

Another visitor to North Vietnam (and also to Red China) in March 1972, folk-singer and identified CPUSA member Pete Seeger, admitted to having made tapes for GI's to be broadcast by *Radio Hanoi*.

Seeger claimed in a *Saturday Review* article:

Monday [March 20, 1972]–I6 do two twenty-minute broadcasts that will be broadcast to GIs over "Voice of Vietnam." I have been thinking all week about what I will say and sing and, after talking with Seymour Hersh [the U.S. writer and author of *My Lai 4*] and Toshi [Mrs. Seeger], decided to stay strictly away from political explanations of any sort.

I start with the song "Turn, Turn, Turn" ….Then I say, "Yes, this is Pete Seeger from Beacon, New York and some of my friends will say 'What the hell are you doing up there?' Perhaps the question is "What are any of us doing in this part of the world?" … [Pete Seeger, "Strummin' Banjo in North Vietnam," *Saturday Review* (May 13, 1972), p. 32].

Prior to Miss Fonda, Seeger was the last reported U.S. national involved in *Radio Hanoi* broadcasts to U.S. servicemen.

The second category of broadcasts, that is. Those originated elsewhere but transmitted from North Vietnam has also been utilized frequently since 1965. Two early broadcasters in this category were black militant Robert Williams and another black Korean War defector Clarence Adams, who taped their messages in Peking for replay over North Vietnamese media. Aimed primarily at blacks and other minorities, these messages called on American servicemen to desert or to demand their return to the U.S. where they were to aid in the "real struggle," that is, in the ghettos of American cities. This divisive theme, as can be seen with the previously-mentioned "live" broadcasts by Cleaver and Lawson, has been continued to the present. In 1967-1969, black militant activists such as Charles Cobb and Stokely Carmichael of SNCC (now SCC), Julius Lester and James A. Johnson made similar appeals to black and minority GI's. With respect to Williams and Adams, however, both men have been permitted re-entry into the United States after making such blatant propaganda.

Several other taped broadcasts made during 1966 were originated in the U.S. One, a Fourth of July Message by an otherwise unidentifiable female, Elizabeth Stafford, declared the war "unjust" in light of the Founding Fathers concepts of freedom and independence, and accused the U.S. of war crimes in Vietnam. Another, a Christmas message by an Ed Anderson, played up domestic problems such as racial strife, hunger and disease along with portraying the "hopeless" war in Vietnam. Finally, the year 1966 saw several broadcasts by "Radio Stateside," which made tapes in Los Angeles for broadcast from Hanoi. Two announcers, Steve Fisher and Joe Epstein, combined music with a highly-slanted analysis of the news, especially on the Vietnam War. Sandwiched in between were appeals for desertion and conscientious objector applications. In particular, the pair asked GI's to contact the heavily Communist-Infiltrated Vietnam Committee which was headquartered at Berkeley, and also the Central Committee for Conscientious Objectors, located is Philadelphia, Pennsylvania. In total, *Radio Stateside* made three known broadcasts (January 4, February 16, and August 17 in 1966), and thereafter ceased operations. According to testimony given during HCIS military subversion hearings in October 1971, this technique was again employed in early 1971 with WPAX, Inc., the brainchild of Yippie leader and "Chicago 8"[24] defendant Abby Hoffman. This time, according to Hoffman, in his "official retirement from the Movement" letter published in the *Guardian* during September 1971, Federal authorities reportedly seized the WPAX tapes at the airport.

The third category consists of U.S. servicemen in the custody of the North Vietnamese and Vietcong. Here a distinction must be made between the broadcasts of American airmen held prisoner in North Vietnam and a select group of U.S. Army and Marine Corps personnel in custody of the Vietcong. For the most part, American airmen who have been captured after being downed over North Vietnam have been permitted to make statements to alert military authorities and next of kin of their present sates. Although some of these messages have included passages that the pilots were "reconsidering" U.S. involvement in Vietnam and their own roles therein, the employment of an ethical technique known as a "broad mental reservation" is fairly obvious. In 1971-1972, some of these messages have become rather propagandistic, but a hard core of "progressives" cannot be detected based on the continual traffic analysis of the *Radio Hanoi* broadcasts.

On the other hand, it is evident that a "hard core" group has emerged among U.S. Army and Marine Corps personnel held by the Vietcong. In this group of about a dozen men is a U.S. Army doctor captured in early 1968. Others are a self-admitted U.S. Army defector to the Viet Cong, two Army aviators, two Army Special Forces personnel and several enlisted members of the Marine Corps. The defector, a black soldier who went over to the Vietcong in May 1968, told American troops this past April:

> Refuse to go out on any type of operation, especially combat, including support of the ARVN who'll only let you down.

In an earlier broadcast in February, this same individual in a joint broadcast with another soldier and a marine endorsed the World Assembly for the Peace and Independence of the Indochinese People and such domestic activities as the six-week series of NPAC/PCPJ demonstrations of March-May 1972, and the earlier protest and "Winter Soldier Investigation" of the Vietnam Veterans Against the War in January and April, 1971, respectively. Since April 1971, this small elite has broadcast continually these propaganda themes to U.S. forces in South Vietnam on a regular basis. Although these broadcasts have generally been timed with major events in the combat zone and on the domestic scene, That is, anti-war activities and the like, the median of broadcasts has been 4-6 per month.

In summary, the Vietnamese Communist manipulation of these three major, types of U.S. broadcasters has, since 1965, provided a steady stream of propaganda directed against American forces in Southeast Asia. In terms of the first category alone, U.S. visitors to North Vietnam have made 82 identified broadcasts. By co-timing broadcasts from all three types, it is apparent that the Vietnamese Communists have attempted to gain credibility for their propaganda by means of a technique called theme reinforcement, whereby various speakers from different backgrounds reiterate the same basic theme time and time again somewhat akin to the Nazi propagandist Dr. Goebbels' dictum: "Truth is merely an oft-repeated lie."

The recent dike bombing theme is a case in point. Besides Ms. Fonda, U.S. prisoners of war, foreign correspondents and a former U.S. attorney general have mutually reinforced the theme that U.S. aircraft were intentionally bombing the dikes in North Vietnam, along with schools, hospitals and populated areas. When the evidence for these allegations are examined closely, however, the conclusive proof becomes quicksilver and would scarcely hold water in any but a highly slanted tribunal of Justice.[25]

As the House Committee's Memo makes clear, this Communist-engendered propaganda had its effect on America's military effort in Vietnam. Fonda's activities, as we shall see in Part II, were considerably more notorious than most others because of her celebrity. She became an even bigger celebrity, in certain circles, when she joined forces with one of the propagandists mentioned in the foregoing Congressional report: the poster boy of the anti-war movement, Tom Hayden. It was Hayden more than anyone else—Indians, feminists, farm workers, the Panthers—who was responsible for providing Fonda with the sense of self that she had been so desperately seeking since childhood. "More than any other American radical, Hayden had become associated with the gradual transition of the New Left from antiwar to pro–Hanoi. He had gone to Vietnam in 1965 and had come back rhapsodizing about the 'rice-roots democracy' he had seen there. What he said then and three years later when he brought out the first American POWs, made him Hanoi's leading spokesman in this country."[26]

Hayden, "Mr. Anti–America," thus played Svengali to Fonda's Trilby.

Hayden's radical résumé reflected his involvement in some of the most notorious radical events of the '60s: the founding of Students for a Democratic Society in 1961; the pilgrimage to Hanoi in 1965; the Newark riots of 1967; the meeting with North Vietnamese leaders in Communist Czechoslovakia in 1967[27]; the student strike at Columbia University in 1968; the street warfare at the Democratic Party National Convention in 1968; and his own arrest and subsequent trial as one of the "Chicago Seven."

Hayden and Fonda, who had met in passing, connected once again in 1972 when Fonda, immersed in her Vietnam mode, was narrating a slide show in Los Angeles. Afterwards, Hayden left the audience and approached her. Whatever Hayden was, he was not stupid. Indeed, without necessarily knowing much about her background, Hayden, though no psychiatrist, had sized up Fonda very well. As biographer Peter Collier wrote,

Hayden saw in Jane someone at the end of her tether. Her hyperkinetic tour of the New Left had exposed her to its ideas and jargon. But now that world view was crumbling and she was as isolated as he.[28] Tom saw her as someone who had been drained by the Movement. He had seen others who gave all they could in hopes of achieving radical salvation but were always found wanting for not giving everything. "Their real solution," he later said of the leftists who had been influencing Jane, "was for her to give everything to them and then commit suicide. And she was headed in that direction.'"

He knew she had been seeing other men of the left, but thought she was being used as a mark on their scorecard and was not getting what she needed from her affairs. He also realized that she had stretched herself across too many political commitments, from feminism to black revolution. It seemed that his own solution — to draw away from the intramural fighting of the left and return to the single issue of Vietnam — might work for her too. He got Jane to agree to look at the slide show on Indochina he had put together.

The slides he brought to her ... were different from her own harshly propagandistic ones. His pictures tried to evoke what he saw as the subtle tragedies behind the long war.[29]

Apparently, Hayden's soft-sell worked. After he and Fonda became intimate, she signed on with him — no surprise to those who knew her well.

A former colleague of theirs noted that to understand Hayden and Fonda, "'all you have to know is that they are both very, very ambitious people. Tom was a big hero to the people who mattered most to Jane. *She still had lingering doubts about herself, and he could dispel them.* I mean, this great intellectual was taking her seriously, so she figured everyone else would have to, too.' And Hayden? 'Jane was still a pretty glamorous creature, and Tom was a fan, let's face it. When they got together, he was broke and she was worth millions. Jane was also a powerful force — she was a hundred times more famous than he was— and he had been out of the spotlight for a while. He wanted the access to middle America that she gave him.' Overriding all else in Jane's mind was one paramount consideration. Sisterhood aside, she needed another mentor, another substitute for her father. Hayden filled the bill nicely."[30]

As a Fonda friend put it: "By the spring of 1972, Jane had reached something of a dead end. She'd tried everything in the Movement and she hadn't found a foothold. She was in a sort of free-fall. People laughed behind her back. She was out of synch. It doesn't sound very flattering, but those of us who knew her well realized that she needed a man to follow."[31] That man was Tom Hayden, and Fonda followed him across the threshold, beyond which lay wartime North Vietnam.

---

1. Collier and Horowitz, *Destructive Generation,* 267.

2. Andersen, *Citizen Jane,* 194.

3. Anderson, *Citizen Jane,* 193. Collier has said "It was at this moment he realized that the New Left had become chic" (Collier, *The Fondas,* 220).

4. Accompanying Fonda on a tour of Indian reservations, college campuses and military installations was her old French Marxist friend, Elisabeth Vailland, whose limited English nevertheless did include the clichéd slogan "All power to the people" (Andersen, *Citizen Jane,* 209).

5. Herman and Downing, *Jane Fonda,* 62.

6. Tom Hayden, among the earliest pilgrims to North Vietnam, and Fonda's next husband, adoringly characterized the Black Panthers as "America's Vietcong" (Andersen, *Citizen Jane,* 213).

7. Andersen, *Citizen Jane,* 213. According to Collier, some of the Panthers called Fonda "a 'rich white bitch' behind her back and bragged about having sex with her." For her part, Fonda is reputed to have said, "[m]y biggest regret ... is that I never got to fuck Che Guevara" (Collier, *The Fondas,* 197).

8. Andersen, *Citizen Jane,* 214.

9. Andersen, *Citizen Jane,* 209.

10. Andersen, *Citizen Jane,* 209.

11. *Hearings Before the Committee on Internal Security, House Of Representatives, Ninety-Second Congress, Second Session,* 7679. This Report will hereafter be cited as *Hearing Report.*

12. *Hearing Report,* 7680.

13. *Hearing Report,* 7680.

14. Collier, *The Fondas,* 194.

15. Collier, *The Fondas,* 199.

16. Collier, *The Fondas,* 201.

17. Herman and Downing, *Jane Fonda,* 66.

18. Collier, *The Fondas,* 208.

19. Andersen, *Citizen Jane,* 230. So, too, were her later Communist friends in Hanoi.

20. Andersen, *Citizen Jane,* 241.

21. In order that Mr. Thach's report be presented exactly as it appears in the *Hearing Report,* no effort has been made to correct typographical and other errors.

22. See Chapter 4 for details concerning these statements, and the Appendix for their complete texts.

23. Not coincidentally, Wald's report of his "interview" with American POWs in Hanoi was the same in form and substance as Fonda's would be several months later. See Chapter 4.

24. The number "8" appears in the *Hearing Report,* although the correct reference is to the "Chicago Seven."

25. *Hearing Report,* at 7688–7694.

26. Collier, *The Fondas,* 220–221.

27. As a result of this meeting, the Viet Cong released three POWs to Hayden in Vietnam. One of those, Dan Pitzer, who had been a captive for five years, said that Hayden "played right into [Hanoi's] hands. Besides, Hayden's visa and passport had been yanked by the U.S. The only way the State Department would let him back in the States without a hassle was with us. *We* were his ticket home—not the other way around" (Andersen, *Citizen Jane,* 270).

28. Hayden had recently been purged from his collective, the Red Family, largely because of accusations of "anti-feminism."

29. Collier, *The Fondas,* 223–24.

30. Andersen, *Citizen Jane,* 251; emphasis added.

31. Collier, *The Fondas,* 219. As recently as early 2001, on Barbara Walters' TV show, Fonda admitted that she had spent her life trying to please men.

Part II

In North
Vietnam

CAPTIVE AUDIENCE:
THE AMERICAN POWs

Ready to die or at least "make them think that I was ready to die" rather than divulge the details of the note-drop scheme, that night Stockdale managed to break a window and with the glass shards chopped his wrists....

By different means—drinking urine, hanging, or chewing the veins of their wrists—the four attempted suicide before [their interrogator] finally relented (Stuart I. Rochester and Fred Kiley, Honor Bound, *488–9)*

By 1962, when Fonda was living the high life in the United States, "more than 10,000 U.S. military personnel were committed to the Vietnam action."[1] By 1964, when Fonda was cavorting with Vadim and assorted others, "U.S. forces would have suffered more than 1,000 casualties," and by the end of that year some three-score Americans would have been captured and/or killed by the Viet Cong in the South.[2] By 1966, when Fonda was being politically seduced by French intellectuals, the North Vietnamese were threatening to try American POWs as "war criminals." By 1968, when Fonda was meeting with American deserters and the Viet Cong in Paris, over 300 fliers were being held in North Vietnamese prisons. By 1970, when Fonda was deep into New Left politics, American prisoners of the Viet Cong had been brutally force-marched from the South all the way to Hanoi. By 1972, when Fonda connected with Hayden, hundreds of American POWs were being held by the North Vietnamese and scores of others by the Viet Cong.

In short, while Fonda was trying to "find herself" by consorting with America's detractors and enemies, Americans were fighting and dying in Vietnam — and becoming prisoners of brutal, often sub-human Asian communists. Unfortunately — or perhaps fortunately — what most Americans know about POW camps that have imprisoned their countrymen comes from Hollywood movies, and then it is usually limited to German POW camps of World War II: guards from Western Europe not unlike the POWs themselves, healthy-looking prisoners, barracks-type shelter, plentiful food, warm clothing —*Hogan's Heroes.*

Putting aside whether or not these depictions have been accurate — Steve McQueen playing with his baseball glove in *The Great Escape*, Frank Sinatra casually scheming to escape in *Von Ryan's Express*, William Holden exuding confidence as he cake-walked through confinement in *Stalag 17*—rarely has Hollywood, even in its superficial way, tried to depict the lot of Americans in Asian captivity. World War II movies like *Bataan, Back to Bataan* and *Corregidor* were mere propaganda which hardly depicted at all the Japanese camps in the Philippines, Japan or Manchuria, let alone revealed their horrors. Postwar films like the glorified *The Bridge on the River Kwai* hinted at the barbarity of the Japanese but did not begin to paint an accurate picture of what it was like for Allied prisoners building the Thailand-Burma railway. The Korean War and its aftermath produced a few pictures such as *Time Limit* and *The Manchurian Candidate* whose sanitized versions of life in Asian POW camps in no way accurately described what it was like for American prisoners of the North Koreans and Chinese. We make this point because in order for Americans today fully to understand the nature and gravity of what Fonda did in Hanoi,[3] her contribution to North Vietnamese propaganda, and the impact she had on the American prisoners held in South and North Vietnam,[4] it is necessary first to understand the state of the audience to whom her broadcasts and other conduct in North Vietnam were directed. *It is necessary to understand — from real-life facts — the inhuman conditions in which the POWs were held, and the barbaric physical and psychological treatment visited upon them by the Viet Cong and the North Vietnamese.*

The problem, however, in understanding, is this: *No matter how eloquent the language, mere words can not adequately convey to civilized readers just how inhumane those conditions were and how barbaric was the physical and psychological treatment.* As Mike McGrath put it in the preface to his book of drawings,

The way we lived in the hell-holes of the Vietnamese prisons is so unimaginable to the average American that words alone are not sufficient to convey the experience. When we returned to the United States, we used the words *shackles, stocks, manacles* and *irons*; yet many Americans could not, or would not, picture what the words meant.... In trying to review my life as a POW, I notice that my drawings are too *soft*; I was unable to portray the actual *hardness* of the conditions we lived under — the dimly lit rooms and claustrophobia-inducing cells; the lack of adequate food which, combined with filth, caused disease and indescribable discomfort. It is difficult to sketch a vitamin and protein deficiency that results in beri-beri; and no picture can convey the impact of constant plagues of lice, heat rash, biting bed bugs, mosquitoes, cockroaches, and rats. Add to this the hostility and brutality of the guards, who had been taught from childhood to hate Americans, and the sum total is an unbelievable existence for hundreds of American fighting men who somehow survived the ordeal.[5]

And that was in the North. We shall soon see what the conditions were in the fetid jungles of the South. Among the captives in the South, the actual death rate was higher in some camps than it was in Hanoi, a number of POWs were executed, and conditions were execrable. Following the Tet Offensive of 1968 and the Cambodian incursion of 1970, scores of POWs were force-marched to Hanoi. Some of them died during those treks.[6]

The POW literature makes a noble and often successful attempt to describe the below-subsistence-level food, the inadequate or non-existent shelter, the less-than-primitive sanitation, the absence of even rudimentary medical care, the near-impossibility of maintaining even a semblance of personal hygiene, and the many other kinds of deprivations the POWs suffered. The literature also succeeds, to a considerable extent, in making real the Communists' psychological warfare techniques, and the captors' cruder use of sadistic torture.[7]

It is this—the state of the POWs whom Fonda and her Communist handlers targeted in South and North—that we will try to convey here, as best we can, given the limitations of language, and the reality of the POWs' situation.

These descriptions cannot do justice to the POW accounts that we are drawing on to convey the situation of those to whom Fonda's broadcasts and other conduct in Hanoi were directed. We can paraphrase, second-hand, but there is no substitute for the eloquence of first-hand POW accounts. Generally speaking, the literature reveals that the experiences of virtually every POW in the South was very much the same as others held there. The same was true in the North. Differences were mostly of degree, not of kind.[8]

Furthermore, although there were similarities between the treatment of POWs in the South and the North, there also were important differences. As Rochester and Kiley summarize in *Honor Bound*, "PWs in South Vietnam had a more precarious experience and usually suffered a worse fate than PWs in North Vietnam, who, although tortured more systematically and more rigidly incarcerated, had food and medical aid more readily available and had important advantages of leadership and organization accruing from a more homogeneous PW population and larger, more concentrated numbers. By the end of 1964, with the guerrilla war intensifying and PW conditions steadily deteriorating in the South, one out of every three Americans taken prisoner by the Viet Cong could expect to die in captivity, a percentage that, with fluctuations, would persist through the decade."[9]

As one survivor of four jungle camps in the South and then incarceration in the North put it,

Life in the south, for those blessed enough to make it out, was a nightmare of hellish proportions that transformed civilized human beings into primal animals struggling to cling to some fleeting sense of what it means to be alive, and why. In some, that tiny ember of hope finally flickered out. At best, it was a half-life because of the traumatic and debilitating experience of having survived the malnutrition, disease, and near insanity that had ultimately killed so many of our fellow prisoners who never lived to make it north, much less make it home as we did.[10]

There was another important difference between captivity in the South and North. As Rochester and Kiley have reported, "[y]et, even as [the ranks of prisoners in the South] swelled [after Tet, in early 1968], the 'Southern' PW's treatment and circumstances did not measurably change. If the story of the prisoners in the North featured slammers, torture, and heroic resistance, the Southern ordeal continued to

be dominated by forced marches, casual brutality, and extreme neglect and deprivation."[11] On the other hand, a 1967 shootdown has said about captivity in the North:

> We went through hell up to September 1969. Ho Chi [Minh] died that month. About a
> month after that, the [North Vietnamese] came around with big smiles. They took off the
> leg irons, manacles, etc. They unblocked the vents and let fresh air in the rooms. They
> medicated our boils and heat rash from the stifling heat. They gave us extra water and a
> pair of socks (first time). We immediately quit bowing[12] … they yelled at us, but did not
> hit us. Prior to this, they would beat a man unmercifully if he refused to bow. In short, the
> prison policy had changed … and it changed in all prisons [in the North], not just with
> one local camp commander. They never tortured (with a few exceptions) as a policy from
> October 1969 until our release in Feb-March 1973.[13]

Thus, while the treatment of American prisoners in the North had improved for
some two years before Fonda's July 1972 pilgrimage to Hanoi, still, when Fonda arrived there were hundreds of POWs in the North who had earlier suffered through
years of abuse[14]; in the South, the abuse was unremitting.[15]

The following, then, by category, are descriptions, and some first-hand testimony,
of what befell many American prisoners of the Viet Cong and the North Vietnamese.
Many of these prisoners had been captives for years before conditions "improved" in
the North, and they and their brethren in the South *were a susceptible captive audience — literally — for Jane Fonda's pro–Communist, anti–America propaganda broadcasts and her other conduct in Hanoi, North Vietnam, in July 1972.*

But before we begin reciting the grim facts of POW existence, which are merely
representative but not exhaustive, we must repeat: The reality for the POWs was necessarily far worse in nature and degree than anything our words can even begin to
convey.[16]

Treatment Upon Capture

Usually, at the point of capture, prisoners were blindfolded, trussed, stripped and
searched.[17] Their equipment and personal belongings were taken, and, more often
than not, they were deprived of their boots. Sometimes they were given Vietnamese
sandals.[18] Most of the time, treatment was extremely brutal. One POW in the South
was tied behind a water buffalo that was then driven through sharp bush, lacerating
much of the prisoner's skin. The same man had an ant nest impaled on his head.
Fighter pilots who had sustained injuries from ejection, often exacerbated from their
parachute landings, had their wounds and broken bones negligently — even sadisti-
cally — worsened by their captors, civilian and military alike.[19] "They tied me with
commo wire, my hands bound behind my back to my feet. Then they tied some wire
around my neck and started dragging. I said my last prayers. Blood spurted from my
mouth; I was strangling to death."[20]

"They kicked me back up to my feet and marched me up and down some steep,
muddy slopes. I fell to the ground and motioned that my wrists were badly cut from

the wet ropes. That was a mistake, because [one of the guards] had them pull the binders tighter! ... They prodded me along until we came to another fast stream. 'This has got to be it, I can't make it across another one. I guess drowning is the way I'm going out,' I thought. ... Curiously, laboriously, I inched my way over slippery boulders toward the far side. It seemed a miracle that I had made it again, as I scrambled up the bank on the other side. I was reaching the end of my strength and endurance. Continuing along, I came to a very steep slope covered with slick, yellowish mud. I tried to climb it, but it was a disaster. I slipped, rolled, and tumbled in the yellow-orange slime. They forced me to rise again and again and continue the climb."[21]

En Route to Incarceration

Threats and interrogation began almost immediately. Since virtually all prisoners in the South had their boots taken from them immediately upon capture,[22] they were obliged to march barefoot to places of internment through the inhospitable jungle. Indeed, some of those who survived captivity in the South went shoeless for as much as five years, or even more, their feet sometimes becoming unrecognizable. On forced marches, they stumbled barefoot, or in Vietnamese sandals, across rivers and swamps, through mud and paddies, over rocks and fragile bridges. POWs were exhibited to angry villagers, usually humiliated and often beaten.[23] They were spat upon. Rocks were thrown at them. Beatings by guards on the line of march were routine. "The soldiers ... took turns to see who could hit my face the hardest. After the contest, they tried to force dog dung through my teeth, bounced rocks off my chest, jabbed me with their gun barrels, and bounced the back of my head off the rocks that lay at the bottom of the ditch. I said my final prayers that night, because I was sure I would not reach Hanoi alive."[24]

As the forced marches pushed further away from the point of capture and deeper into the jungles of the South, the POWs were deprived of any meaningful food, rest, sleep and shelter. At night, they were tied or chained to immovable objects. We were "tied with commo wire in the most painful way imaginable. My forearms were held parallel to the ground while elbows were pressed to my sides and drawn to the rear. The wire was then wound tightly around biceps and elbows, duck-wing fashion and continued behind me to tie Williams and, in turn, Cannon and Strickland. Anyone who failed to maintain the pace would torture the others by pulling the wire tighter. ...The trail was muddy and slippery. ...I was groaning from the most intense pain of my life. I didn't think I could go much farther. I wanted to stop and let them shoot me. I lost all desire to live."[25]

Unlike in the South, often after a trek through remote villages of the North, airmen captives were thrown into vehicles for the trip to Hanoi.[26] "Back in the jeep I realized that I was no longer tied, but I still couldn't move my paralyzed arms. ...A guard got in on either side of me, and on the all-night ride the one on my right beat my ribs

continually with his fists. ...Early in the morning we stopped, and I was blindfolded
and left in the truck for a few minutes. One of the soldiers came back and completely
enshrouded me in a blanket.... Soon I was gasping and struggling for every breath.
I began to pray for help, but I didn't think that the Vietnamese knew that I was going
down for the count. I wasn't sure that they gave a damn either."[27]

Food

Food in the South was often in short supply even for the Viet Cong themselves,
who were fighting a moving guerrilla war and thus usually not near supply bases. The
VC scavenged as they went along; most of the food that they had stored in places like
caves had become spoiled and inedible. POWs in the South supplemented their diet —
rice, often uncooked and contaminated with rodent feces—with rats, eels, snakes,
lizards and any other living creature that they could get their hands on, including
camp mascots such as dogs and cats, and the occasional chicken or ferret. There was
little or no protein in the prisoners' diet. Being fed pig fat was cause for celebration.
Once, when guards slaughtered a sow, "[t]he prisoners' portion was, predictably, the
head. We ate every morsel of meat we could scrape from her skull."[28] What food
there was often came crawling with maggots. Malnutrition was the norm, often actual starvation. Most POWs in the South existed at marginal subsistence for years.
"The pittance [of rice] that the guards poured out from a dirty metal container each
day for the prisoners was infested with bugs and rat feces. As our hunger began to
blunt our strength and our senses, we soon neglected the simple routine of sifting the
disease-bearing filth from the rice."[29]

The food situation in the North was not much better. The first airman captured was
fed food that "was sickening — animal hooves, chicken heads, slimy bits of vegetables, cold
and rotten fish, unidentifiable chunks of meat covered with hair. In a few weeks, vomiting constantly and suffering from bloody diarrhea, he lost almost forty pounds."[30] As the
American flier recounted it: "Sometimes I lifted the cover off a plate and found a chicken
head floating in grease, or in a slimy stew or soup smelling of drainwater. At other times
an animal hoof, perhaps of a cow or pig, with the hair still attached, came mixed with
pieces of carrots or turnips. Six-inch prawns, complete with eyes, were served floating in
a dirty, brackish liquid. More than once a blackbird lay feet up on the plate, its head and
feathers intact and the eyes open. I dug through the feathers and pulled the skin apart to
pry off the small portions of meat. Often this meant chewing the meat off the attached
skin. Then I'd take the few chunks of dry bread and soak up the greasy liquid. My insides
churned and my body shook. This was always the prelude to fits of vomiting. Sometimes
it happened so quickly that I heaved all over the plate. But extreme hunger led me to try
again and I often ate the serving, splattered with my own vomit, to satisfy the craving
for any kind of sustenance."[31]

Later, the food "improved": watery soup, fish heads, wormy bread. Usually rice.

At one time, POWs at an installation in Hanoi only had watery soup to eat for six months, and what they thought was rye bread was actually bread with vermin crawling in it. The POWs often thought they were eating one thing, but actually were eating another because of the darkened condition of their cells. Light bulbs were usually turned off during the day while vents and windows were sealed shut in an effort to prevent communication among the POWs. So they often could not see what they were eating.

"Just as routine were the bugs and insects we ingested with the rice and water. The last meal of the day frequently came when it was already dark, particularly in the winter, and while we ate we would hear the telltale crunch as our teeth bit through the hard outer coverings of live roaches. Sometimes a guard close by would respond to our cussing and shine a light in our direction. That was when we got close-up looks of the insect-infected rice and the live bugs struggling to crawl out of the cups of water."[32] Water often looked and smelled like sewage, and sometimes was. As Denton reported, "When a member of a North Vietnamese political delegation visited Denton and referring to the fertilizer floating in his soup bowl, remarked contemptuously to the American, 'Do you know that you are eating shit?,' Denton retorted that he hoped there was 'some protein in it.'"[33]

As horrendous as the food was, there was never enough of it. "But despite the filth, as soon as the guards turned away or left [the area where dishes were washed], I'd pick up the scraps and devour them. There were times when I found banana peels that had turned black. They would be thrown in a corner, where I knew rats had nosed over them. If the guard wasn't looking, I would put them under my shirt, take them back to my room and eat them."[34]

"I lost fifty pounds in the first three months of my captivity. Many others lost considerably more. It was not unusual for a man who was over six feet tall to weigh as little as 120 pounds."[35]

Sanitation

In the South, latrines consisted of holes in the ground. Dried banana leaves served as paper. Caged prisoners sometimes had cans to defecate in; sometimes not. Chronic diarrhea and dysentery caused most prisoners to defecate scores of times each day. Rats and rat feces were everywhere.[36] If cooking implements weren't washed, insects and rodents would finish what was left, and if rice wasn't washed before cooking much of it consisted of rat feces.

In the South, "[d]uring the rainy season, downpours continued for weeks on end, leaving the camp a slimy wallow of mud mixed with human excrement left where the dysentery-stricken men stood because they could not reach the latrine pit in time. For the first several months, even during the dry season, we had to walk barefoot through that stinking filth because the guards refused to allow us any sandals."[37]

Even though in the North prisoners were housed in actual buildings, open cesspools and pigpens stood just outside cells. Sewers ran into drinking wells. Rain brought dirty water flooding into some cells, bringing dead vermin with it. The metal dishes prisoners ate on were licked clean during the night by rodents. Defecation was into buckets, carried from the cells to be dumped outside, or into holes in the ground. Mostly, the buckets were too small, regularly overflowing. In McGrath's words, "The turnkey would open our door at seven o'clock every morning. He would then quickly step back as the penetrating stench from nine sweating bodies rushed out the door. With all the windows bricked up or blocked off, the smell became almost unbearable. The first man out would pick up the reeking slop buckets, almost always filled to the brim. The rest of us would stagger out, thankful for a breath of fresh air."[38] Alvarez recalled, "The stench was with us all the time. We had long since accepted as normal having to sit a few feet away from each other when one of us had a bowel movement, which was often because we always seemed to come down with diarrhea. There was never enough water to wash the odor off our hands. And though we took daily turns dumping the bucket and swishing the inside with sticks and straw brushes at the well near the bottom of a hill, they never supplied us with any disinfectant. As the tin buckets were not replaced, they developed a hard coating of crap that no amount of cleaning could remove. Though it was the source of the interminable smell, we had to live with the bucket in our sealed quarters day in and day out. The odor was just as bad immediately outside our doors because, cows, pigs and chickens drank from the concrete vats and rats frequently drowned and floated in the slimy water where we shaved and washed out cups and plates."[39]

Medical Care

In the jungle, scurvy, jaundice, dysentery, malaria, fungus infections, bleeding gums and edema were rampant, with virtually no medication to deal with them. Cerebral malaria would cause convulsions and death. Pneumonia was not uncommon. Beriberi, caused by inadequate vitamin B-1, made POWs' limbs, stomachs and other body parts swell to hideous sizes because of water build-up. One POW's stomach looked as though he'd swallowed a basketball. Another's testicles were the size of baseballs. In the jungles, wounds and broken bones—incurred in combat, from capture, or as the result of torture — more often than not went untreated. There was no way to treat gangrenous wounds. Maggoty wounds were either untreated, or dealt with insufficiently. For invasive medical procedures in the South, like removing shrapnel, there was usually no anesthesia available. In the South, "medical care was no better than the French had experienced under the Viet Minh, and those PWs who died in captivity likely perished as often from neglect as from willful mistreatment or execution. ...[A]s Viet Cong attitudes hardened and medical supplies became scarcer, injuries and illness would increasingly go untreated. The VC would later refuse the

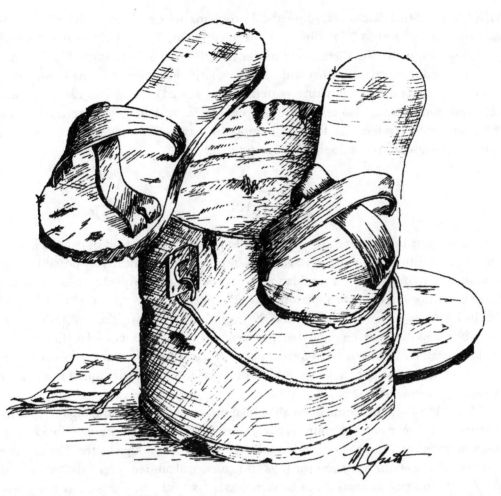

"Slop bucket used for toilet facilities. Because the top edge was often jagged and rusted, the prisoners would use their slippers — made of rubber tires — as a makeshift seat." (Drawing by John M. McGrath, *Prisoner of War: Six Years in Hanoi*.)

repeated pleas of captured Army doctor Floyd Kushner, the only physician among the American prisoners in Southeast Asia, to administer aid to wounded and sick comrades."[40] Indeed, Dr. Kushner has stated that one Private, one Private First Class, two Lance Corporals and four Sergeants "died in my arms."[41]

Generally, Vietnamese physicians were poorly trained, making whatever treatment they provided POWs problematic. Often, wounded prisoners received no care at all, lying in their own urine and feces. John McCain, whose ejection and fall into North Vietnam and subsequent capture caused massive injuries, "was not washed once in six weeks and endured an agonizing two hours writhing on a crude bed while a doctor tried to set the bones in his right arm without the use of an anesthetic. Finally, the attendant settled for wrapping him in a body cast."[42] McGrath said that in Hanoi, "I begged the Vietnamese to set my broken arm and relocate my dislocated shoulder. My requests were ignored. ...I thought the pain would drive me insane."[43]

Why? As Jim Stockdale was told, medical problems are cared for "only after political problems are solved."[44] Robbie Risner remembered, "I was lying on my stomach groaning with pain. The Vietnamese officer told the doctor he thought I had kidney stones. The doctor raised his fist and hit me a sharp blow right over the kidney. The last thing I remembered was pain so intense that I passed out. When I came to, I was vomiting and choking. No one would help me from the truck. They refused to use the stretcher to carry me in. I began inching my way out. On my hands, knees and stomach, I crawled to the door of the hospital."[45]

Hygiene

Sanitation and hygiene are related. To the extent that instead of proper sanitation there is filth, excrement, sewage, rats and the like, it is nearly impossible for a prisoner to maintain even a semblance of proper personal hygiene. Because of the harsh conditions in the South, prisoners were often covered with lice, skin boils and flea infestations, and they experienced the nightmare of having their wounds being eaten by maggots. Dysentery and diarrhea were rampant, prisoners defecating dozens of times each day, those unable to make it to the primitive latrines routinely defecating in their pants. At best, they could wash themselves and their clothes in a nearby stream — if there was one.

Most POWs, South and North alike, had not used hot water during their entire captivity — in some cases as many as five or more years. "You were given only a minimum amount of time to wash, and usually there was not enough water. The garbage was kept in the washrooms and the pigs and chickens had free run of the garbage. If a man was too sick or weak from broken bones, as I was, he simply did not get to wash his body or his clothes until he was strong enough to make it to the washroom under his own power. Some men were placed in irons and left to live in these open washrooms as a form of punishment. They had neither mosquito nets nor protection from the elements."[46] POWs restrained in leg stocks — not an uncommon fate in both the jungles of the South and the prisons of the North — faced a Hobson's choice of unremitting pain from the unrelieved bodily need to evacuate waste, or releasing their urine and stool (often constantly diarrheic) where they would lie for hours or sometimes weeks. As bad as this was for men confined by themselves, often POWs were held in stocks next to each other, compounding the debilitating experience.

In the South, "[t]he epidermis cracked open with water-blister-type sores that first ran clear serum and then pus. Scratching was almost sexual in its relief but only made the disease worse. The pus dried, gluing our pajamas to our backsides. The pain was horrible. Eighteen of us were jammed together on the bed. It was excruciatingly hot. But we had to sleep under our blankets to ward off hordes of mosquitoes. Men cried out at night, 'Kill me! I want to die!' ...The disease was combined with our growing dysentery and malaria. The hooch smelled like a septic tank. It was best not to get up at night unless absolutely necessary. Probably you would step in excrement while walking down the aisleway."[47]

While the living conditions in the prisons of the North were not nearly as primitive as in the jungle camps of the South, they were no picnic. Indeed, the deterioration in personal hygiene was a direct result of the primitive sanitation situation in the Northern prisons described above. For example, soon after the war heated up, toward early 1966, POWs could wash, at best, every couple of weeks—sometimes only every few months. McGrath again: "After about a month, I was able to sit up to urinate into a rusted-out bucket. I had a high fever and dysentery. Boils and infections covered my body."[48] Alvarez: "I was sick with diarrhea and dysentery, passing blood in my vomit and stool for the first six weeks [of my captivity]. One day as I squatted in the unfamiliar position in the latrine, the crap splashed all over my feet. From then on I took to using the jagged-edged bucket in the corner of my room. Even though I swilled it daily in the vat outside, the stench lingered pervasively in my cell and on myself."[49]

Confinement

In both the South and the North, the POWs were *de facto* confined less by the physical structures in which they were held than by the locations of their imprisonment. In the South, physical places of confinement ran the gamut: sheds; huts; caves; holes; bamboo huts with thatch roofs; bamboo cages too small for a POW to stand or lie down; larger bamboo cages in which a prisoner could sit up and lie in, but not stand; sometimes, "adequately" sized bamboo cages. But the real confinement in the camps of the South came from where they were situated: surrounded by dense impenetrable jungle, amidst hostile native populations (like the Montagnards). Escape was theoretically possible, and some made it. However, most American prisoners were held captive by their environment. Even if normal security mechanisms—chains, guards, dogs, booby traps—could be surmounted, "the would-be escapee still had to navigate dense jungle without a compass or provisions, typically minus shoes, and in a debilitated state. 'You can walk out of the camp,' 1968 escapee James Rowe later contended. 'But they don't really worry about you getting away. They found that everybody that tried ... either blundered into more troops, ran into another camp, or become [*sic*] disoriented.' Proceeding overland through thick brush during the rainy season, Rowe said, 'you leave a path that looks like Fifth Avenue....' [The Mekong Delta] 'is probably the most hostile natural environment that an American could face.'"[50]

Much the same was true in the North. Although Hanoi's Hoa Lo prison was in the traditional mold of colonial lock-ups, with high, thick, concrete walls topped with glass shards, guard towers and barbed wire, it was virtually in downtown Hanoi, the capital of North Vietnam. Other prison facilities in and around Hanoi were much the same.[51] It is not surprising that even though a few POWs managed to extricate themselves from prisons in Hanoi, none got very far. Rochester and Kiley quote Red McDaniel as follows:

Even if we did make it out of the compound, the people in Hanoi were dedicated to tracking down any foreigners and were promised $1,500 by the government for every American flyer they caught. It would be tough trying to get through that kind of "police force." What's more, the average North Vietnamese is about five feet two inches tall, with black hair, yellow-skinned, slant-eyed. How would I, at six feet three inches, now about 160 pounds, with red hair, fair-skinned, and round-eyed, fit into that population if I tried to use its traffic patterns to get to the sea?

And there was another problem, that of environment — the miles of jungle, the thick, cruel bush that a man would have to negotiate to get out. To illustrate the nature of the land we were living in, [one of our guys] killed a poisonous snake in our room one night, and in the morning when we emptied our toilet bowls, we hung it up on the fence. We watched that snake periodically through the door peephole, and in three hours it had been completely devoured by insects. Nothing was left of it — nothing. We knew the same thing could happen to us if we tried to make it 110 miles to the sea.[52]

McGrath was correct when he observed, "Few people can comprehend what it is like to be in solitary confinement for months or years at a time. Each minute of the day painfully drags by as you try to make your mind think of something new. A few men were in solitary for as many as four years! One of our senior officers … was in solitary confinement for 58 months. Most men were confined for a number of months, usually immediately following capture."[53] Even worse than solitary was solitary in the dark: "The Vietnamese boarded his windows and left his cell darkened for 10 months. Experiencing panic attacks and fits of crying and screaming that he attempted to keep from the guards by burying his face in a blanket to muffle the sounds, by the time he [was moved] he was 'like a man hanging on to a cliff by his fingernails.'"[54] Another POW, "[f]or seven weeks … battled rats, roaches, and an existential loneliness in complete darkness, his 'black bubble' finally pierced by the tapping of [another POW] who 'soothed' him back to sanity with news and 'time hacks' on the hour, as he had lost track of day and night."[55]

Cold and sweltering heat were constant companions. "With the onset of winter … insulation became as worrisome a concern as ventilation. Their earthen bunkers had tin roofs that afforded little protection from the raw chill. 'We were cold and hungry all the time,' [a POW] wrote, the emaciated bodies battered by the freezing temperatures…. 'The drizzle and chill were constant, and sometimes a storm would fill the cement gutter and cold, dirty water would flood into the cells,' carrying all manner of dead vermin…. By late spring unrelenting sun and humidity once again converted the unventilated cells to 'steam closets.' …[One POW] remarked, 'The tin roofs overhead served as solar conductors and radiated heat that broiled us in our cells…. Suffocation seemed a very real possibility.' [Another POW] added, 'We crept to our cell doors and sucked like animals for air….'"[56]

Hazards

While in view of the too-real, life-threatening dangers that American prisoners faced in their Southern and Northern captivity, it may seem odd to speak of "hazards." Still, they existed, and in their own way they were sometimes equally dangerous to the safety and lives of the POWs.

For example, even if the Viet Cong in the South wished to treat its American POWs in a more-or-less civilized manner (for indoctrination, propaganda or other reasons), still, the VC's constant movement while fighting a guerrilla war and the normal perils of the jungle itself made for a dangerous situation. Even worse than the disease, the heavy rains, the jungle rot, the lack of food, the undrinkable water, the indigenous insects and animals, the drastic swings in temperature and the lack of sunlight through the rain forest canopy was the omnipresent danger of death or maiming from American military action itself: the horrendous B-52 bombing, strafing by our own helicopter gunships, friendly artillery fire. "The B-52 attacks had begun to escalate in early 1971, and howitzers were pouring shells into the hills not far from us. A few rounds came close enough to send hot, jagged shrapnel screaming over our heads and shearing off limbs of trees nearby."[57]

Although the hazards were different in the North, they still existed: "accidental" maiming or death from beatings; succumbing to disease from malnutrition and infection; going insane from debilitation, boredom, solitary confinement, beatings, torture. And, as in the South, being annihilated by one's own bombing—not that some of the prisoners didn't welcome the B-52s: "Just after dark the air-raid sirens went off.... Then came the bombs, and by the long volley of explosives, we knew immediately that the birds were B-52s. ... The sky lit up, and we all jumped up onto the pad to look out.... The [B-52s] came in several times that night, and when the bombs impacted nearby, we hugged the walls in case the jail was hit. ... God, we were excited! ... laughing, crying, yelling, 'Hit the bastards, Dick [Nixon]! Give 'em hell!'"[58] Nevertheless, the B-52 raids over Hanoi put the POWs there in significant danger.[59]

Indoctrination and Propaganda

The French experience at the hands of the Viet Minh and the treatment of American POWs in Korea — where prisoners were most useful for purposes of indoctrination and propaganda — was repeated with American POWs in Vietnam, with, as we shall see in the next two chapters, the Communists using Jane Fonda and others to further their ideological goals. Accounts from both the jungle camps of the South and the walled prisons of the North are consistent in their description of endless lectures, self-criticism sessions, group discussions, writing of personal histories and anti-war sentiments, teaching of Vietnamese history, and the like. The goal was to obtain pro–Communist, anti–South Vietnamese, anti–American, anti–war statements that could be used in the North Vietnamese worldwide propaganda campaign.

Even primitive jungle villages had large multi-kilowatt speakers incessantly blaring out propaganda. It was no different in the prisons of the North.

Day after day, with up to five hours of programming daily, the green boxes poured out a stream of Voice of Vietnam radio broadcasts, propaganda pronouncements delivered by impassioned Vietnamese or disaffected Americans, and distortions of the news or personal apologies read by the prisoners themselves under pressure. ...Taped appeals from prominent American peace advocates, many of them visitors to North Vietnam — personalities such as Jane Fonda, Joan Baez, Stokely Carmichael, and Ramsey Clark — at once incensed and demoralized the prisoners.[60]

Psychological Warfare

The purpose of Communist psychological warfare operations against American prisoners in Vietnam was to soften them up in order to create collaborators, and to obtain from those collaborators and from recalcitrant POWs, pro–Communist, anti–American, propaganda statements, in writing and on tape, for use in the North Vietnamese's international propaganda war. American prisoners were called "criminals" and "air pirates." They were told that the Geneva Convention did not apply to them because they weren't prisoners of war — and, as such, they could be summarily shot. In 1966, the Communists threatened to hold "war crimes" trials. Taking a page from tactics the Chinese had used on American POWs in Korea, Communist captors in Laos, South Vietnam and North Vietnam would try to crush a prisoner's resistance by hinting, or actually saying, that he would soon be released, but not releasing him, then again suggesting release, then again reneging — the process repeated over and over. As in the South, the North Vietnamese played this "early release" game, implying (sometimes saying) that "progressive" prisoners might be released early. Only a few were.[61]

Solitary confinement was a powerful weapon: A Special Forces captain, captured in 1964, had contact with another American military POW only once in nearly nine years. Even in the North, where eventually there were hundreds of POWs, total isolation from other prisoners was an oft-used tactic to break men psychologically. One Air Force colonel, for example, spent over three years in solitary. Some prisoners were isolated for five or more years.

Threats of execution were common, sometimes being carried to the point where a firing squad would pull triggers on empty chambers. Mail — sending and receiving it — was used as a weapon. Prisoners were allowed to know that they had received mail and parcels, which were then looted by the guards or withheld entirely in order to bring additional pressures on the captives. The quantity and quality of food was routinely manipulated in order to encourage or discourage prisoners. So, too, with soap, the occasional toothbrush and toothpaste, and everything else that the prisoners craved, as well—even paper, desperately needed after frequent defecation.

"Privileges—sunlit cells, outdoor exercise, opportunities for bathing—were alternately bestowed and rescinded in a usually fruitless but nonetheless unsettling effort to regulate prisoner behavior. ...Even in such mundane matters as dress, the Vietnamese may have employed subtle methods to demean or demoralize the Americans: sometime in late 1966 a uniform with broad red or plum and gray vertical stripes became the standard prison issue, an outfit so clumsy and degrading that [one PW] referred to it as 'the clown suit.'"[62]

Restraint

Leg stocks were a favorite method of restraining POWs. In the South, they were often crudely hand-made, too small to accommodate the ankles they secured. So ankles would bleed, become infected and then swell, their unnaturally enlarged size making the already unbearable pain now excruciating. "Most onerous were the heavy U-shaped irons shackled to their ankles and worn 15 or more hours a day except at Tet and Christmas. Weighing 10 to 20 pounds and connected by a sliding bar, the restraints were a major impediment to sleeping and even the most perfunctory moving about."[63]

Chaining POWs, especially in the South, was common. One POW was fitted with an iron collar around his neck. A failed escape attempt in the South brought one prisoner three months in stocks. Manacles, used frequently, inflicted excruciating pain, causing wrists to become cut and infected: "They locked our ankles into leg irons ... and handcuffed our hands behind our backs.... For a solid week we could neither roll over on our bellies because our feet were locked in position, nor lie down on our backs for fear of tightening the handcuffs. The answer was to turn our torsos slightly to try and rest on our sides. But there was no solution to the greater problem of Tom's diarrhea. By sitting up and painstakingly working the bowl upwards, I tried to edge it closer to him. [But] ... unable to contain himself, he had to let the excrement splash out. Unable to wipe himself because his arms were handcuffed, Tom lay covered in his own filth."[64]

Torture

Despite the "public relations" risk attendant on torturing prisoners, *the primary purpose for torturing them, especially in the North, was to obtain written and taped statements for use in the Communist's crucially important international propaganda war against the United States*—a war, as we shall see in the next two chapters, that Jane Fonda helped the North Vietnamese wage.

After repatriation in 1973, it was estimated that nearly every American POW in North Vietnam experienced some kind of torture, usually to extort propaganda. Alvarez recalled:

They herded me into the notorious Blue Room and locked the door. In this small enclosure of blue-painted walls, the feeble bodies of American pilots confronted the simple instruments of betrayal: the stick pen, the bottle of ink, the blank paper — all placed neatly on the plain wooden table. Here was where principles and valor buckled under to limitless physical strain. Here was where honor was measured by days of endurance.[65]

"The techniques varied from use of the ropes[66] to cuffs of a ratchet type that could be tightened until they penetrated the flesh, sometimes down to the bone; aggravation of injuries received at ejection or upon landing,

Wrist and leg shackles. (Drawn by John M. McGrath, *Prisoner of War: Six Years in Hanoi.*)

such as twisting a broken leg; forcing a man to sit or kneel for long periods of time without food or sleep; beatings with fanbelt-like whips and rifle butts; the application of an assortment of straps, bars, and chains to body pressure points; and prolonged solitary confinement, often while in darkened quarters and/or in leg irons and manacles. Just as ... the prison waste buckets, designed for Orientals, were too small for the American anatomy, so, too, were ankle stocks and wrist cuffs undersized — making even simple shackling painful and torture that much more excruciating."[67]

As we suggested earlier in this chapter, these words by Rochester and Kiley — illustrative of the torture techniques — do not begin to describe the reality of what American prisoners of the Communists had to bear. "The atrocities committed by the North Vietnamese are too numerous to depict in [McGrath's book of drawings, *Prisoner of War*]. There are reports of men who were burned with cigarettes. At least one man had bamboo slivers pushed into his finger. Some men reported that they underwent electrical shock torture. ...One of my friends told of being forced to walk on his knees through broken glass."[68]

The POW memoirs contain horrendous descriptions of what they had to endure. A civilian prisoner in Laos was buried alive, up to his head. For a week he remained there, numb and without food, with insects crawling over the only part of his body that was exposed. When his captors dug him out, for a while he was virtually paralyzed.

Another memoir reports a tale of horror in the North: "They stripped me of my clothes and began to beat me with a whip made from an auto fan belt fastened to an eighteen-inch piece of bamboo. I squirmed as they beat me. They tied my elbows behind my back and then my wrists and feet. I was still able to squirm around. This time they put me face down on the floor, placed an iron bar across my neck, and a guard stood on either side of the bar. They beat me on my buttocks and legs. They were careful not to hit me where scars might show. The lashes drew large blood blisters. The beating lasted until 4:00 P.M. on the first day. I was urinating, defecating blood, and throwing up on the floor. They stopped and made me kneel for the next eighteen hours. Two guards and an officer were left in the room with me. I was slapped or kicked awake when I dozed off. I was beaten for the next five days, given nothing to eat or drink and not allowed to sleep."[69]

Perhaps the worst torture the North Vietnamese inflicted was "the ropes":

Let me try to tell you what it really feels like [wrote Larry Guarino] when they tightly bind your wrists and elbows behind your back with nylon straps — then take the strap and pull the arms up, up your back, to the back of your head. ...Well, imagine this with both arms tied tight together — elbow to elbow, wrist to wrist — and then, using the leverage of his feet planted between your shoulder blades, with both hands, he pulls with all his might, 'til your arms are up and back over your head down between your feet, where your legs are between iron bars. The pain is literally beyond description....

Besides the pain itself, you are tied up so tight that your windpipe becomes pinched and you breathe in gasps. You're trying to gulp in air, because your wind passage is being shrunken. Your throat, in a matter of 30 seconds, becomes completely dry....

"The ropes" torture. (Drawing by John M. McGrath, *Prisoner of War: Six Years in Hanoi.*)

After about 10 or 15 minutes in this position, tied up so tightly, your nerves in your arms are pinched off, and then your whole upper torso becomes numb. It's a relief. You feel no more pain.... The breathing is still difficult, but the pain is gone. You've been anesthetized. However, when they release the ropes, the procedure works *completely* in reverse. It's almost like double jeopardy. You go through the same pain coming off the ropes as you did going in.[70]

As Rochester and Kiley have noted, "the ropes" were not the only torture device used by the Communists in North Vietnam. Guarino again:

I continued to kneel from seven that morning until just after noon, when a goon squad came in. One of them pulled my pants down, then kicked me over on my belly. They spread-eagled me and tied my arms and legs with ropes. A couple of people stood on my hands, and someone beat me with a fan belt. ...Then back on my knees I went. I tried to rest by falling down now and then, but the guard would force me back up at bayonet point. ...They added a blindfold. ...The goon squad returned and repeated the fan-belt beating, each time increasing the number of strokes. Between the interrogations and the beatings, I had to stay on my knees, until about six in the evening. Then they sat me on the wooden stool and harassed me all night long, refusing to let me shut my eyes. My legs and feet began to swell due to restriction of circulation from the [leg] irons. Three mornings later, I was getting nutsy because I had been awake seventy-two hours. ...I was on my knees from six A.M. until six P.M. Sometimes I was reaching for the sky, other times it was hands tied, or thumbs wired behind me. Most of the time I was blindfolded, and always in the leg irons. ...I don't ever remember having to go to the toilet at all. ...All night long they kept me awake, sitting up on the little stool. ...The goon squad came and beat me again. This was my fourth or fifth beating with the fan belts. The first few times I was hit I cried out, because the sensation was so unusual and so horribly painful. There is a severe burning feeling when you are hit, and it feels like your buttocks have been set on fire. I tried not to scream... . [The guard] put the bottom rung of the stool across my neck and pinned me down, while the others stretched me out with the ropes... . I never remembered any more than ten to fifteen strokes before I passed out.[71]

Here is another description:

I still marvel at their ability to torture, without conscience or remorse, an injured man almost to the point of death. I had a severed humeral head ... and the humeral head of the left arm was severely dislocated and shoved next to the ribs and scapula. My knee was dislocated. I had compression fractures in at least two areas of my back. The back fractures left me powerless to move my head or hold my head up when they sat me up. My chin hung down on my chest. The pain in my left arm was agonizing. Yet they brutally tortured me for three days by twisting my good arm behind my back until my right shoulder and right elbow were dislocated. I tried to scream, but they had stuffed dirty rags between my teeth and into the back of my throat. I gagged and snorted and blew snot from my nostrils in a desperate attempt to get enough air to breathe and stay alive. The flames of pain in my brain from the injuries in both arms is just a distant memory now, but it surely hurt then. After the three day intense hourly sessions, they left me lying on the floor for the next 12 days to see if I lived or died. I couldn't sleep as every time I passed out from exhaustion, my broken left arm slipped from the grip of my right hand ... and I would begin screaming in pain. I had to stabilize the left arm at all costs. I couldn't lay it down in any position, even on my chest. I had to hold it and stabilize it at all times. By the end of that 15 days with no sleep I was stark raving mad and in delirium. I couldn't remember days or sometime distinguish days from nights...so I made a mark on the wall each sunrise. My calendar worked well as my days matched the date when I later made contact with other prisoners. I had to stabilize my arm for the next several months.... Luckily I found a nail in a wall and tied my wrist in an upright position to the nail. This allowed me to fall into deep sleeps while in a delirious state. Then the dysentery started ... shitting 40 times a day, living in my own filth. Well, you get the idea. They were bastards. Some of us were lucky to live. Others died.[72]

McGrath reports similar barbarity: "The unbearable pain of torture invariably brought screams from the prisoners. To prevent the screams, the Vietnamese guards would stuff dirty rags into your mouth with a rusty iron bar that would chip the teeth and tear the skin off the roof of the mouth. If you resisted by gritting your teeth, the guard would continue to shove until your teeth broke or you opened your mouth."[73]

And, finally, this is what was done to Bud Day, an American airman who would later be awarded the Medal of Honor and who after General Douglas MacArthur, became the most decorated military man in our nation's history:

[The interrogator] tore my towel in half lengthwise. When he couldn't stuff half of it into my mouth, he tore it again. He jammed about a quarter of it in and then wrapped my face tightly with the rest of it.

The guard produced a set of traveling leg irons about four feet long and roughly forced the "U" bolts above my ankles, slipping the bar through the ends, behind my ankles. He padlocked them and ordered me to drop my pants.

Producing a set of figure-eight screw down manacles, he screwed them tightly on my wrists, forcing my poorly-healed arms together at an impossible angle. The manacles began to cut and gouge my wrists immediately, causing scabs that remained for several years. My hands began to swell and throb.

While standing with my buttocks bared, my trousers around my ankles, the guard told me to lie on the floor, face down. Two guards were in the room standing against the opposite wall, each holding a thirty-inch length of fan belt in his hand. The belt was knotted so it would not slip from the hand of the beater. [The interrogator] gave the order to begin the beating.

The entire scene was so bizarre, so totally out of the days of Mongol Hordes, that it boggled my mind. Springing off the opposite wall in succession, the guards charged at me, screaming like banshees, whips raised high above their heads. Carried by momentum, they would smash the whip across my buttocks, lower back, or upper legs. Cutting, searing, tearing, dehumanizing pain racked my body and assailed my mind with a series of shrieking tormented pleas for relief.

Again I shook my head.

[The interrogator] told the beaters to go ahead. The whips cut, seared, gouged, and burned the bleeding, swelling flesh on my buttocks. A trickle of blood coursed its way down from buttocks to legs and dripped on the floor. The first sharp cracks of the whips changed into juicy-sounding *splats*.

[The interrogator] would put a question to me; I would refuse to answer. He would order the guards to smash me. My mind raced from pillar to post searching for possible answers, refuges, dodges, and courage. Cutting, knife-like pain ripped through the swollen meat, down through the legs, up through the spine to the brain. Involuntary animal-like noises boiled out of my throat. Blood trickles and fright argued with reason and resolve. "Jesus, sweet Jesus. Courage ... please?"[74]

Suicide

When human beings are brutalized like this, it is not surprising that their thoughts frequently turn to ending the torment even at the cost of their lives. Guarino remembers, "I saw that one of the torturers had left a stretch rope under the desk, If I could just manage to wrap it around my neck, then climb up on the wooden stool and reach the metal brackets that the windows were hung on, I might be able to get the other end of the rope looped over, then fall off the stool and hang myself. Then I saw that the brackets were held only by wood screws that might pull out. The hemp rope also looked frazzled and could snap immediately from my weight. I didn't want to botch the job that badly. No, I decided, hanging wasn't a good choice."[75] The POW then tried, unsuccessfully, to slash his wrists—a fruitless act that brought only more torture.

Upon arrival at the Hanoi Hilton, many POWs were in such bad shape they would have welcomed death: "I was delirious with pain. I was suffering from a badly dislocated and fractured left arm, two fractured vertebrae and a fractured left knee. The Vietnamese dislocated both my right shoulder and right elbow.... I wished I could die! When the Vietnamese threatened to shoot me, I begged them to do it. Their answer was, 'No, you are a criminal. You haven't suffered enough.'"[76]

A Marine held prisoner for four years tried to take his life by biting at his wrists. Unsuccessful, he tried to cut them with the excrement-encrusted sharp-edged cover of his defecation pail. Two airmen suffered such excruciating pain from manacles that they tried suicide by repeatedly pounding their heads against a stone wall. The POW who had been buried alive by the Pathet Lao tried unsuccessfully to strangle himself with a rope that had been tied around his neck. An airman who wrongly believed he had violated the Code of Conduct, by giving up what was actually meaningless information, tried unsuccessfully to hang himself by his own pajamas. And these were just some of the attempts.[77]

The Consequences

Human beings cannot be treated in the manner just described without extremely serious consequences to their mental, psychological and physical wellbeing. While it is true — even miraculous — that many of those who suffered at the hands of the South and North Vietnamese Communists came through their ordeals relatively intact in mind and body, others were not so lucky. Some perished in the jungle camps of the South. Others died from brutality and disease in the prisons of the North.

Still others — until they, too, recovered or died — became the living dead. Here are just six examples:

He was "a hulk of human wreckage" one PW said of another. "He had lost 100 pounds, developed a pronounced stoop from long intervals of enforced squatting, and been ravaged by a series of infections and ulcerations. ... So severe was his ring-worm–type infection that one hand had swollen to four or five times its normal size...." Within a month, this American prisoner died in the jungles of the South.[78]

"I looked over and saw a man with gray hair, going bald fast, with a beard and a hairy chest. His arm was in a sling. He was big and looked like a starving ape. I said, 'Christ Almighty! Two years [here] and look at him!'"[79]

"He looked shriveled. He snuffled like a kid. ... He looked very old. Old and tired. He had a runny nose and seemed as helpless as a little child. I remembered how he had kept fighting after he was wounded, how he pulled us through those first days after our capture."[80]

One senior POW "had been reduced to 'a blind, crippled, animal, shitting on the floor'...."[81]

"His weight had dropped to 100 pounds (from 160) and his feet were so inflamed from beriberi that he was sleeping less than an hour a day and, despite the freezing temperatures, could not bear to have a blanket on them."[82]

One POW had been "kept in the dark so long that his eyes were going bad. His teeth were loosening and falling out. His hair, once thick and black, came out by the handfuls whenever he ran his fingers through it."[83]

A POW who had spent years in the South and was later marched to Hanoi described the reaction of a fellow prisoner in the North when the latter first saw the former: "Though he later learned that I was only thirty-eight, [the latter] thought that I was an old man. My gray-streaked hair and grizzled stubble beard, with a gaunt face whose eyes seemed lost in their deep black sockets, gave him this impression. [The Southern POW's] legs were so infirm that I virtually staggered into the room. When I smiled in greeting to the young aviator, [he] noticed several teeth missing in front.... 'My God,' thought the twenty-three year old Navy officer, 'he [the POW from the South] looks like the Count of Monte Cristo'...."[84]

"It had been five-and-a-half years since I last saw my face," Alvarez wrote. "I approached like a man entranced, as if transfixed by the image of my own face growing larger with each step forward [toward a mirror]. My God! Could that be me! Delicately, as if afraid my skin might crumble, I touched my stubby cheeks and felt my chin and then my eyes. I dragged my fingers over the furrowed lines. Something inside me recoiled from the image in the mirror. Good God! I looked so old! With shock and astonishment I saw the flecks of gray in my hair. I could not believe it. I was only thirty-two.... Inside I did not feel the weight of age, but I had only to look at that face staring back at me to see the ravages of time and the wear and tear of captivity. ... I studied the drawn cheeks and looked deep into the lackluster eyes. They were drained and tired, colorless and empty. Gone were the flashes of youthful animation and the healthy tone of a younger skin. ... I trembled much like any youth might have upon waking from a nightmare to find that the glimpse of his own aging face was not a dream but a reality."[85]

In some ways worse than suffering personal horrors was seeing how those horrors had turned men into zombies. Despite his own suffering, Robbie Risner was heartbroken at the sight of living dead men:

An American stumbled out of [one of the cells] in his shorts. He was so emaciated that he looked like one of the Dachau inmates. Though over six feet, he weighed about a hundred pounds. He staggered with weakness and could hardly maintain his balance. ...[Another POW] was not only emaciated, like the other two, but he appeared to be in a trance. Looking only at the sky, he kept his arms in identically the same position at all times, rigidly pressed to the sides, never moving. It was as though he was hypnotized, just walking around and around. Sometimes when he went to the wrong place, the guard would come and get him as you would a little child, and head him back.[86] At repatriation, all three of these POWs were listed as having "died in captivity."

Bud Day had similar feelings at the sight of John McCain:

I was brought to earth by the sight of McCain. I was appalled at his condition. I knew ... that he was a young man. I was confronted by a white-haired skeleton. There were deep, sunken pouches under his eyes, which popped bug-like from their cavities. His body was pathetically emaciated. He looked exactly like a survivor of Dachau. I guessed his weight at 100 pounds or less. ... John was in an immense body cast.... His right arm was propped up, sticking out of the cast like a broomstick arm protruding from a snowman. It angled out crazily. One did not have to be a doctor to recognize another butcher job. His right knee had been torn apart. ...His leg was nearly stiff, with only the faintest bit of movement possible at the knee. His left arm and shoulder were broken and neither had been set nor attended to. He could not wash, relieve himself, or do any normal function of life without assistance. Without someone to feed him, he was a dead man. John's head and body were filthy. Food particles and juices covered his chin, neck, and sideburns. He had not been cleaned after bowel movement.[87]

This, then, was the treatment, and the conditions of captivity, of many American POWs whom Jane Fonda would attempt to influence by her propaganda broadcasts and other conduct when she suddenly appeared in North Vietnam, on July 8, 1972.

These, then — brutalized, debilitated American prisoners of war — were, literally and figuratively, Jane Fonda's captive audience for her performance in wartime North Vietnam.

---

1. Rochester and Kiley, *Honor Bound*, 58.

2. Rochester and Kiley, *Honor Bound*, 58.

3. See Chapter 4.

4. See Chapter 5.

5. John M. McGrath, *Prisoner of War, Six Years in Hanoi*, ix.

6. Jeremiah A. Denton, Jr., with Ed Brandt, *When Hell Was in Session*, viii.

7. There is an abundance of Vietnam POW literature, much of which describes the conditions in which American prisoners were held and the brutality to which they were subjected by the Viet Cong in the South, and by the North Vietnamese above the Demilitarized Zone. See, for example, this book's bibliography and on the Internet, www.lbjlib.utexas.edu/shwv/mb/pow.html and www.eos.net/rrva/nampow/nampowbooks.html.

8. Frank Anton, *Why Didn't You Get Me Out?* 42–3.

9. "For the entire length of the Vietnam conflict, including short-term confinements early and late in the war, the mortality figure for prisoners held in the South would be closer to 20 percent, as compared with 5 percent in the North" (Rochester and Kiley, *Honor Bound*, 67). In fairness, however, it should be noted that in the South, as well as in the North, there were instances, albeit rare, of decent treatment afforded POWs, including sustenance, shelter and medical care. "I braced my legs against the far bunk and yelled in total panic. Just then, I saw the friendly guard who had given me the blanket that night in [a different lock-up]. He was standing just outside, looking through the peep [hole in the door]. His eyes were filled with tears; they were running down his face. He stuck his fingers through the bars of the peep, meaning for me to touch him. I did, and his touch, the touch of another human being, was reassuring. He stayed for a long time, but eventually he had to leave to take care of his other duties. I was again desolate and frantic, but at least no longer claustrophobic. The nice guard came several times. Knowing I was in danger of losing it altogether, he tried to encourage me. Once he pointed to the other bunk, meaning soon I'd get company. Another time he held up five fingers, meaning five more sleep downs [confined there] until a move. Another time he motioned down, down with both hands, then put his face against two clasped hands, meaning lie down and sleep. He tried his best for me..." (Guarino, *A P.O.W.'s Story*, 46). Another POW told an equally poignant story on the PBS documentary *Return with Honor*. After being shot down, parachuting, and landing, he was sitting on the ground, his back against a tree. His leg was dislocated. Using hand signals, he communicated to his guard that the boy should pull on the airman's dislocated leg out and thus realign the bones. The young guard somehow understood. He sat opposite the American, braced himself, and yanked on the dislocated leg. It popped back into place. Thus, despite other serious injuries, the flier went on the road to Hanoi and into a long captivity less crippled than he would have been but for his guard's act of kindness. In the prisons of the North, that could make the difference between survival and death. (POW Mike McGrath's statement made in the PBS documentary *Return with Honor*, which aired on November 13 and 14, 2000.) Admiral Denton has written that en route to Hanoi in a Jeep, he was "aflame with pain from the waist down. I settled back as best I could. The driver was obviously

trying to go easy over the bumps in deference to me, and I was thankful. [But this] was one of the few acts of compassion that I would experience in North Vietnam." Later, literally just inside the gate of Hoa Lo prison, the Hanoi Hilton, the driver helped Denton out of the Jeep and "patted me gently on the stomach and gave me a sympathetic look. But first he looked around to see if anyone was watching" (Denton, *When Hell Was in Session*, 19, 27).

10. Anton, *Why Didn't You Get Me Out?* 42–43.

11. Rochester and Kiley, *Honor Bound*, 446–47.

12. Up until then, the American prisoners were required to bow in the presence of their guards. Failure to do so would be punished by, at least, beatings. "After two months I was strong enough to lift my slop bucket and limp into the toilet dump area. My arm was in constant pain and I had to move very slowly.... I passed a guard without bowing. The guard hit me in the solar plexus and almost floored me. It was all I could do to stagger back to my room" (McGrath, *Prisoner of War*, 26).

13. Email from former POW, in the possession of the authors.

14. There were "more that 300 downed U.S. airmen who entered captivity before or during the middle years and lived to return home in 1973" and who were held in North Vietnam when conditions changed in late 1969, and who remained there when Fonda showed up in July 1972. Rochester and Kiley, *Honor Bound*, 479.

15. Although it will never be possible to fully convey with words the bestial nature and extent of torture inflicted on American prisoners by the Viet Cong and North Vietnamese Communists, some measure of it may be understood by the fact "that not one amputee, not one mental case, not one cosmetically displeasing prisoner was returned to the United States" when American POWs were repatriated in the 1973 Operation Homecoming (Day, *Return with Honor*, 190). Since it has been well documented that there were those among the POW population who had lost their mental faculties and limbs, it requires little imagination to know what happened to them at the hands of their brutal captors, and thus why they were not repatriated.

16. It should again be emphasized that while the prisoners' situation in the South remained mostly the same throughout their captivity — with, to be sure, some periods being worse and some a bit better — POW treatment and conditions in the North improved somewhat in the later years of their confinement, especially after the death of Ho Chi Minh in the fall of 1969, and then

as repatriation neared. There was some improvement in food, medical care, conditions of restraint and confinement, and indoctrination, and some lessening of the North Vietnamese need for propaganda. Certainly, torture as a policy changed. However, given the age and primitive condition of the prisons in the North, not much could be done about problems of sanitation, personal hygiene and vermin infestation. Nor about the danger to the POWs of American bomber strikes in the Hanoi area, especially at the power plant. In addition, it should be noted that while the following descriptions paint a deservedly and accurately horrendous picture of the POW's treatment and the conditions of confinement, there were some exceptions from time to time, from prisoner to prisoner, and from one place of detention to another.

17. Jim and Sybil Stockdale, *In Love and War*, 103.

18. See, for example, Robinson Risner, *The Passing of the Night: My Seven Years as a Prisoner of the North Vietnamese*, 10. Even the type of sandals given to POWs was directly related to the nature of their captivity. In the South, the sandals had heel straps so that the POWs would be able to walk. In the North, the sandals lacked heel straps, so that the POWs would be able only to trudge.

19. McGrath, *Prisoner of War*, 2.

20. Zalin Grant, *Survivors: Vietnam P.O.W.'s Tell Their Stories*, 20. This POW was captured in the South.

21. Guarino, *A P.O.W.'s Story*, 11. This POW, a fighter pilot, crashed in the North.

22. See, for example, George E. Day, *Return with Honor*, 5.

23. Day, *Return with Honor*, 53.

24. McGrath, *Prisoner of War*, 4.

25. Grant, *Survivors*, 53.

26. Stockdale, *In Love and War*, 113.

27. Guarino, *A P.O.W.'s Story*, 14.

28. Anton, *Why Didn't You Get Me Out?* 89.

29. Anton, *Why Didn't You Get Me Out?* 53.

30. Rochester and Kiley, *Honor Bound*, 90.

31. Everett Alvarez, Jr., and Anthony S. Pitch, *Chained Eagle*, 68.

32. Alvarez and Pitch, *Chained Eagle*, 165.

33. Rochester and Kiley, *Honor Bound*, 153–154.

34. Risner, *The Passing of the Night*, 101.

35. McGrath, *Prisoner of War*, 98.

36. "By the light of the moon I saw the courtyard teeming with rats! In their frenzied scurrying they swarmed over the bushes and low trees.... There were so many of them that their movements sounded like a collective hum. The terror never abated, knowing that these monstrous rats used

my cell as a thoroughfare between the main court-yard and the entrance to the sewers. In the months ahead it was difficult to sleep as they removed all my makeshift efforts to block the floor-level holes." Alvarez and Pitch, *Chained Eagle*, 66.

37. Anton, *Why Didn't You Get Me Out?*, 43–44.

38. McGrath, *Prisoner of War*, 48.

39. Alvarez and Pitch, *Chained Eagle*, 165.

40. Rochester and Kiley, *Honor Bound*, 65.

41. Email in the possession of the authors. Dr. Kushner added: "The VC forbid the men from calling me Doc, and made me the latrine orderly to break down rank structure. I was officially forbidden from practicing medicine. …I was not allowed to practice medicine unless a man was 30 minutes away from dying, then they came down with their little bottles of medicine and said 'Cure him!'"

42. Rochester and Kiley, *Honor Bound*, 361.

43. McGrath, *Prisoner of War*, 20.

44. Stockdale, *In Love and War*, 158.

45. Risner, *The Passing of the Night*, 158.

46. McGrath, *Prisoner of War*, 16.

47. Grant, *Survivors*, 159.

48. McGrath, *Prisoner of War*, 8.

49. Alvarez and Pitch, *Chained Eagle*, 68.

50. Rochester and Kiley, *Honor Bound*, 231–32.

51. The name "Hanoi Hilton," while literally referring to the Hoa Lo prison in Hanoi, has in popular usage become a generic term for various places of incarceration in and around Hanoi. Those included, but were not limited to, the Zoo, Alcatraz, the Plantation, the Powerplant, the Briarpatch, Camp Faith and Son Tay. A place called Dogpatch was some hundred miles north of Hanoi, close to the Chinese border. To make matters more confusing to the non-expert in POW matters, most of these places had sub-descriptions. For example, Hoa Lo prison had POW-named sections called New Guy Village, Heartbreak Hotel, Camp Unity and Little Vegas (which in turn had sections called, predictably, Stardust, Desert Inn, Thunderbird and Riviera). Ironically, today most of the large Hoa Lo prison has been torn down and replaced by an actual Hilton hotel.

52. Rochester and Kiley, *Honor Bound*, 481.

53. McGrath, *Prisoner of War*, 12. Denton has written that "eventually, [he] would become the first military prisoner in North Vietnam to spend more than four years in solitary. Only five men were to achieve that unpleasant distinction" (Denton, *When Hell Was in Session*, 73). At the prison called "Alcatraz," where Denton spent just over two years, "The cells were tiny: a standing area 47 inches square, plus a raised pallet area the length of a man's body. The pallet was nothing more than

bamboo strips laid side by side. Mine had a nail that protruded near my right shoulder blade. There was no window, and the only ventilation was from a few small holes drilled in a steel plate door, which was recessed. A dim bulb, ten watts or less, provided the only light. Most of the time there was only darkness and silence" (Denton, *When Hell Was in Session*, 147).

54. Rochester and Kiley, *Honor Bound*, 313.

55. Rochester and Kiley, *Honor Bound*, 349.

56. Rochester and Kiley, *Honor Bound*, 334–35.

57. Anton, *Why Didn't You Get Me Out?* 104.

58. Guarino, *A P.O.W.'s Story*, 328–29.

59. The danger was especially acute for POWs who were stashed at a North Vietnamese power plant, and there used as hostages against bombing raids. Nevertheless, pinpoint attacks were made against the power plant target.

60. Rochester and Kiley, *Honor Bound*, 180.

61. Although strict orders were issued by senior POWs against accepting early release, a few prisoners took the North Vietnamese offers and were repatriated before 1973. On the other hand, Seaman Douglas Hegdahl was ordered to accept early release because, in what would be a bonanza of information for POW families and intelligence officials, he had memorized the names of hundreds of POWs being held in Hanoi.

62. Rochester and Kiley, *Honor Bound*, 125–26.

63. Rochester and Kiley, *Honor Bound*, 330.

64. Alvarez and Pitch, *Chained Eagle*, 176.

65. Alvarez and Pitch, *Chained Eagle*, 169.

66. "…[G]uards forced him face down on his bunk, set his ankles into [iron leg] stocks, and bound him tightly with rope at the elbows. The long end of the rope was then pulled up through a hook attached to the ceiling. As a guard hoisted the prisoner, he lifted him off the bunk enough so that he could not relieve any of his weight, producing incredible pain — with shoulders seemingly being torn from their sockets — and horribly constricting breathing. (An alternate technique was simply to set the prisoner on his bunk or the floor, arch his back with a rope stretching from the feet to the throat, and place pressure on the back until his mouth was practically touching his toes.)" (Rochester and Kiley, *Honor Bound*, 145.)

67. Rochester and Kiley, *Honor Bound*, 147.

68. McGrath, *Prisoner of War*, 60.

69. Grant, *Survivors*, 303.

70. Rochester and Kiley, *Honor Bound*, 147–48.

71. Guarino, *A P.O.W.'s Story*, 202–04.

72. Email from former POW, in the possession of the authors.

73. McGrath, *Prisoner of War*, 84.

74. Day, *Return with Honor*, 156–158. This description of torture continues in Day's book for

some *six more pages*. The torture itself lasted for days on end, with virtually no respite. No civilized person can possibly read of the nature and extent of torture inflicted on Col. Day without experiencing horror and rage. Day has reported that "[a]ll told, 26 men had been beaten to the verge of death" (Day, *Return with Honor*, 169). Larry Guarino somehow endured 390 days of "hard torture." Not surprisingly, the North Vietnamese's sadism was not limited to their human subjects. "There were two groups of mongrel dogs in camp, those that the 'V' [the North Vietnamese] fed and who barked with Oriental animosity at the POWs, and those that were fed and handled by the POWs, and who barked at the 'V' with Oriental anger. The dogs all resembled Chinese Chows.... The pro–American dogs were ordinarily the first slain in the frequent forays for food, for the 'V' enjoyed dog meat. As we were peeping into the yard one sunny morning, we were flabbergasted to note that a young female worker, a food handler, was masturbating a male dog with enthusiasm. The dog was also enthusiastic until the young woman lighted her cigarette lighter and put the flame directly against the animal's penis! ... Another fun diversion for the 'V' was to catch the baby rats or mice that abounded in the camp. The rat was soaked in either gasoline or lighter fluid, and then torched with a cigarette lighter. This event always drew a sizable crowd, and the air would be split with shrieks and cheers as the animal raced desperately around until its tiny legs were burned off, and it fell squealing to the ground. The most dreadful spectacle of all was the foray after the dogs, ducks or turkeys. The dogs, at least, seemed to sense their impending doom. Normally, the 'V' would stride into the yard without the slightest notice of an animal, and should a dog venture within kicking distance, he could expect a jolting boot on one end or the other. Apparently, it was their belief that the meat would be more edible if pounded thoroughly before cooking. On slaughtering days, the 'V' would pick up a piece of brick or rock in one hand and attempt to coax the dog into lethal range with a crust of bread. The dogs were, of course, distrustful, but, like POWs, they were also hungry. Once the dog was enticed into range, he would be dazed with a well-thrown rock, and the entire camp contingent would join in pursuing and stoning it to death. It was considered a meritorious achievement to be the lucky fellow who would disable the dog by breaking its first leg, but even

better to be the one who broke the second. After all, *anyone* could cave in the skull when it was immobile" (Day, *Return with Honor*, 119). Pigs fared no better. "The guards made horrible sport out of butchering their food. When they killed a pig they first punched its eyes out so that it would stand still, then they beat it to death. Cows suffered a like fate. They tied them with ropes strung all over like a spider web, and then beat them to death with an ax. The women killed the dogs for meat by hanging them in a grotesque position and then beat them with sticks. All the while, the guards and women laughed as though they were at a sports event" (Ralph Gaither, as told to Steve Henry, *With God in a P.O.W. Camp*, 128).

75. Guarino, *A P.O.W.'s Story*, 205–06.

76. McGrath, *Prisoner of War*, 6.

77. Short of suicide, some POWs tried to injure themselves so that their disabilities would prevent them from being forced to write propaganda material or record propaganda statements. For example, so he could not be forced to make propaganda tapes, one POW "decided that I would try to ruin my voice by hitting my larynx. I began pounding my throat as hard as I could. My eyes watered and sometimes I saw stars. I gave frequent judo chops to the throat that were very effective as far as judo goes. I choked and struggled to get my breath. My neck swelled up, but it did not affect my voice. I did not know if I was hitting the right spot, but anyway, it did not work. I could still talk. Then I thought about the acid that I had heard about. I knew I could not get hold of pure acid, but my bar of soap had a tremendous amount of lye in it; so much that it would almost eat up the skin. I took my cup and filled it with a third cup of water, and part of a bar of lye soap. I crumbled, mashed and stirred it into a mushy, mucky substance. Then I began gargling with it. It burned the inside of my mouth like fire, almost cooking it, and I accidentally swallowed some" (Risner, *The Passing of the Night* 112).

78. Rochester and Kiley, *Honor Bound*, 236.

79. Grant, *Survivors*, 113.

80. Grant, *Survivors*, 140.

81. Rochester and Kiley, *Honor Bound*, 308.

82. Rochester and Kiley, *Honor Bound*, 296.

83. Rochester and Kiley, *Honor Bound*, 517.

84. Rochester and Kiley, *Honor Bound*, 511.

85. Alvarez and Pitch, *Chained Eagle*, 218–19.

86. Risner, *The Passing of the Night*, 200.

87. Day, *Return with Honor*, 105.

4

"ADHERING TO THEIR ENEMIES"

Our country has no capability to defeat you on the battlefield.
But war is not decided by weapons so much as by national will.
Once the American people understand this war,
they will have no interest in pursuing it.
They will be made to understand this.
We will win this war on the streets of New York.
(Jim and Sybil Stockdale, In Love and War, *181)*

This is Jane Fonda speaking from Hanoi... (Hearing Report, *7647)*

On July 11, 1972, a confidential cable from the American embassy in Vientiane, Laos, to the Secretary of State in Washington, the United States delegation at the Paris peace talks, the Commander-in-Chief of Pacific Forces and our embassy in Saigon, South Vietnam, revealed the following:

Subject: Travel to NVN: Jane Fonda
   As Dept is likely aware from press reports, actress Jane Fonda arrived in Hanoi 8 July via Aeroflot from Moscow. *Subject was not carried as passenger on Aeroflot manifest* deposited during Vientiane transit morning July 8 nor did she disembark to transit lounge.[1]

Fonda had left the United States, traveled to Paris and, fittingly, flown from there to Moscow. Boarding an Aeroflot flight in the Soviet capital, apparently incognito, she remained on the airplane when it landed in supposedly neutral Laos, and exited only when she arrived in Hanoi, North Vietnam. "Clad in black pajamas [typically worn by the Viet Cong in the South] and a white tunic, Jane stepped off her Aeroflot jet on July 8, 1972.... She arrived, she told her uniformed, helmeted hosts, with 'greetings' from revolutionary 'comrades' in America."[2]

Fonda had come to Hanoi — as had Hayden, Joan Baez and other Americans before her — willingly and knowingly to provide grist for the North Vietnamese propaganda mill, an operation that had been in place for decades. In fact, when ranking U.S. Naval POW Jim Stockdale was dragged before an assemblage of top North Vietnamese officers and an interpreter-announcer from the English-language propaganda program, "Voice of Vietnam":

The unwary announcer started addressing the important one as "Vien" until [one of the interrogators] came forward and whispered to him what I suppose was a reminder that criminals like me were never to hear a proper Vietnamese name. But I had all I needed. "Vien" had to be Nguyen Khac Vien, a name with which I had become familiar through my research in graduate school. Vien is a medical doctor and a longtime resident of Paris. He is a master Communist propagandist, a better-than-average writer in English, and an intellectual of sorts, a former acquaintance of Albert Camus. He led the Viet Minh propaganda and agitation campaigns and demonstrations in Paris and in the French countryside during 1953 and 1954, efforts that had a part in discouraging the French people and French government from pursuing their war in Asia. Moreover, Vien is known to be a longtime close personal friend of Premier Pham Van Dong. During our ensuing talk through the radio-announcer interpreter, it became clear that as far as Vien was concerned, the master game plan for this war had been well in the works for a long time: It was to be a replay of the Dien Bien Phu era, *including the propaganda-induced political disillusionment of the Western adversary*.[3]

Indeed, from the very beginning of Ho Chi Minh's Viet Minh resistance to French rule, the guerrillas' command structure "was divided into a military arm and a political-psychological warfare arm, with the political commander, Ho, supreme."[4]

As we noted in the previous chapter, despite the "public relations" risk of torturing American prisoners of war, the North Vietnamese chanced it because of the high value they placed on propaganda.[5] At no time was this more apparent than in 1967, when the Communists opened yet another POW facility in Hanoi — this one "*devoted specifically to the production and dissemination of propaganda*."[6] Among its several prisoner-given names, it is probably best known as the "Plantation." "The Vietnamese converted a portion of the facility into a Potemkin village of sanitized cells, garden patches, and scrubbed corridors that would serve as a showplace for displaying the captives to visiting delegations and conducting photo sessions and other propaganda activities."[7]

The POWs, however, were not going to play Hanoi's propaganda game. As we have seen, they resisted torture as best they could. Another method of thwarting the Communists' propaganda plans was self-defacement.

Stockdale was convinced that officials at the Hilton were after him to make a movie for PW consumption in which he advised junior officers to cooperate with the captors. To defeat the plan, he tried fasting, then disfigured himself by chopping his hair and scalp with a razor and, when the Vietnamese requisitioned a hat, pounding his face with a stool and against the wall until he was unfit to be photographed or filmed. ... But the best counterextortion technique proved to be the self-defacement. Painful as it was — he had to "freshen" his bruises with his fists to keep his eyelids swollen and cheekbones mashed — it allowed him to regain some measure of control from his tormentors.[8]

Yet, in the face of the heroic, mostly successful efforts of American POWs to deny the North Vietnamese their much-needed propaganda victories — by taking indescribable torture, by voluntarily defacing themselves, by seeing the Plantation for what it was and acting accordingly and by every other means open to them — Jane Fonda handed her Communist hosts a pro–Communist, anti–American propaganda coup.

Why? Again, Fonda biographer Peter Collier understood what was driving the actress-turned-militant: " When she arrived in Hanoi, Jane was as malleable as she had been when she returned to the United States after her Paris exile two years earlier — ready to find her relevance in the use others could make of her."[9]

And use her, to good effect, the "others" — the Communists — would. Indeed, as we shall see in this chapter and even more in the next, the use to which the North Vietnamese put Fonda — with her knowing consent and active participation — gave them what they needed: legitimacy and favorable propaganda.

Once Fonda was in Hanoi, her Communist hosts laid on a full schedule for their American comrade who had come halfway around the world to assist them in their international propaganda efforts.[10] Fonda's North Vietnamese itinerary is reproduced here verbatim as it appears in the *Hearing Report*, except for material indicated as having been omitted or added.[11]

July 8	Arrival in Hanoi.
July 9–11	Visit to Hanoi "War Museum" ... and Bach Mai ... to view alleged bomb damage to the hospital there.
July 12	Visits to Nam Sach district ... and Hong Phong Village to view bomb damages to dikes and populated areas.
July 13–16	Unknown activities, but Fonda later claimed to have "traveled hundreds of miles throughout the bombed regions" in the days preceding her Hanoi press interview of July 19 with Jean Thoraval (a French AFP reporter who with several other Western correspondents, has promoted allegations that the U.S. is deliberately bombing the dikes and areas with non-military targets).
July 14	First [probably live] Fonda broadcast to GIs via Radio Hanoi.
July 17–18	Visits Nam Dinh district, described as a main textile center of North Vietnam, to observe alleged bomb damage to "non-military" targets.
July 17	Second [live] broadcast to GIs via Radio Hanoi in which she described previous visits to Bach Mai Hospital and Hanoi War Museum.[12]
July 18	Interview with captured U.S. Airmen in Hanoi.
July 19	Interview with AFP correspondent Jean Thoraval (cf. above) which is mainly an anti-U.S. denunciation of the war and, conversely, a propaganda piece to stress the "determination" of the North Vietnamese to resist. Fonda added that she was forced to take refuge at a road-side shelter during a U.S. raid of July 18.
July 19	Third [live] broadcast to GIs via Radio Hanoi.
July 20	Press Conference at "Hanoi International Club" where she described her visits to the countryside since July 8, her earlier meeting with U.S. PWs and concluded with her usual anti-U.S. diatribe.
July 20	Radio Hanoi broadcast, described as a Vietnamese translation of a Fonda statement, on the North Vietnamese "liberation" of Quang Tri Province and how the ARVN [Army of the Republic of (South) Vietnam] counteroffensive was doomed to failure; fourth [live] broadcast to GIs explaining U.S.-SVN (South Vietnam) violations of the Geneva Accords of 1954.
July 21	Fifth and sixth [live] broadcasts to GIs, both aimed at U.S. fliers, on alleged war crimes and veiled suggestions to refuse to fly further combat missions.
July 21	Fonda meets with North Vietnamese Nguyen Duy Trinh where she claimed to have "witnessed U.S. crimes in Hanoi ... Hai Hung, Ha Tay and Nam Ha provinces" and expressed thanks to him for distinguishing between "U.S.

imperialists" and "The American people who are friends of the Vietnamese
people in the struggle for peace and democracy." Fonda also told the Vice
Premier that "she was convinced that under the wise leadership of the
Vietnam Workers Party and the DRV [Democratic Republic of Vietnam]
Government the Vietnamese people will certainly win brilliant victory."

July 21   Fonda [probably taped] broadcast to "the Vietnamese people."
July 22   Fonda departed Hanoi. "Seeing her off at the airport," a Radio Hanoi
               broadcast noted, "were members of the Vietnam Committee of Solidarity
               with the American People and the Vietnamese Film Artistes Association";
               stopped at Vientiane, "escorted by a French photographer."
July 23   Arrives in Paris via Moscow on *Aeroflot* flight; delayed tape broadcast to
               "South Vietnamese Youth" on alleged represssions of the Thieu government
               and the VC [Viet Cong] struggle against it.
July 24   Seventh Radio Hanoi broadcast to GIs (noted as having been recorded July
               16, 1972).
July 25   Press Conference in Paris.
July 27   Arrival in New York.
July 28   New York Press Conference. Basically the same rhetoric as the Paris press
               meeting.
July 28   Eighth broadcast to GIs (delayed tape ca. July 18–19).
July 29   Delayed tape (in English) to "Saigon Soldiers."[13]
July 29   Arrival in Los Angeles.
July 31   Attended Los Angeles premiere of "F.T.A." and announces she is
               "abandoning her career" until after the November election "in order to
               campaign against the Vietnam War."

In the years since Fonda's July 1972 pilgrimage to Hanoi, there have been many reports of what she did there. Some have been accurate, some not. *Since our opinion that
she could have been indicted and tried for treason rests mostly on Fonda's actual pro–Communist, anti–American, propaganda broadcasts and her other conduct in North Vietnam,
it is essential to get the facts down correctly.* Principally, Fonda's activities in North Vietnam fell into four categories: (1) broadcasts— some live and some taped — under the aus-
pices of Radio Hanoi; (2) meetings with senior Communist officials; (3) tours of civilian and military sites; (4) an "interview" with seven American prisoners of war.

To set the record straight, let's begin with the broadcasts, which, outside a few
government agencies, have never been heard in the United States in their entirety. Indeed, few people outside of government have ever even read the transcripts. There
are two categories: (1) Fonda's broadcasts to American military personnel, and (2)
her broadcasts targeted to others. The list of Fonda's broadcasts is reproduced here
verbatim, except for material indicated as having been omitted.[14]

To American Military Personnel[15]

Date/Time	To Whom Addressed
July 14, 1972	"All of you in the cockpits of your planes … in the 7th Fleet"
July 17, 1972	"U.S. Servicemen"
July 19, 1972	"American Servicemen"
July 21, 1972	"U.S. Pilots"

July 22, 1972	"U.S. Flyers and Airmen"
July 20, 1972	"the U.S. men who … have been sent here to fight"
July 24, 1972	"U.S. Pilots and Airmen"
July 25, 1972	"U.S. Pilots and Airmen"
July 28, 1972	"U.S. Servicemen"
July 30, 1972	"American GIs"
August 15, 1972	"American Servicemen"
(Recorded July 20, 1972)	
August 22, 1972	"American Servicemen"
(Recorded ca. July 22, 1972)	

To Others

July 20, 1972   Re North Vietnamese Army liberation of Quantri Province
(Hanoi domestic service in translated Vietnamese)
July 20, 1972   Recorded passage from her Hanoi Press Conference Statement
(English to Europe, Africa and Mid-East)
July 21, 1972   "Message to South Vietnamese People"
(Liberation Press Agency [clandestine] in English to Eastern Europe and Far East)
July 23, 1972   "Letter to Southern Youths"
(Translated Vietnamese to South Vietnamese)
July 26, 1972   "Talk with Saigon Students"
(English to American Servicemen involved in The Indochina War)
July 29, 1972   "Message to Saigon Soldiers"
(English to South East Asia)
August 1, 1972   "Fonda … message to Mme. Binh in Cuba" sends her a
                       "warm kiss"
(Liberation Radio [clandestine] in Vietnamese to South Vietnam)

From this list of broadcasts, it is apparent that Fonda was addressing not only every American serviceman and woman (enlisted and officer) on the ground in Vietnam and on ships off the coast, but also South Vietnamese soldiers and civilians as well. Her broadcasts were beamed to the jungles of the South, the prisons of the North and even to Eastern (that is, Communist) Europe.

To the extent there is sympathy among Americans for Fonda's activities in North Vietnam, it is probably because they have never known what she actually said in Hanoi, and what was attributed to her.[16] The list follows:

- American pilots were bombing non-military targets, such as hospitals, villages, schools, factories, pagodas, theaters and dikes.[17]
- Americans were using "illegal, outlawed weapons," including chemical bombs and chemical toxic gases.
- Ordering the use of, and using, these weapons makes one a "war criminal."
- In the past, users of such weapons were "tried and executed."
- The Vietnamese people were peasants, leading a peaceful bucolic life before the Americans came to destroy Vietnam.

- The Vietnamese seek only "freedom and independence," which the United States wants to prevent them from having.
- The Vietnamese fighters are her "friends."
- The million infantry troops the United States put into Vietnam, and the Vietnamization program, have failed.
- The United States seeks to turn Vietnam into a "neocolony."
- Patrick Henry's slogan "liberty or death" was not very different from Ho Chi Minh's "Nothing is more valuable than independence and freedom."
- Her meeting with seven "U.S. aggressor pilots" found them "healthy and repentant."
- Nixon violated the 1954 Geneva Accords.
- Vietnam is "one nation, one country."
- The Communists' proposal for ending the war is "fair, sensible, reasonable and humanitarian."
- The United States must get out of South Vietnam, and "cease its support for the ... Thieu regime."
- "I want to publicly accuse Nixon here of being a new-type Hitler whose crimes are being unveiled."
- "The Vietnamese people will win."
- "Nixon is continuing to risk your [American pilots'] lives and the lives of the American prisoners of war ... in a last desperate gamble to keep his office come November. How does it feel to be used as pawns? You may be shot down, you may perhaps even be killed, but for what, and for whom?"
- "Can you justify what you are doing?"
- Nixon "defiles our flag and all that it stands for in the eyes of the entire world."
- "Knowing who was doing the lying, should you then allow these same people and some liars to define for you who your enemy is?"
- "If they told you the truth, you wouldn't fight, you wouldn't kill."

- "Our parents were having to pay in order to finance, to buy weapons for the French to kill the Vietnamese people."
- American troops are fighting for ESSO, Shell and Coca-Cola.
- "Should we be fighting on the side of the people who are, who are murdering innocent people, should we be trying to defend a government in Saigon which is putting in jail tens of thousands of people into the tiger cages, beating them, torturing them…. And I don't think ... that we should be risking our lives or fighting to defend that kind of government."
- "I am very honored to be a guest in your country, and I loudly condemn the crimes that have been committed by the U.S. Government in the name of the American people against your country."
- "We have understood that we have a common enemy — U.S. imperialism."
- "We have followed closely the encroachment of the American cancer in the southern part of your country, especially around Saigon. And we hope very soon that, working together, we can remove this cancer from your country…."
- "We thank you [the Viet Cong and North Vietnamese] for your brave and heroic fight."
- "Nixon's aggression against Vietnam is a racist aggression, [and] the American war in Vietnam is a racist war, a white man's war…."
- Soldiers of the South Vietnamese army "are being sent to fight a war that is not in your interests but is in the interests of the small handful of people who have gotten rich and hope to get richer off this war and the turning of your country into a neocolony of the United States."
- "We read with interest about the growing numbers of you [South Vietnam Army troops] who are understanding the truth and joining with your fellow

countrymen to fight for freedom and independence and democracy. We note with interest, for example, that as in the case of the 56th Regiment of the 3d Division of the Saigon Army, ARVN soldiers are taken into the ranks of the National Liberation Front, including officers who may retain their rank. We think that this is an example of the fact that the democratic, peace-loving, patriotic Vietnamese people want to embrace all Vietnamese people in forgiveness, open their arms to all people who are willing to fight against the foreign intruder."

- "We know what lies in store for any third world country that could have the misfortune of falling into the hands of a country such as the United States and becoming a colony."
- "The only way to end the war is for the United States to withdraw all its troops, all its airplanes, its bombs, its generals, its CIA advisors and to stop the support of the Thieu regime in Saigon...."
- "There is only one way to stop Richard Nixon from committing mass genocide in the Democratic Republic of Vietnam, and that is for a mass protest ... to expose his crimes...."
- "In 1969–1970 the desertions in the American army tripled. The desertions of the U.S. soldiers almost equaled the desertions from the ARVN army...."
- Although "we do not condone the killing of American officers ... we do support the soldiers who are beginning to think for themselves."
- American soldiers in Vietnam discovered "that their officers were incompetent, usually drunk...."
- "Perhaps the soldiers ... who have suffered the most ... [are] the black soldiers, the brown soldiers, and the red and Asian soldiers."
- Recently I talked to "a great many of these guys and they all expressed their recognition of the fact that this is a white man's war, a white businessman's war, that they don't feel it's their place to kill other people of color when at home they themselves are oppressed and prevented from determining their own lives."
- "I heard horrifying stories about the treatment of women in the U.S. military. So many women said to me that one of the first things that happens to them when they enter the service is that they are taken to see the company psychiatrist and they are given a little lecture which is made very clear to them that they are there to service the men."
- "I think Richard Nixon would do well to read Vietnamese history, particularly their poetry, and particularly the poetry written by Ho Chi Minh."

On that literary suggestion, we can end this summary of Fonda's propaganda statements in Hanoi.

Fonda's own words, and the thematic analysis that follows, make plain beyond any reasonable doubt the intent and import of her statements. They contained lies about the United States, its leaders, their motives and their acts. They maligned the President of the United States. They spouted the Communist propaganda line in every respect. They sought to undermine the morale and military effort of our soldiers in the field and our prisoners in jungle camps and North Vietnamese prisons.

And her words even encouraged mutiny and desertion.

That there was a consistent pro–Communist, anti–American, propaganda theme to virtually everything uttered by Fonda in her broadcasts from Hanoi, that Fonda's statements reveal a clear intent to aid the North Vietnamese and injure the United States, cannot be disputed. Indeed, a research analyst[18] for the House Internal Security Committee prepared the following "Theme Analysis" of Fonda's Hanoi statements for the Committee in July 1972.[19] Its conclusion clearly identifies what she was trying to accomplish in North Vietnam. The Theme Analysis is reproduced here verbatim, except for material indicated as having been omitted.[20]

THEME ANALYSIS OF FONDA STATEMENTS TO MEDIA FROM HANOI

The recent visit of American film actress Jane Fonda to North Vietnam during the period July 8–22, 1972, has received widespread media coverage both in the United States and North Vietnam. Of special interest to this [House Internal Security] Committee are Ms. Fonda's six personal broadcasts via Radio Hanoi to American servicemen stationed in South Vietnam and elsewhere in Southeast Asia, all of which contain intrinsic textual passages that these messages were purposely so intended. In addition, several other Radio Hanoi broadcasts (both English-language and in Vietnamese) carried excerpts of her statements, along with "third person" reportage by Soviet (TASS) and French (AFP) radio commentators from Hanoi.

1. "Hanoi VNA International Services in English, 0246 GMT 14 Jul 72" Fonda statement preceded by Vietnamese broadcaster noting that the message was addressed to "all the U.S. servicemen involved in the bombing of North Vietnam." Fonda's own statement included a description of alleged U.S. bombing of dikes in the vicinity of NAM SACH (60 km. E of Hanoi) on the Red River on July 12 just before her visit to that area. After a quasi-humanitarian appeal on how that district was strictly an agricultural area, and devoid of military targets, she accused the U.S. of "terrorist tactics" because of the bombing raids of July 12. In making her appeal to U.S. servicemen, she asserted: "I (?implore you), I beg you to consider what you are doing. In the area I went yesterday it was easy to see that there are no military targets, … no important highway, … no communications network, … (and) no heavy industry…. All of you in the cockpits of your planes, on the aircraft carriers, those who are loading the bombs, those who are repairing the planes … please think what you are doing.

2. "Hanoi in English to American Servicemen Involved in the Indo-China War, 1300 GMT 17 Jul 72" Fonda statement began:

> This is Jane Fonda speaking from Hanoi, and I'm speaking particularly to U.S. servicemen who are stationed on the aircraft carriers in the Gulk [sic] of Tonkin, in the 7th Fleet, in the Anglico[[21]] Corps in the south of Vietnam

After a rather pointed diatribe about U.S. producers of military weaponry, Ms. Fonda then accuses the American military leadership of employing "illegal" weapons, such as "toxic chemicals." guava/spider/pineapple bombs, and combinations of napalm, phosphorous and thermite. She concludes: "And the use of these bombs or the condoning the use of these bombs make one a war criminal."

Endorsing the current Democratic Party nominee as "an example of the overwhelming, overwhelming feeling in the United States among people to end the war" who also "represents all that is good to these people ... an end to the war, or end to the bombing," Fonda asserted that it was not "in the interests" of U.S. troops to attack North Vietnam.

Fonda then described the alleged bombing of the BACH MAI hospital which she visited earlier that day. After claiming that a bomb had hit the center of the hospital, "obviously dropped there on purpose," she added: "With the kind of bombs, the kind of techniques that have been developed now, you know, particularly you pilots know that accidents like that don't happen.... Why do you do this? Why do you follow orders telling you to destroy a hospital or bomb the schools?"

Obviously begging the question by compounding a false supposition with another, Fonda goes on to relate the use of "plastic" pellets (which, in her expert knowledge of medical technology, "doesn't show up on X-rays") which preclude extraction, and "chemical bombs," which causes pregnant women to produce "deformed babies."

In essence, this message employs quasi-humanitarian "scare" tactics and hyper-legal rhetoric which, while not openly advocating U.S. servicemen to disobey orders, certainly distorts the actual nature and purpose of U.S. air operations to a degree that if a serviceman believed all of her *a priori* arguments, then he could have only one logical alternative, That is, to refuse to participate in bombing raids. *The message, therefore, represents a highly subliminal appeal to servicemen to disobey orders, etc.*[22] evidently prepared by professional propagandists.

3. "Hanoi in English to Europe. Africa and the Middle East, 2000 GMT 19 Jul 72." This a North Vietnamese broadcast with excerpts of another Fonda "address to American servicemen" describing her visit to the textile center of Nam Dinh on July 18, which did not appear in FBIS for some reason. Fonda then described the ruins of the hospital, schools, churches, recreation centers and the textile factory in Nam Dinh, all of which were allegedly targeted by U.S. fliers in spite of the fact that "no military targets" exist in that city. In addition, she alleged that the nearby dike system had "large fissures" from several bombing raids. Following this, she then appealed to U.S. troops:

> What are your commanders telling you? How are they justifying this to you? Have you any idea what your bombs are doing when you pull the levers and push the buttons?

This message, in brief, is of the same type of that of July 17 (No. 2 above).

4. "Hanoi In English to Southeast Asia, 1000 GMT 21 Jul 72." Introduced as a "recorded message ... to U.S. pilots involved in the Vietnam War," this broadcast generally denounced the U.S. employment of antipersonnel bombs which "were outlawed by the Geneva Convention of 1907." She also reiterated the "plastic pellet" story. More important, Fonda asked U.S. fliers:

> How does it feel to be used as pawns? You may be shot down ... even be killed, but for what, and for whom? ... We are afraid of what, what must be happening to you as human beings. For isn't it possible to destroy, to receive salary for pushing buttons and pulling levers that are dropping illegal bombs on innocent people without having that damage your own souls?

Carrying this subliminal, quasi-humanitarian appeal further, Fonda continues:

> Tonight when you are alone, ask yourselves: What are you doing? Accept no
> ready answers fed to you by rote from basic training on up, but as men, as
> human beings, can you justify what you are doing? Do you know why you
> are flying these missions, collecting extra combat pay on Sunday? ...I know
> that if you saw and if you knew the Vietnamese under peaceful conditions,
> you would hate the men who are sending you on bombing missions.

5. "Hanoi in English to American Servicemen Involved in the Indochina
War, 1300 GMT 22 Jul 72." In this broadcast, Fonda appealed to everyone involved in the bombing raids over North Vietnam, including specifically naming
six U.S. aircraft carriers, "the Anglico Corps" and USAF B-52 and F4 "Phantom" crews. She then accuses President Nixon of lying to the American people
about Vietnam, and to American servicemen about the real purpose of the raids
on North Vietnam. Switching her appeal to U.S. troops, she again became
rhetorical and asked:

> All of you ... know the lies. You know the cheating on the body counts,
> the falsified battle reports, and the number of planes that are shot down
> and what your targets really are. Knowing who was doing the lying, should
> you then allow these same people and same liars to define for you who
> your enemy is. Shouldn't we then shouldn't we all examine the reasons
> that have been given to us to justify the murder that you are being paid to
> commit. If they told you the truth, you wouldn't fight, you wouldn't kill....
> You have been told lies so that it would be possible for you to kill.

Although more detailed analyses of Fonda's Hanoi propaganda statements are
found in the next chapter, which addresses her statements' impact, it is useful to em-
phasize a related point here. Consider some of the statements made by this young actress who lacked political sophistication, who was ignorant of history, who had an almost non-existent knowledge of international affairs, and who probably had never
before written anything more complicated than a check: "neocolonialism," the 1954
Geneva Accords, what constituted a military target, different types of aircraft and ordnance, the "Anglico" reference and more. It is obvious that in Hanoi, Jane Fonda was
acting as a willing tool of the Communists, to a considerable extent simply reading
"canned" material created by professional Communist propagandists (albeit perhaps
with an occasional ad lib). Indeed, some of the words and syntax are those of a person or persons for whom English was not a first language, and it is doubtful that the
political language came from Fonda herself.[23]

It is apparent from Mr. Thach's analysis that Fonda's broadcasts had a central
pro–Communist, anti–American, theme and that by those statements she intentionally sought to undermine the United States' military effort in Indochina. But Fonda's
broadcasts were not her only statements in aid of the North Vietnamese. In addition
to the live broadcasts made by Fonda on Hanoi Radio, and replayed endlessly not only
throughout Vietnam but also within the Northern prison camps, she made many
other statements while being escorted around the city and its environs to view what

her hosts claimed were bombed-out civilian installations like schools and hospitals. Examples abound. She was taken to a hamlet called Hong Phong, and afterward the North Vietnamese issued a news release saying that the day before Fonda's visit, American bombing had killed two elderly people — and adding that "Jane Fonda felt great indignation at the U.S. attack on civilian populations."[24] As some of her propaganda broadcasts indicated, she "was taken to see dikes allegedly destroyed the day before. 'In her assessment,' read the Hanoi news release, 'the U.S. had made deliberate attacks on dikes to jeopardize life and terrorize the people.' At a press conference she said that every evidence of bombing that she had seen was directed at a nonmilitary target."[25]

As to Fonda's tours, it is noteworthy that virtually on her first day in Hanoi she was taken to the North Vietnam Communists' "War Crimes" museum which displayed ordnance and artifacts allegedly used by American forces in Vietnam. When, in early 1970, Everett Alvarez, Jr., the first airman–POW in Hanoi, was taken to the museum, he saw his own helmet and uniform and photographs and equipment of other captured pilots.[26] Apparently during her visit to Hanoi, Fonda had told her hosts that every American should tour the museum.

As a result, the North Vietnamese made most of us captive POWs visit the museum against our will. ...In regard to the visit to the War Crimes Museum; yes my room was forced to go there along with other rooms. ...On the night we were forced to visit the War Crimes Museum we were driven by a bus to the site a few miles from the Hanoi Hilton. We knew as soon as we got there that something different was in the mill. There were quite a few extra guards and a large table where they had us sit down. Candy and cigarettes were available — this meant that they were trying to be nice. We thought that we saw some cameras behind the screen and were immediately suspicious. The Vietnamese officer told us that we were in the War Crimes Museum and that they were going to allow us to visit it. Being the ranking officer (SRO) I replied that we had no interest in seeing the display and wanted them to return us to the camp. This did not set too well with them. When everyone at the table stayed in position (I was really proud of my men) they again ordered us to rise and tour the displays. We still did not respond. Three of the soldiers grabbed me knowing that I was the SRO and the spokesman and wrestled me to the floor. The next man in the line was [Big Bill], he was quite big and tough as he had played tackle for [a college] football team. They grabbed him and started to force him to the ground. It took about five of them and it got quite rough. I feared that they would break some of Bill's bones, etc and since we had made the point that we were being forced to attend, I gave the order to Bill to stop resisting and for the remainder of the troops to go on the tour without any further resistance. I did this so that my men would not be injured for it was obvious to me that they had the available manpower to handle any resistance from us. And we had made the point that they were forcing us to visit the facility. As we approached each station we turned our backs to the display and gave the one finger salute to any cameras that might have been recording our visit. It was very obvious by our gestures and positioning that we were not there willingly. They would get no propaganda value from our visit. Shortly after the tour began and it was obvious that they had failed to show willing viewers we were taken back to the prison.[27]

But even worse than her "War Crimes" museum tour, Fonda's most notorious visit was to the site of a Communist anti-aircraft gun, which was used to blast American pilots and their planes out of the sky. Even many of Fonda's supporters were shocked and disgusted to see the helmeted Fonda smiling, clapping, shaking hands and otherwise fraternizing with the weapon's crew. Film of this episode makes clear beyond any doubt whatsoever that Fonda was enjoying herself greatly; indeed, she looks nearly orgasmic.[28] Fraternizing with the gun crew was obscene enough. But then Fonda climbed into the anti-aircraft weapon's control seat, put her eye to the sight, and feigned taking a bead on imaginary American aircraft. The Communist crew smiled and applauded. The North Vietnamese propagandists had a field day, and French and other cameramen distributed the film worldwide. The photo's caption reads: "American actress and activist Jane Fonda is surrounded by soldiers and reporters as she sings an anti-war song near Hanoi during the Vietnam War in July 1972. Fonda, seated on an anti-aircraft gun, is here to 'encourage' North Vietnamese soldiers fighting against 'American Imperialist Airraiders.' She is wearing a helmet and Vietnamese-made ao-dai pantaloon and blouse." Seventeen years later, Fonda was still trying to explain away her conduct, apparently not understanding that what she said then simply reinforced what she had done in 1972 in Hanoi. Here's what a Fonda interviewer wrote in 1989:

"And merely visiting the gun on that trip was not in itself unusual or shameful," she says. "It was a very normal thing for people visiting Vietnam to be taken to an air-defense installation. Hundreds of people had gone and done the same kind of tour. You visited military installations and when you were there you wore a helmet wherever you went."

Still, in that notorious film clip we see her in her helmet, striding up to the gun turret, then suddenly breaking into this rapturous grin and waving her arms as if she's making a theatrical gesture of hailing the deadly weapon. Next she's bouncing up to take a seat on the firing chair behind the barrel of the gun, smiling and waving as if she were blowing kisses.

What was that show-biz–like song-and-dance gesture she made before the gun? It was a song, in fact, that led to the gesture, she explains. While it looks as if she is hailing or blowing kisses to the gun, that arm-waving gesture was actually a show-bizzy flourish to an American song she was singing to the gun crew in exchange for a song they had sung to her.

"There was a group of young soldiers, 17 or 18 maybe, and they sang me their national anthem," she says. It was translated for her and she was struck by the fact that it contained a passage from the American Declaration of Independence: "We hold these truths to be self-evident." Caught up in her naive enthusiasm for the solidarity of spirit between the American Revolution and the Vietnamese struggle, she responded with theatrical gusto when the gun crew asked her to sing them an American song.[29]

In addition to this photo-op, there were many others—with "workers, peasants, students, artists and dancers, historians, journalists, film actresses, soldiers, militia girls, members of the women's union, writers"[30]—especially when Fonda met and socialized with high-ranking North Vietnamese officials. At the end of her trip, she spent some time with Nguyen Duy Trinh, Vice Premier of North Vietnam. Fonda "told him that she was deeply impressed by the Vietnamese people's determination to emerge victorious. She also told the Vice Premier that his people would 'certainly triumph' over the Americans."[31]

Even worse than Fonda's broadcasts, her photo-op tours and her chumminess with North Vietnamese Communists, was her encounter with American POWs being held captive in Hanoi. Since one of the two essential elements of the crime of treason is "adhering" to the enemy — that is, committing an "overt act" — it is unfortunate that there has been so much erroneous reportage about Fonda's interaction with American POWs in Hanoi. The fact is that Fonda is not guilty of certain acts attributed to her, but she is certainly guilty of others.

Let's set the record straight. It has been reported on the Internet in recent years that POWs surreptitiously slipped Fonda messages which she turned over to the North Vietnamese. That story is false.[32] Also untrue is that any POW died for refusing to meet with Fonda.[33]

It is true, however, that POWs were unwillingly made to meet with Fonda. One prisoner didn't even know where he was being taken:

I was informed ... to get ready to leave. We were put on a bus, blindfolded and driven away. Others were loaded on the bus at another stop and the bus left again. We were unloaded, lined up and had the blindfolds removed. We were then taken into a room and seated. The next thing that occurred was the appearance of Hanoi Jane and she began to speak.[34]

But there's more to this story, which reveals just how much Fonda was in the sway of Communist propaganda experts.

Fonda ... was doing a script, at one point she got lost in what she was saying, went back and used *exactly* the same words again for about two sentences to get back on track. I never got a chance (nor did I want to) say anything, it was a listen and be on display thing ... anything else would have brought on problems.[35]

What did she say? Pointing at a chart,

Jane Fonda's theme was that we [the United States] were committing genocide on the Vietnamese people. She also asserted that we were bombing the dikes which was against the rules of war.[36]

At this staged performance, Fonda was parroting a theme provided her by Communist North Vietnam propagandists, one entirely consistent with broadcasts and other statements she had already made in Hanoi.

Needless to say, Fonda quickly lied about her meeting with the Hanoi Hilton POWs, continuing to parrot the North Vietnamese propaganda line:

This is Jane Fonda speaking from Hanoi. Yesterday evening ... I had the opportunity of meeting seven U.S. pilots. Some of them were shot down as long ago as 1968 and some of them had been shot down very recently. They are all in good health. We had a very long talk, a very open and casual talk. We exchanged ideas freely. They asked me to bring back to the American people their sense of disgust of the war and their shame for what they have been asked to do.

They told me that the pilots believe they are bombing military targets. They told me that the pilots are told that they are bombing to free their buddies down below, but, of course, we all know that every bomb that falls on North Vietnam endangers the lives of the American prisoners.

They asked me: What can you do? They asked me to bring messages back to their loved ones and friends, telling them to please be as actively involved in the peace movement as possible, to renew their efforts to end the war.

One of the men who has been in the service for many, many years has written a book about Vietnamese history, and I thought that this was very moving, that during the time he's been here, and the time that he has had to reflect on what he has been through and what he has done to this country, he has— his thought has turned to this country, its history of struggle and the people that live here.

They all assured me that they have been well cared for. They — they listen to the radio. They receive letters. They are in good health. They asked about news from home.

I think we all shared during the time I spent with them a sense of — of deep sadness that a situation like this has to exist, and I certainly felt from them a very sincere desire to explain to the American people that this was is a terrible crime and that it must be stopped, and that Richard Nixon is doing nothing except escalating it while preaching peace, endangering their lives while saying he cares about the prisoners.

And I think that one of the things that touched me the most was that one of the pilots said to me that he was reading a book called *The Draft*, a book written by the American Friends Service Committee [Quakers], and that in reading this book, he had understood a lot about what had happened to him as a human being in his 16 years of military service. He said that during those 16 years, he had stopped relating to civilian life, he had forgotten that there was anything else besides the military and he said in realizing what had happened to him, he was very afraid that this was happening to many other people.

I was very encouraged by my meeting with the pilots [because] I feel that the studying and the reading that they have been doing during their time here has taught them a great deal in putting the pieces of their lives back together again in a better way, hopefully, and I am sure that when — when they go home, they will go home better citizens than when they left.[37]

This live broadcast by Hanoi Jane, directed to American troops, free and captive, throughout North Vietnam, was blatantly false.

- The prisoners were not "all in good health."
- Fonda did not have "a very long talk" with them.
- The meeting was not "very open and casual."
- They did not "exchange ideas freely."
- The prisoners did not express "their sense of disgust of the war and their shame for what they have been asked to do."
- They did not ask Fonda to encourage their "loved ones and friends … to please be as actively involved in the peace movement as possible."
- They did not assure her "that they have been well cared for."
- They did not express "a very sincere desire to explain to the American people that this was a terrible crime and that it must be stopped, and that Richard Nixon is … endangering their lives while saying he cares about the prisoners."

These lies were simply more canned North Vietnamese propaganda, broadcast in furtherance of Fonda's intent to damage the United States and help the North Vietnamese.

Can it be said that these lies, and the rest of what Fonda said and did in Hanoi, could have been construed by a jury as having provided "aid and comfort" to our North Vietnamese enemy? We'll have the answer in the next chapter. For now, suffice it to note the words of an American POW who would later become a United States Congressman: In the summer of 1972, "the voice of Jane Fonda hung in the air over Camp Unity. Our camp guards and the commander were overjoyed to have a celebrity of her status come over and align herself with their 'humane cause.' I'll never forget seeing a picture of her seated on an antiaircraft gun, much like the one that had shot my plane out of the air and given seven years of my life to the North Vietnamese prison system. I stood in front of her photograph in a quiz [interrogation] room and stared in disbelief until the twisting in my gut made me turn away."[38] While Sam Johnson was revolted by Fonda's visit, a prominent North Vietnam colonel—"journalist" Bui Tin—saw the value of her presence in Hanoi: "That visit and the support it showed had great impact on the Vietnamese people.... We realized that there were two Americas—one who dropped bombs on us, and the other who had sympathy."[39]

As Colonel Bui Tin's "sympathetic" comrade boarded a Soviet "Aeroflot jet in Hanoi for the flight to Paris ... [s]he hugged her Vietnamese hosts. As a pledge of solidarity, they gave her a ring made out of the wreckage of a downed U.S. plane."[40] Soon after, Fonda continued to parrot the North Vietnamese propaganda line, intentionally lying about her meeting with the American POWs. *The Washington Post* reported that at a stopover Paris press conference,

Jane Fonda, back from Hanoi, said today that a group of American war prisoners asked her to tell their parents and friends to work for the victory of Sen. George McGovern because "they fear if Nixon stays in office they will be prisoners forever."

The actress said at a news conference that seven prisoners she met gave her messages for scores of people urging them to defeat President Nixon in the November election.

The prisoners, wearing purple and red striped uniforms, were shown in a 20-minute silent color film with Miss Fonda...

The rest of the film, emphasizing what the actress considers to be deliberate American attacks on the North Vietnamese dike system, showed her in black native pajama pants and a black T-shirt touring paddy fields and wading through bomb ruins.

The actress acknowledged that she had made daily radio broadcasts over Hanoi radio aimed at American servicemen...

The longest-serving prisoner she saw had been in Hanoi since 1967, the most recent since last month. "They assured me that they were in good health," she said. "When I asked them if they were brainwashed they all laughed. Without exception, they expressed shame at what they had done."[41]

From Paris, having spent nearly a month in North Vietnam consorting with America's enemy—by making broadcasts, by meeting with senior Communist officials, by touring civilian and military sites, by "interviewing" American prisoners of war — Fonda returned to New York. She landed at Kennedy Airport — reportedly wearing the black pajamas and coolie hat of the Viet Cong.[42]

1. Emphasis added. A copy of this cable is in the possession of the authors.

2. Andersen, *Citizen Jane,* 253.

3. Stockdale, *In Love and War,* 179; emphasis added. The "We will win this war on the streets of New York" statement, quoted above, was made to Stockdale by one of the Communist North Vietnamese's chief propagandists.

4. Rochester and Kiley, *Honor Bound,* 3.

5. In Korea, "while maltreatment had often enough been the lot of prisoners of war … [t]he Korean experience added a new dimension – the comprehensive exploitation and indoctrination of the Americans in furtherance of the enemy's political aims. As official U.S. writings later stated, the Communists made the prison compound an extension of the battlefield, and their treatment of prisoners was 'but another weapon in the worldwide war for the minds of men.' In the camps, political and ideological warfare continued, directed against the prisoners and through them, against world support for the United Nations' effort" (Vernon E. Davis, *The Long Road Home: U.S. Prisoner of War Policy and Planning in Southeast Asia,* 7).

6. Rochester and Kiley, *Honor Bound,* 340.

7. Rochester and Kiley, *Honor Bound,* 341. Not surprisingly, in this respect, the Plantation was not unlike the Nazis' Theresienstadt ghetto. "Situated near the Czech city of Prague, it served a dual function. An assembly center for transports of Czech Jews to Auschwitz, Theresienstadt also was a 'model' to reassure foreign governments and international welfare agencies that Jews, especially elderly ones from Germany, were living in a decent place. … Most were eventually deported and murdered" (Richard L. Rubenstein and John K. Roth, *Approaches to Auschwitz, the Holocaust and Its Legacy,* 254).

8. Rochester and Kiley, *Honor Bound,* 337.

9. Collier, *The Fondas,* 225. Fonda's need to be of use to others was not limited to her North Vietnam pilgrimage. Indeed, on Barbara Walters' February 9, 2001, TV show, Fonda admitted that she "needed to be needed." Collier's use of the term "malleable" was an accurate characterization of Fonda, for on the same TV show she made several admissions to the same effect: "I became what my father wanted"; "I became whatever the man wanted me to be"; and her last husband, Ted Turner, "got used to me being malleable."

10. Fonda's itinerary in North Vietnam was pieced together from various descriptions in the press, and her own statements at press conferences held in Hanoi on July 20, Paris on July 25, and New York on July 27. Doubtless, intelligence sources contributed information.

11. In order that Fonda's North Vietnamese itinerary be presented exactly as it appears in the *Hearing Report,* no effort has been made to correct typographical or other errors.

12. One consequence of Fonda's visit to the so-called "War Crimes" museum is discussed later in this chapter.

13. At this entry, the *Hearing Report* raised the question of why an English-language tape would be aimed at "Saigon Soldiers," and asked whether the broadcast could also have been "meant for American ears with respect to desertion?" (*Hearing Report,* 7641).

14. In order that the list of Fonda's broadcasts be presented exactly as it appears in the *Hearing Report,* no effort has been made to correct typographical or other errors.

15. *Hearing Report,* 7642.

16. The complete texts of Fonda's broadcasts in Hanoi, and the statements attributed to her at press conferences and related events by the North Vietnamese (for example, "In her opening statement Jane Fonda pointed out…" *Hearing Report,* 7652) are reproduced in the Appendix exactly as they appear in the *Hearing Report* of the House Committee on Internal Security, September 19, 1972.

17. Of all Fonda's statements, this is among the worst. One pilot explains: "Our ROE [Rules of Engagement] specifically prohibited attacks on dikes, pagodas and hospitals. In fact they went so far as [to] call for us not to make any attack on a 'legitimate' target that would possibly endanger those three if we missed our targets by bombing long, short or wide of them. I'm not suggesting that we wanted to attack pagodas or hospitals, but in announcing that self-imposed limitation, we tied our hands. The enemy knew that ROE. So guess where a lot of the AA [anti-aircraft] sites were emplaced. Yup. On those very dikes and near those very pagodas and hospitals that were prohibited, indeed, protected by our own ROE." Email in the possession of the authors.

18. Joseph E. Thach, author of the "Memo Re Radio Broadcasts from North Vietnam by U.S. Citizens" set forth in Chapter 2.

19. The analysis of five of Fonda's principal broadcasts from North Vietnam are reproduced here *verbatim*.

20. In order that Mr. Thach's analysis be presented exactly as it appears in the *Hearing Report*, no effort has been made to correct typographical or other errors.

21. Mr. Thach's Theme Analysis contained a footnote explaining the term "Anglico": "*Anglico is a current military term which stands for 'Air-Naval Gunfire Liaison Company,'* a shore detachment composed of U.S. Marines and Sailors which direct air and artillery strikes from off-shore Navy ships. The usage of this acronym, hardly a familiar term even within the U.S. armed forces, implies that this particular message is a highly sophisticated appeal prepared by professionals [in] the field."

22. Emphasis added.

23. A good example is Fonda's use of the term "neocolony." That, and associated terms like "neocolonialism," have been favorite buzz words of the Communists for decades. As Isaiah (Ike) McMillan, a prisoner of the Viet Cong in the South later incarcerated in North Vietnam, stated, "The North Vietnamese also explained about colonialism. They told us about the British empire and pointed out the difference between the British method and the American method, which they called *neocolonialism*" (Grant, *Survivors*, 291; emphasis added).

24. Collier, *The Fondas*, 225.

25. Collier, *The Fondas*, 225.

26. Alvarez and Pitch, *Chained Eagle*, 218.

27. Email from the narrator, in possession of the authors.

28. On Sunday, November 19, 2000, the E! Channel presented a two-hour biographical documentary on Jane Fonda in which the anti-aircraft gun film clip was shown. That presentation also featured sound bites of some of Fonda's North Vietnam broadcasts. The voice was unquestionably hers.

29. *Chicago Tribune*, interview of Jane Fonda by Ron Rosenbaum, January 20, 1989 (excerpted from *Vanity Fair*).

30. *Hearing Report*, 7671.

31. Andersen, *Citizen Jane*, 256.

32. See *www.Hanoijane.net* for a statement by Mike McGrath, president of NAM-POW rebutting this story.

33. It has been reported in the media and on the Internet that two POWs were tortured in an effort to force them into meeting with Fonda. However, despite considerable effort to find independent corroboration of these stories, we have been unable to do so. Accordingly, in assessing Fonda's conduct in North Vietnam, we cannot base any of the case against her upon either of these stories.

34. Email in the possession of the authors.

35. "Problems" is a euphemism. Lack of cooperation at this show interview would surely have resulted in more torture. The source of the former POW's quoted words is an email in the possession of the authors.

36. Email in the possession of the authors.

37. *Hearing Report*, 7670. Back in the United States, Fonda telephoned the wife of one of the POWs: "She called me after that meeting to let me know [my husband] was fine. I said I just didn't see how he could be fine held in prison, kept from his country, his home and his family. She hung up on me." Email in the possession of the authors.

38. Sam Johnson and Jan Winebrenner, *Captive Warriors: A Vietnam POW's Story*, 264.

39. Andersen, *Citizen Jane*, 256–57. When Fonda departed Hanoi, seeing her off were members of the Vietnam Committee of Solidarity with the American People and the Vietnam Film Artistes Association.

40. Andersen, *Citizen Jane*, 257. There is no way to know whether an American airman perished in the crash of the aircraft from which Fonda's souvenir was made.

41. *The Washington Post*, July 26, 1972.

42. The day after arriving in New York, Fonda held another press conference, continuing her attacks on the United States and her defense of the Viet Cong and North Vietnamese. Within a month, she was back on the platform, this time in San Francisco. Among other statements, Fonda said that the Communists "are fighting for us, and their victory is our victory" (F.B.I.–prepared transcript of F.B.I.–recorded tape of Fonda's speech, in the possession of the authors). Fonda's attacks on American POWs continued until after their repatriation in 1973. When the last accounted-for American POW was out of Vietnam, officially April 1, 1973, stories of the brutal treatment to which they had been subjected began to surface. True to form, Fonda castigated them. Hanoi Jane called these Americans — who had suffered indescribably, and walked into freedom with their heads held high and their wounds, psychological and physical, mostly hidden from public view — "'liars, hypocrites, and pawns.' She was livid at the charge that these men had been tortured: 'Tortured men do not march smartly off planes, salute the flag, and kiss their wives. They are liars. I also want to say that these men are not heroes.' One of the first contingent of POWs said that, indeed, he had not only been tortured, but that the Viet-

namese had tortured him — broken his arm — for the specific purpose of forcing him to see her during her visit to North Vietnam. Jane's response was a shrug: 'Nobody's perfect, not even the Vietnamese'" (Peter Collier, *National Review*, July 17, 2000). This POW's statement has not been corroborated. Fonda's impugning of POW torture stories persisted: "At home, there were some Americans who refused to believe that POWs were tortured. Others believe that their torture was somehow justified. In 1973, shortly after the American POWs were repatriated, anti-war activist Jane Fonda, after hearing reports, of Americans tortured in the camps in North and South Vietnam, commented to *Newsweek* reporters: "There was most probably torture of POW's[,] guys who misbehaved and treated their guards in

a racist fashion or tried to escape were tortured. Some [U.S.] pilots were beaten to death by the people they had bombed when they parachuted from their planes. But to say that torture was systematic and the policy of the North Vietnamese is a lie" (Robert C. Doyle, *Voices from Captivity*, 192, citing *Newsweek*, April 16, 1973, 51). See also "Jane Fonda and Tom Hayden — Candid Conversation, "*Playboy* (April 1974): 67. Interestingly, in *Reunion* Hayden writes, "Instead of trying to heal the wounds of war, Nixon chose the POWs as his true heroes.... Nixon resurrected an old rage still close to my surface. Asked for a reaction by reporters, I recall snapping back that the POWs were 'liars, hypocrites, and pawns in Nixon's effort to rewrite history.' Jane remembers that it was actually she who made the comment" (Hayden, *Reunion*, 454).

"GIVING THEM AID AND COMFORT"

The international publicity surrounding her trip may have helped prevent U.S. plans for bombing the dikes of North Vietnam (Tom Hayden, Reunion, 450)

We know that the Communist North Vietnamese were conducting an international propaganda war, especially aimed at the "hearts and minds" of the American people and their military forces in Vietnam. We know that indispensable foot soldiers in the propaganda war were disaffected Americans, preeminent among them Jane Fonda, who journeyed to the very heart of the North Vietnamese homeland to serve their cause. We know that Fonda made pro–Communist, anti–American broadcasts and engaged in other conduct — aimed at our troops, free and captive — intending to contribute to the Communists' effort to further their propaganda campaign, to improve their military position, and thus to injure the United States.

Did Fonda succeed?

When we focus on what the North Vietnamese needed from their propaganda campaign — namely, to portray themselves as victims of post–Franco aggressive American neocolonialism, to legitimize their attack on the South, to undermine our military effort in defense of the South and, in Jim Stockdale's words, achieve "a propaganda-induced disillusionment of the Western adversary"[1] — it readily becomes clear that Fonda's activities in Hanoi were directed to those ends. Indeed, during a September 1972 shootdown's "initial interrogation, while they were trying to convince me that the war was bad and that the American people were against it, the [North Vietnamese] repeatedly reminded me that *even 'the great Jane Fonda' labeled us as war criminals*, so I should admit my crimes and receive more lenient treatment."[2]

It is indisputable that American prisoners in South and North Vietnam were forced to listen to Hanoi Jane's pro–Communist, anti–American propaganda broadcasts.

- "Jane Fonda's tape was played in my camp repeatedly…"[3]
- I heard "her taped broadcast advising us, 'You are war criminals and should be tried as such,' and to 'do everything you can to help the (North) Vietnamese!'"[4]
- "Inside the famed 'Hanoi Hilton' POW camp, Fonda's words were broadcast over loudspeakers day and night until,

in the words of one prisoner, 'we almost went fucking crazy. It's difficult to put into words how terrible it is to hear that siren song that is so absolutely rotten and wrong.... It was worse than being manipulated and used. She got into it with all her heart. She wanted the North Vietnamese to win. She caused the deaths of unknown numbers of Americans by buoying up the enemy's spirits and keeping them in the fight. That's not what you'd expect from Henry Fonda's daughter."[5]

- Fonda's tapes were played not only in the Hanoi Hilton itself, but in virtually every other Communist prison. One of the POWs who was forced to meet with Fonda has said, "One of the most demeaning and infuriating results of this criminal act she performed [the meeting] was the fact that the V [North Vietnamese] played statements by Hanoi Jane on the prison radio for days following her appearance."[6]

- "When the [North Vietnamese] announced on the radio (Radio Hanoi, which was piped to speakers high in our cells, so we couldn't cut them, and which was played at 6:30 AM and 8:00 PM daily) that there was going to be a visit to Hanoi from these two (Ramsay Clark and Jane Fonda), by name, we discussed it in our daily communications time (during the noon siesta, when there was only an occasional roving guard coming into the cell block) and graded this as being an A-visit. We had started grading the visits from groups, according to the importance given them by the [North Vietnamese]. We knew these two would be given the red carpet treatment, and they were. ...[After repatriation] I was asked to be interviewed on a national TV broadcast, by Harry Reasoner. I was asked how I felt about Jane Fonda, and I replied, 'The kindest thing I can say about that is that I'm not fonda Jane.' To this day, I get a sick feeling in the pit of my stomach, whenever her name comes up ... including right now, as I write this!"[7]

Col. Larry Guarino remembers Fonda's visit very well:

The Box [loudspeaker] hailed the arrival of a famous American movie actress who had "come to Hanoi to demonstrate her friendship with the Vietnamese people and her opposition to the illegal immoral, and unjust war." The Box also told us that "their friend Jane Fonda" had met with some American prisoners, to talk about the war and their treatment ... The Vietnamese played a tape, which they said had been made by Fonda and a group of young American women, demonstrating against the war outside the main gate of the U.S. Army base at Fort Dix, New Jersey. We were all sitting on the pad listening to the women singing, in lusty voices, a song entitled, "Fuck the Army!" Actually, they didn't sing it, they screamed it. *We sat there in shock, trying to adjust to the harsh realization that these were our own American women! We couldn't believe that they would involve themselves in such filth to show their dissension and encourage our soldiers to desert!*[8]

When POWs had a choice whether to listen to Fonda's propaganda, which was not often, predictably they refused, although there was a price to pay. One POW recalls, "About 100 of us were in a compound near the Chinese border in 1972.... One day all of the cells were opened in our building ... and we were ordered out of our cell and marched over to some outside area to listen to a tape of [Fonda] spewing garbage about the war. I do recall she was using every bit of her acting training to convince the listener of her anti-war, anti-American opinions. After a few minutes of listening I asked the guard if we had to stay and listen to that tape. He surprisingly said, "No," so I went back to the building/cell. Shortly thereafter everyone else had returned to their cells and we were 'punished' for our transgressions by being locked up for 7-10 days without being permitted outside to bathe/wash clothes or have a lamp in the cell. Previous camps had bare light bulbs in the cells which were on all the time. This camp had none. Our only light was what came thru the small windows during the day and an oil lamp made out of an empty tuna fish type of can."[9] Another report from the camp on the Chinese border confirms that the North Vietnamese were intent on exposing the POWs to Fonda's propaganda:

They brought Sony tape recorders that were battery operated, and we all had to sit around and listen to tapes that were done expressly for us by [Clark] and Jane Fonda ... basically telling us what a bunch of good guys the North Vietnamese were, and what a bunch of jerks we were. We ought to be sorry, and we ought to protest the war, and rise up and criticize the war, and these kinds of things. It just really pissed you off if nothing else.[10]

Fonda's propaganda junket to North Vietnam had an adverse impact not only on the American POWs held captive there, but also on those who were still free: "I wasn't yet in Hanoi when Fonda made that infamous visit in July 1972," one of the last shootdowns remembers. "I offer you a thought that might prove appropriate to consider while you evaluate the impact of her actions. There were a lot of us who were also still flying combat missions in July of 1972. As one of them (I was shot down in September), I shall never forget the picture in *Stars and Stripes* of her sitting in a NVA [North Vietnam Army] AA [anti-aircraft] gun looking through a gun sight, or the words she spoke. Great stuff to see, hear and read as you man up for a combat mission. My point is this: the true costs Jane Fonda inflicted on our country and people in that war go far, far beyond those which could be construed as the misguided pontifications of a Hollywood diva. She truly caused significant pain and suffering to those who honorably served this country.... Clearly, those already in North Vietnamese prisons bore the brunt ... but her actions were also ... deliberate stabs in the back to those of us still fighting our country's bidding in cockpits, ships and foxholes."[11]

Understandably, the POWs subjected to Fonda's diatribes—broadcast not only to them, but throughout North and South Vietnam and around the world—reacted strongly.[12] After all, she had accused them of gratuitously killing innocent civilians, of using illegal weapons, of being war criminals, of fostering the imposition of neocolonialism, and more. At the same time, she had attacked their Commander-in-Chief, and lauded the Viet Cong and North Vietnamese. Worse, Fonda had implied that American soldiers should desert and mutiny. This was the precise propaganda line the North Vietnamese had been putting out for years, but now it was coming from an American actress who possessed worldwide celebrity, and whose celebrity guaranteed that her statements and other conduct in Hanoi would garner international publicity, as they certainly did.

As to the effect of Fonda's activities in North Vietnam on the home front, an American law professor writing about the esoteric subject of "protest travel" has inadvertently provided us with further evidence of the value to the Communists of her trip to Hanoi. "High-profile 'protest' travel, such as that of actress Jane Fonda and others to North Vietnam during the undeclared war, provides an apt illustration: their travels conveyed a message that urged [the American] people to question government policy. Their meetings with North Vietnamese leaders humanized the enemy, challenging the public to think the unthinkable: Perhaps we can talk to them, perhaps they don't have horns and tails after all."[13]

Fonda's trip to Hanoi sent a message not only to the American public, but to the North Vietnamese as well. Here is an exchange between *The Wall Street Journal* and Col. Bui Tin, a dedicated Communist cadre for most of this life, and one of the first officers of the North Vietnamese army to enter Saigon on the day it fell.

Q: Was the American antiwar movement important to Hanoi's Victory?

A: *It was essential to our strategy.* Support for the war from our rear [from China] was completely secure while the American rear was vulnerable. Every day our leadership would listen to world news over the radio at 9 a.m. to follow the growth of the American antiwar movement. *Visits to Hanoi by people like Jane Fonda ... gave us confidence that we should hold on in the face of battlefield reverses.* We were elated when Jane Fonda, wearing a red Vietnamese dress, said at a press conference that she was ashamed of American actions in the war and that she would struggle along with us.

Q: Did the politburo pay attention to these visits?

A: Keenly.

Q: Why?

A: Those people represented the conscience of America. The conscience of America was part of its war-making capability, and we were turning that power in our favor. America lost because of its democracy; through dissent and protest it lost the ability to mobilize a will to win.[14]

There is perhaps no better testimony to how Fonda's activities in North Vietnam may have inhibited U.S. war policy than that provided by Tom Hayden: "The international publicity surrounding [Fonda's] trip may have helped prevent U.S. plans for bombing the dikes of North Vietnam."[15]

To examine the success of Fonda's pro–Communist, anti–America propaganda efforts on behalf of the North Vietnamese, the House Committee on Internal Security at the time of the September 1972 hearing obtained the analyses of three experts on enemy propaganda and psychological warfare. The pertinent testimony of Edward Hunter and reports of Francis M. Watson, Jr., and Brigadier General S.L.A. Marshall is reproduced here verbatim, except for material indicated as having been omitted.

ANALYSIS OF JANE FONDA'S ACTIVITIES IN NORTH VIETNAM[16]

Edward Hunter[17]

I had the opportunity as part of my responsibility in World War II to review and analyze enemy propaganda for the U.S. Government. This came in many forms, from radio broadcasts directed at Allied forces and publics, to enemy films and photos, devised to weaken and subvert morale on our side....

Troops ordinarily discount anything known to come from the enemy's side. They know that the enemy has a harmful intent in telling it. The enemy knows this, and so a number of devices are concocted to lend credibility to what emanates from its territory....

The enemy seeks to add credibility to its propaganda, too, by putting an American citizen before the microphone, and by having him or her address the American troops. ...When the American citizen, especially one with the glamour and the prestige value of a Jane Fonda, can travel back and forth between the United States and the enemy capital without interference or arrest by the American authorities, the effect on military morale is bad to devastating.

What comes from a source on one's own side commands attention, under any circumstance. When the enemy can obtain the assistance of a national of the country it is fighting, to propagate its material in his or her own country, and also to broadcast it personally over the enemy's radio, going to its capital city to do so, it has achieved a form of war propaganda for which as yet there is no professional term—except, perhaps, the old fashioned word, treason....

The effect on Americans stationed in the Asian theatres, within hearing distance, or in reach of propaganda leaflets, pamphlets, or other materials in which her statements are quoted, are obviously expected to be injurious to stamina and morale. The question is only whether the communists have achieved this objective. A study of this approach, that takes advantage of our leniency unparalleled in military annals, shows that damage must certainly have been inflicted by it. Indeed, Fonda's impact is certainly greater than the achievements of a Tokyo Rose in World War II, or even a Hanoi Hanna of the early period of the Vietnam warfare. Fonda has taken this technique a big step forward, proportionate to the new "psywar" dimension in modern warfare, by being able to operate both on her own soil and in communist areas. Once we entered World War II, neither Germany or Japan had this advantage.

Jane Fonda seriously assaulted the stamina of any fighting American listening to her highly dramatic and professional war propaganda. An incalculable number of Americans must have been more or less shaken. The impact of war propaganda is frequently a delayed reaction, that rises to the surface during a period of fatigue, frustration or personal danger. Jane Fonda's emotional outpourings were particularly attuned to this characteristic.

I have just read and analyzed the text of the numerous statements, interviews and broadcasts made by Jane Fonda during her July, 1972 trip to North Vietnam. This survey will therefore be limited to her activities, and her impact, particularly on American troops in Vietnam. Her broadcasts to the American forces and the Vietnamese and her declarations made during that journey continue to be put on the air, directed at U.S. troops and the Vietnamese, after her departure. The enemy obviously recognizes this as highly suitable for exploitation as propaganda weaponry against the Americans, the South Vietnamese, and others helping us.

1. Identification—Jane Fonda is not restricted to the scene of her operations, on enemy soil, as was Tokyo Rose, sure to be arrested and prosecuted upon her return to the United States. She is able to pursue her propaganda work in her native land, this is the target of communist international operations, while supporting Hanoi's position on every issue. The mind of an American soldier in Vietnam is attacked this way from front and rear.

The enemy is not only in front of him, but behind him, in his homeland. At the same time, those whom he is fighting are being portrayed to him as not really the enemy.

If this weren't so, they obviously would be arrested, wouldn't they! This is the confused picture that is being presented to the typical soldier, who is forced to do the fighting and the dying.... Such broadcasts and other activities of Fonda constitute a propaganda pressure in which foe becomes friend, making foes of one's friends....

2. *Coordination*—Jane Fonda's broadcasts and declarations parallel, in the points she stressed and in what she did not mention, precisely what the enemy was insisting upon, or ignoring....

3. *Reinforcements and Orchestration—Two of the most forceful tactics in a propaganda warfare assault on troops require precisely the contribution made by Fonda.* The one is reinforcement. When a soldier hears something from his own as well us the enemy's side, this is the strongest possible reinforcement....

4. *Professionalism—Jane Fonda's broadcasts and other declarations made in North Vietnam fit neatly into the up-to-the-minute, Communist Party line, and were tactically adapted to the most recent developments in the fighting and "peace" sectors. They were visibly the product of communist psychological warfare planning. Their wording was highly professional in structure and aims. Her varied talks and statements dove-tailed, with her arguments adapted to different audiences. Her operations were those of a team member in the enemy's "psywar" organization.*

Any soldier who listened, or read her crisp, dramatic presentations, could not help but be at least subtly affected, in present or future attitudes....

...The enemy's success in enlisting Americans who possess what is called "prestige value" to help in the execution of its propaganda warfare catches the target soldier off balance. He does not anticipate being deceived and lied to by fellow Americans. His stamina, therefore, is more likely to be shaken. In war time, this is tantamount to being wounded. A psychological casualty is as advantageous, or more so to the enemy as any other kind. The enemy finds its best use for such as Jane Fonda in this area of service.

Her broadcasts and statements at Hanoi reinforced and coordinated major issues that the communists are propagandizing in the United States and elsewhere....

She supported the communist claims by clever use of calculating selected material such as the Pentagon Papers. She simply did not mention the invasion across the DMZ (demilitarized zone) by most of the North Vietnamese Army, but by reverse logic, she accused the United States of being the invader.

5. *Reverse Logic—Rarely did even Goebbels go to greater extremes of calculated distortion and propaganda lying against the United States than Fonda did during her brief month of North Vietnamese vituperation against her native land.* She kept sounding the Red note of inevitable American military defeat and inevitable Red victory—a win policy becomes the desirable goal for the communists, whereas a no win policy has to be America's destiny. Indeed, she called on

Americans to help this process along, of achieving a Red victory and American defeat.

She supported, in this contest, Hanoi's insistence on American submission to each of its demands....

Subtly, she supported the build-up by the Reds of an Orwellian basis for the concocted charge of genocide against the United States, that we can surely anticipate, if Red psychological warfare deceptions enable communist conquest to succeed. She repeatedly used such terms as crimes, heinous crimes, and criminals—all referring to Americans and the United States. She had only the greatest praise for the North Vietnamese. *Her accusations against us actually surpassed those of Tokyo Rose.*

Certainly, anyone who recalls the text of Tokyo Rose's broadcasts must admit that Jane Fonda's goes far beyond what Tokyo Rose said, certainly in the actress' condemnation of the United States.

An up-to-the-minute propaganda service was rendered to the enemy by Fonda. Frequent references to the fighting at Quang Tri, the provincial capital in South Vietnam that was captured by the North Vietnam divisions in their dash across the demilitarized zone—demilitarized unilaterally, only to our side—demonstrates this.

Communist atrocities against the Quang Tri residents are an international scandal. So was the set-back to the communist divisions. Red troops, fleeing from the city, slaughtered civilian men, women and children indiscriminately along with South Vietnamese prisoners. Residents of the city significantly fled toward the South, into Saigon-controlled areas, and away from the North and Hanoi-controlled territory, even when it was American planes that were bombarding the Red troops. Nobody wanted to stay with the communists.

Yet Fonda took this opportunity to demonstrate her loyalty to the communist side. She referred to the strategic hamlets in the South where the refugees were being given a haven as "concentration camps". She indulged in the big lie that the "liberation troops"—meaning the Red divisions—occupied the province "in cooperation with the peasants.... All the people in the province arose like birds breaking out of their cages."

These lies by an American citizen whom every movie goer knew, whose prestige had only just been shockingly enhanced by receipt of a top Hollywood award, were translated into Vietnamese. They could not be without impact on those who heard her in the South. She shifted the facts, in her English text for Americans, away from Red terror and the flight from the Reds, and the Red set-backs, to which she made no reference. She spoke, instead of the thousands of years the Vietnamese fought for "freedom and independence" and identified this with the present fighting by the invading communists in their occupation of Quang Tri.

She made a hero out of the Vietnamese hijacker. Nguyen Thai Binh, who was killed trying to seize a plane at Saigon to go to Hanoi after returning from his education in the United States. He "wanted to do nothing more than to return to his people and fight for freedom and independence for his country," she said in a Hanoi broadcast beamed to "the Saigon students."

"We have a common enemy—U.S. imperialism", she declared, identifying herself in plain English with the enemy. "Imperialism" is a present day code word used by Reds when they specifically mean United States.

This broadcast declared that the American people were demanding acceptance of Hanoi's demands, and that "we identify with the struggle of your people," referring to the communist side. The Vietnamese who hear this—and many Americans too—knowing that she passed freely between the United States and enemy territory, implementing her self appointed task, *could only be confused, certain that for her to be able to do this, there must be powerful influences in the American Government—wittingly or unwittingly—supporting this.* Vietnamese must remember that treason inside the French Government facilitated France's defeat in Indo-China, and cannot help but equate the situation today. *Too many parallels exist. Americans hearing her preach this way can only have their doubts and frustrations increased.*

When an American travels to an enemy capital, and coordinates his or her declarations with enemy needs and claims, what else can it be but conspiratorial, and what other description can apply but treasonable? Of course, this has to have a detrimental influence on stamina and morale. This impact is increased and given a respectability when the propagandist is able to go back and forth between her own and enemy soil. A legitimacy is given by government in this way to whatever she says as if it had secret approval. What other impression can a soldier, for whom facts stand out starkly—you either live or you die—be expected to get?

My propaganda analysis of the Fonda broadcasts from Hanoi were made in the same manner as I analyzed propaganda in World War II for the Government. *What I have found in her work was irrefutable evidence of intent to assault the morale and stamina of the American fighting man and the South Vietnamese soldier.* Her outpourings also were translated into Vietnamese, and beamed at the South Vietnamese troops and civilians alike, to soften both up for fifth columnism and treason.

The information that an American of glamour such as Jane Fonda, was telling them that they were on the wrong side, that they should be distrusting and opposing the Americans, and rejecting their own elected government in favor of the Viet Cong and the North Vietnamese communist forces, could even have a decisively detrimental impact in some minds. Jane Fonda's broadcast of July 21 from Hanoi to U.S. pilots was typical, in this framework.

This was essentially a wedge-driving or splitting job, with this added subtlety. She, as an American, simultaneously identified herself with the American pilots and with the side they were fighting. Quite specifically, she identified the U.S. pilots with herself against their higher officers and against the American government. This was a tactical transfer—a transfer tactic—in which sides were transposed, the enemy becoming our own side. Indeed, this was a highly professional piece of "psywar" propaganda.

Indeed, it is so concise and professional a job that I most strongly doubt that she wrote it herself. She had to have been working on it with the enemy. Her movements and utterances disclose skilled indoctrination—a brainwashed mind—but even so, her work in Hanoi could not have been an unassisted effort.

The listener, charmed by the voice of the "famous actress" hearing it come so appealingly from the enemy capital at Hanoi, might well have his own thoughts of war guiltily shifted entirely to himself and to the military machine to which he was attached, making it seem as if these were the source of the fighting and the cruelties of war, being convinced that the other side really consisted only of peaceloving people, busily building up, as she said, a free country, who "cannot understand what kind of people would fly over their heads and drop bombs on them." Such inside-out logic is constructed in an appealing manner, so as to exploit the target-recipient's best traits. What can be made to sound more rational, particularly to a calculatingly confused war-weary mind?

No hint was contained in anything she said of any invasion having taken place of South Vietnam, or of any attack from the North across the officially agreed-upon demilitarized zone. No hint that this was accompanied by a terror campaign planned by communist "psywar" tacticians with cruel fitness. Hers was a sob-sister-type of appeal, skillfully and professionally designed to inject guilt feelings into the minds of the American officers and men. "Tonight, when you are alone, ask yourself, what are you doing?" she asked dramatically. "Do you know why you are flying these missions, collecting extra pay on Sundays?"

Yes, indeed, pay for this sort of national task, much more so, overtime pay, did seem incongruous. The injection of the element of financial compensation in terms even of overtime pay subtly suggested to the American pilots that they were hired hands, killing as a job, comparable to gangsters who collect from their bosses to "rub-out" some civilian. Indeed, she used this term, "your bosses", with its sinister connotation, declaring that they had created militarily useless instruments of torture that were being employed against "babies and women and old people" alone. Her words well fitted the actress role in which she was raised.

She referred in this way to "pellet bombs," containing "plastic pellets," which she said "cannot destroy bridges or factories … they cannot pierce steel or cement." The listener would have to shake himself to recall that there were any communist soldiers using any sort of weaponry at all, especially any devilishly cunning booby traps, or that any military supplies were being sent by the Reds into South Vietnam. Her description was of an idyllic countryside, despoiled by us. "I know that if you saw and if you knew the Vietnamese under peaceful conditions, you would hate the men who are sending you on bombing missions," she declared. Thus subtly, she injected hate of their own side.

Her strictures, in common with communist-type propaganda in general, were adapted to long range, world-wide aims, as well as to short-range, local objectives. Her message undercut the use of tactical weaponry developed for our forces, while at the some time supporting the campaign to induce our scientists to sabotage the development of advanced defense production. She referred to people "whose minds think in terms of statistics, not human lives," who "are proud of this now perfection"—that she described as "rough-edged plastic pellets." She closed this broadcast with the declaration, "I believe that in this age of remote controlled push button war, we must all try very, very hard to remain human beings."

Who could argue with this? Except that it related to an extraneous state of affairs, apart from the warfare being fought at that moment, in which all the aggressions actually were those of the communists, who ware implying, through her, in effect, that any defense against the rapist, the mugger, and the invader constituted the assault, not the acts themselves. This is the "psywar" contest in which Fonda represented world-wide communist corrosion of will and character in those being set up as their next target.

Her broadcast, referring to the enemy side, portrayed all of it as people who do not differ "from our own children, our mothers, or grandmothers." The fatigue and understandably frustrated mind of a pilot, fresh from a mission over North

Vietnam, cannot be considered wholly invulnerable to such plaintive appeals from such an American source, particularly in view of the anti-anticommunist policy that permeated most of what he read that issued from his own country, and seemed to be official government policy, as if Fonda only were echoing American official and intellectual views.

The communists were being given all the advantage by default. Jane Fonda being allowed to assault every phase of our society specifically, *by name*, whereas even the words communism, and treason, were practically taboo on our side....

Here, in front of me, is another Fonda broadcast from Hanoi, of July 30, about 1500 words long, announced as "An address to American GIs in South Vietnam." Her appeal to the American flyers had been directed toward breaking their will to hit the targets assigned to them. *This appeal to GIs encouraged them to disobey orders ... desert, and generally take the side of the enemy.* Her broadcasts to the GIs were more brashly worded than to the usually better educated pilots. She preached subversion with subtlety, using as a vehicle the descriptions of what she said other supposedly rebellious American soldiers were doing, dramatically leaving the impression that such insurrection is right and good, and that those hearing her should go and do likewise.

Even those who listened to her out of curiosity, to hear a glamorized film star in a real life role, sure that they could not be influenced, could be softened up by it to accept the same line when they came across it elsewhere reinforced and orchestrated in our customary channels of communications. We would be foolish to discount this impact simply because we cannot pin down what will bring it to the surface later on, when and where.

Jane Fonda's July 30 broadcast to the GIs was in unabashed support of the campaign to destroy the American forces, particularly the U.S. Army, from within. This has been an enemy tactical objective that was built up out of the antidraft movement.

The broadcasts in which she was introduced as talking to Saigon students, was adapted to that age level, which provides the fighting forces of the country, almost wholly so now that the American and other foreign troops are leaving. *The patent objective too, was to encourage treason in faculties and student bodies, a prime target of world-wide communism. The age of the American troops made them particularly vulnerable to this approach.*

At the start of the broadcast, she said, "I loudly condemn the crimes that have been committed by the U.S. Government in the name of the American people against your country," thus supporting the Red splitting tactic that differentiates between the American people and their government. She subtly proceeded along this line, as if what she termed "the repression by the U.S. Government and the Saigon clique" were recognized facts accepted by the peoples of both countries.

Her broadcast gave a shocking insight into the conduct of the American-educated Vietnamese student-hijacker. She told of talking to the Vietnamese students in the United States—one can imagine what she told them!—and of their longing to return "to a peaceful Vietnam."

"For the time being," she said, "they feel that their duty is to remain in the United States and do their political work among the American people."

She subtly put over a particularly cunning piece of enemy propaganda pressure by this approach. She casts suspicion on every patriotic South Vietnamese student in the United States by classifying them all as pro-Red conspirators.

One of the major propaganda gimmicks of the Reds, wherever their people are living a particularly onerous life in a controlled environment that excludes information from the outside, is to portray conditions in the non-communist world as even worse. The truth about the incomparably better life led by people in the United States than elsewhere can hardly be suppressed, so particular attention is paid to whatever isolated case can be drawn on to dispute this fact.

When Jane Fonda can come out and say over the air, as she did that July 26, from Hanoi, describing the United States as a country where "people have no reason for living", it is a particular propaganda gain for the Reds. Those inside communist quarters who are thinking of resistance can be discouraged from undertaking it, and in frustration, may even turn their hatred against America, which they then see as letting them down. *This is a long-time Red propaganda operation to which Jane Fonda contributed her prestige and dramatic skill.*

She engaged in a transfer tactic, too, telling the South Vietnamese that their troubles were due to the United States. She described it as "the American cancer in the Southern part of your country."

Indeed, one would have to go with a hair comb through the rantings of Lord Haw Haw to find much, if anything, equivalent in spleen against the Allies in World War II equivalent to Jane Fonda's tirades against the United States.

Obviously addressing those who are engaged in guerrilla warfare and in other forms of terrorism in South Vietnam, whose booby traps and ambushes have dismembered and disfigured so many American and Vietnamese, she told them: "We thank you for your brave and courageous and heroic fight."

Her report on American prisoners of war followed the long established routine by which a few were trotted out for abject interviews, obviously cowed and rehearsed. The Hanoi regime, in support of this P.O.W. operation, extracts weeks of favorable nation-wide publicity in the United States by releasing, at long intervals, three American prisoners—always three.

Accordingly, a statement broadcast of a "press conference" by Fonda on July 20 records her as saying: "There were seven prisoners that I talked to, some of them who had never spoken to Americans before, and they all expressed regret about what they had done, and they said they had come to recognize that the war is a terrible crime that must be ended immediately."

This must have been a cruel ordeal for the P.O.W.s. The questioning by an American actress who was taking the enemy's position on all things assaulted whatever stamina they had been able to maintain, and to have seemed to confirm the communist propaganda that their country was letting them down, and of invincible Red victory.

Her July 30 broadcast that encouraged mutiny in the American forces generalized with the remark: "In America we do not condone the killing of American officers; we do not condone the killing of anyone."...

These remarks followed her statement that new American recruits in South Vietnam "were separated from the guys who had been there for a while behind barbed wire so they wouldn't find out what had been going on. The men had to turn in their arms at night. Why? Because there were so many U.S. officers being killed. Fragging—the word fragging entered the English language. What it meant was that the soldiers would prefer to roll a fragmentation grenade under the tent flap of their officer, if he was a gung-ho officer who was going to send them out on a suicide mission, rather than go out and shoot people that they did not feel were their enemy."

One hardly needs knowledge of communist double talk to see through these sentences, particularly when they emanated from the enemy capital at Hanoi, uttered by an American known to be favoring the Hanoi cause.

The deteriorating effect on morale and stamina of the Fonda broadcasts should not be underestimated, nor the delayed impact of her tactically chosen subject matter, and its relationship to the major issues with which the Marxists network was concerned.

She went farther, in her assaults on her own country in this Vietnam warfare than Tokyo Rose or even Lord Haw Haw in World War II. The prestige value to the enemy of her as a movie star gave her activities an added impact that none of her predecessors in wartime broadcasting from enemy capitals possessed.

The fact that she can engage in such corrosive activity with impunity, and be accorded a respectability by the press that is without precedent in the annals of warfare, and be able to travel freely to the enemy capital and back is worth Army divisions to the foe. We can be sure they know this, and are determined to take full advantage of it.

Francis M. Watson, Jr.[18]

The enclosed selection of broadcasts, attributed to actress Jane Fonda, were reviewed as you requested. Frankly, although I have pored over literally thousands of pages of underground press material in the past few years, *I have found little that I felt qualified more precisely as purely psychological warfare than these....*

I have to discount Miss Fonda's words as constituting an anti-war protest, not only because they were allegedly directed toward U.S. military forces in the field—a group hardly in a position to act on anyone's protest without disobeying the orders they are operating under—but because she says as much in her text. In other words, she is not addressing her remarks toward influencing the voting behavior of fellow citizens, or toward legislators who are passing on military appropriations, etc., or the President, Secretary of Defense, or even commanders in the field; *she is, in her own words addressing herself to men at the operational level of military units and suggesting to them that they not follow their orders.*

As I noted in the beginning, her techniques, phraseology, and themes are more comparable to combat propaganda operations, designed to encourage misbehavior on the part of troops, than anything else I can think of. For example, her words seem to fit the following passage rather well:

> ...Another major direction of the propaganda effort is to emphasize to the enemy soldier the dangers of combat. Such an appeal, combined with a questioning of the worth of his country's war aims, is designed to encourage the enemy soldier to be particularly cautious and to malinger and to avoid danger at every opportunity, thus reducing the combat effectiveness of his unit. [p 12, U.S. Army FM 33-5, January 1962]

Perhaps more specifically to the Vietnam situation, *I see the texts of these broadcasts as falling quite handily into the statement of a primary psychological goal of insurgent forces* as stated in the 1966 edition of this same manual:

> ...to convince the world and the local population that the motives of nations assisting the threatened government are false. Through national and international media, the insurgent will attempt to malign the motives of all assistance to the local government. Economic exploitation, neo-colonialism, genocide, and capitalism seeking

raw materials and markets are some of the numerous themes used to elicit sympathy and support. [p. 35, U.S. Army FM 33-5, October 1966]

Certain passages in Miss Fonda's material call to mind descriptions of propaganda aimed at the French in the Algerian experience:

> ...Frenchman were told that the war waged by France was unjust, that the FLN was justified in fighting for independence, that the very principles invoked by the FLN were learned from the French Revolution, etc... [p 279 *Undergrounds in Insurgent, Revolutionary, and Resistance Warfare,* Special Operations Research Office, The American University, November, 1963]

Similar material, of course, can be found in the literature on most revolutionary operations in the past fifty or sixty years. The Huks in the Philippines, for example, used some of the same themes.

Getting directly to the resemblance of Miss Fonda's material and traditionally accepted psychological warfare techniques and the prospects of this material affecting troop morale, let me call attention briefly to the origin, history, and theory of this branch of military tactics. As pointed out in U.S. Army manuals, these techniques are as old as recorded history, but came into habitual use in the U.S. services in World War I. There, these efforts focused on surrender appeals to hungry enemy soldiers in trenches. In World War II the techniques were further perfected and broadened, but still, as far as combat troops were concerned, the propaganda appealed heavily to hungry or beleaguered troops or forces whose chances of victory and eventual return to their homeland were rather easily shown to be poor. And, more often than not that has been the case, the propagandist could see a host of personal deprivations among the enemy troops he could seize upon. Even the Tokyo Rose type of effort, at the strategic level, dwelled on the length of time troops had been away from home and played upon their being out of communication with their families and the home scene.

Look at Vietnam....

...in the broadcasts it is easy to spot attacks on what is the basic element of any healthy, well-attended fighting man's spirit—the justice of his cause. Obviously, a man who is hungry enough, will kill just to eat—a frightened man will kill to preserve his own life, etc.—a man who is not so deprived or so threatened must believe in his cause in order to take another human life. Keep pounding at him with arguments otherwise—supported by evidence that the obvious enemy is not the only one who says this—and you begin to get to him.

Then, inject the "war crimes" fear—the "even you may have to answer for this behavior later!!" Use as a background the "women and children" plea, support it with the "I am seeing it with my own eyes, and I am an American, too" credibility potential, and lace it with allusions to the beauty of the women and the pastoral nature of the country side. Come in with the "inhumanity of buttons and levers" against an enemy you don't have to face, and the tearing of flesh with plastic and metal. *It is all in Miss Fonda's text and it is just as it should be, from the standpoint of good propaganda operations.*

Finally, there are some distinct advantages to Jane Fonda, American movie star, and frequent personality around Army posts, as a speaker. She is immediately known. She is glamorous. She has all the trappings of self-sacrifice, and she has rapport. She knows youth and she knows the Army. In this respect she is better than any Tokyo Rose history has ever known—she is a walking encyclopedia of current, cultural and technical intelligence on the U.S. military and the young people who occupy so many of its ranks. She is even an expert on the anti-military movement. She mentions that and thus provides a readily available philosophy and group-association for her listeners.

Just in case all of these things will miss some people, she puts in the personal risk, the prisoner-of-war threat, and the people back home crying over the men overseas, and tops that off with hints that there won't be a job or a place in life for the returning veteran. It is quite complete.

Again, *these broadcasts are, in my opinion, good, military propaganda.* Whether or not they affect troop morale is a matter of assessment, but there is nothing wrong with the design.

Brigadier General S.L.A. Marshall, USA (Ret.)[19]

You wrote me asking my judgment as to the likely effect of the Jane Fonda broadcasts out of North Vietnam on U S service people stationed in that area.

There is no question about the intent of the Fonda broadcasts. The evidence prima facie is that the purpose is to demoralize and discourage, stir dissent and stimulate desertion. But then, that is not the question you posed.

Would it have any one or all of these effects provided the words of the broadcaster were heard by a vulnerable individual? Here I speak of the Fonda production as a whole. *There is no reason to doubt that it would.* To be effective, what is said has to be credible. When the propagandist speaks in the idiom of the audience to whom the words are directed, and in reporting as an eye-witness, cites facts, objects and circumstance with which the listener is likely to be familiar, that meets all of the requirements that insure maximum belief.

I would speculate that Miss Fonda gets help in the preparation of her broadcasts. They are expertly done and are models of their kind.

All of this having been said, as to the main question of whether she did material damage to the well-being of forces in Asia, or for that matter, in the ZI, I am unable to answer.

I would stand on the general proposition that in the occurring circumstances, when any fellow citizen is permitted with impunity to go to such extremes, men and women in the serving forces feel resentful, and in the overwhelming majority, to the degree that they believe they have been let down by government because it does not act, their own feelings of loyalty become taxed. The hurt here is long-term and indirect.

I do know we have an extremely sensitive situation in Indo-China, one probably without precedent in our history. On returning there in July 1970 to get a measure of troop morale and discipline, the Chief of Staff, USA, felt so much alarm at what he found that on getting back to Washington he visited the President to warn him that "anything might happen." That would include large-scale mutiny. Where the balance is just that delicate, any act of aid and comfort to the enemy of the United States could become the fatal straw.

With these analyses on the impact of Fonda's broadcasts from North Vietnam, we conclude Part II of this book. We can now turn to the law of treason and its application to Jane Fonda's activities in North Vietnam.

1. Stockdale, *In Love and War*, x.

2. Email in the possession of the authors; emphasis added. He continued: "[S]everal weeks after I was put in isolation," in the fall of 1972, "an officer came into my cell and asked if there was anything I wanted ... so I said I would like something to read. Almost immediately I received a copy of Tom Hayden's book ... with the admonition that he was Fonda's husband, and that if I read it I would learn the errors of my way."

3. Email in the possession of the authors from a POW Navy pilot.

4. Email in the possession of the authors from a POW Air Force pilot. How did the pilot know that the speaker was Fonda? "[T]he camp commander or one of the English speaking interrogators announced who it was and that the tape had been made exclusively for POWs ... although they never used the term POWs, usually criminals, air pirates, etc.... I believed it was Fonda at the time, and still do. The tape was played through the speakers in each cell."

5. Andersen, *Citizen Jane*, 225.

6. Email in the possession of the authors.

7. Email in the possession of the authors. "Right now" was January 26, 2001.

8. Guarino, *A P.O.W.'s Story*, 321–22; emphasis added. Other POWs have informed us that they, too, heard Fonda's broadcasts, either live or on tape. One has written us that he heard the Fort Dix tape, and that "I did recognize her voice on tape and she was introduced."

9. Email in the possession of the authors.

10. Oral history of Ralph T. Browning, page 37. See note 12 below for other oral histories.

11. Email in the possession of the authors.

12. It was common for the POWs who were exposed to Fonda's broadcasts to want her punished for what they deemed illegal behavior. For example, nearly 20 years later, one former prisoner stated, "I really sort of feel like she should have been tried on some kind of ground for having exceeded the acceptable limits...." This statement — by former POW William J. Reich — and others to the same effect, appear in oral histories given by POW graduates of the United States Air Force Academy to Dr. James C. Hasdorff. Mr. Reich's quotation appears at page 43 of his October 2, 1992, oral history. Nearly two score of these oral histories are archived in the Special Collections department of the United States Air Force Academy library in Colorado Springs, Colorado. The impact of Fonda's 1972 sojourn to North Vietnam remained strong even 20 years later, with some of the former POWs' oral histories containing statements to the effect that they continued to boycott

her films, and that her videotapes should not be sold in military facilities. See, for example, the following oral histories: Thomas G. Storey (October 9, 1972, page 89); Paul A. Kari (April 5, 1992, page 61), "In fact, all these people kept the war going because the Vietnamese people knew if they could get the American people to lose their will to fight, they would win. And every time something like this happened [visits from anti-war activists], it just put another nail in our coffin. I was there for seven years and eight months because creeps like this, Fonda and [former United States Attorney General Ramsey Clark], were over there. It's one reason I'm not a General; it's one reason I'm not in the Air Force; it's one reason I got my vision damaged. There are a lot of reasons, and it makes me very angry that they weren't strung up"; Edward J. Mechenbier (June 20, 1991, page 58), who made the point that if one had been shot down in 1967 or earlier, he would have been unaware of the virulent anti-war movement, and thus overwhelmed when a celebrated American actress showed up in Hanoi to denounce the United States; Ben M. Pollard (May 11, 1992, page 94), "The [Fonda] tape was terrible on the morale of the camp. I thought it was terrible. Yes, there is nothing I can say except total contempt. You know, it's one thing to be anti-war in the United States. It's totally different to be in the arms of the enemy in Hanoi and saying detestable things about your country. Frankly, I hope he [Clark] and Jane Fonda fry in hell..."; Myron L. Donald (September 26, 1991, page 54), "Jane Fonda came traipsing in and said, 'Gee, I would like to see the POWS.' We didn't want to be seen with her. Even standing next to her looks like we're supporting her horseshit. Well, the Vietnamese had told all these people [anti-war visitors] that we were all opposed to the war and this and that, so they've got to find somebody. If nobody would do it, they'd go in and kick the crap out of somebody until they would do it. So Jane Fonda's visit ... directly caused a lot of guys to get the shit kicked out of them..."; John L. Borling (July 1, 1991, page 25), "The anti-war activities were very distressing, had a very negative effect on POW morale."

13. Jeanne M. Woods, "Travel That Talks: Toward First Amendment Protection for Freedom of Movement," 65 *George Washington Law Review* 106 (1996), note 175. At the time of this article's publication, Ms. Woods was associate professor of law at Loyola University School of Law in New Orleans. It is naïve and obscene for Prof. Woods to have believed that Fonda's trip to Hanoi somehow "humanized" for the American public the enemy who, among other atrocities, treated

American prisoners of war in the manner described in the previous chapter.

14. "How North Vietnam Won the War," *The Wall Street Journal*, August 3, 1995; emphasis added.

15. Hayden, *Reunion*, 450. Although Fonda's statements strongly implied that U.S. bombing of North Vietnamese dikes would be some sort of atrocity, the fact is that "destroying dikes to weaken North Vietnam's economy would have been not a war crime, but an attack on a legitimate military target. The British destroyed German dams in World War II, and the NATO bombing of Serbia in the Kosovo war also targeted its economic infrastructure" (*National Review*, February 19, 2001).

16. *Hearing Report*, 7581–7602. In order that Mr. Hunter's testimony and Mr. Watson's and Gen. Marshall's reports be presented exactly as they appear in the *Hearing Report*, no effort has been made to correct typographical and other errors.

17. The *Hearing Report* set forth Mr. Hunter's credentials as follows: "Mr. Hunter served as a propaganda specialist with the Office of Strategic Services during World War II. Later ... he went to the CIA when it was organized.... He also served the U.S. Government abroad as a propaganda specialist, including the Korean war theater. He learned about the new techniques from the inside. He is a leading authority on the techniques of Communism. He put the word 'brainwashing' into our language.... His basic books on the subject are classics, and include 'Brain-Washing in Red China' and 'Brainwashing: Pavlov to Powers.'... He has served as a consultant and as a staff member for various members of the Congress and Congressional committees, as a psychological warfare specialist in the Pentagon, and for various government agencies at home and abroad." Emphasis in Mr. Hunter's Report added.

18. The *Hearing Report* set forth Mr. Watson's credentials as follows: He "is a graduate of the University of Georgia where he received both a BS in Education and a Masters degree in journal-ism. In the early 1960s he was Deputy Manager of an information analysis center for the American Institutes for Research where he conducted research in insurgency and propaganda techniques and revolutionary tactics. He became a specialist in media analysis whereby public opinion trends may be determined from newspapers and other information sources. In 1970 he became chief analyst for a Washington, D.C., firm named National Media Analysis where he studied the so-called 'underground' press and edited published reports detailing the propaganda impact of such newspapers with respect to revolutionary and protest movements in the United States...." Mr. Watson's report was addressed to Dr. Joseph Thach, Research Analyst, Committee on Internal Security, House of Representatives. Emphasis in Mr. Watson's Report added.

19 The *Hearing Report* set forth Gen. Marshall's credentials as follows: "The author of more than 25 books, Brig. Gen. S.L.A. Marshall, USA (Ret.), has been a military writer both in and out of uniform since 1922 after service in World War I during which he rose from infantry private to lieutenant. ... During World War II, Marshall first served as Chief of Orientation for the Army and later was named by Chief of Staff George C. Marshall as one of three officers to establish the Army's historical division. Marshall left active service after World War II but returned to uniform in 1948 to assist in formation of the North Atlantic Alliance. He served in Korea during the war there from 1950 to 1953 and was later an Army observer of conflicts in Sinai, Lebanon, the Congo and Vietnam. Marshall retired in 1960 as Deputy Chief of Information of the Army but returned to Vietnam in 1967 as a columnist, historian and training advisor to Army historians. He is presently the author of a newspaper column on military affairs that is syndicated by the Los Angeles Times and Washington Post." Gen. Marshall's report was addressed to Robert M. Horner, Chief Investigator, House of Representatives Committee on Internal Security. Emphasis in General Marshall's Report added.

Part III

TREASON

Constitutional Treason

*As there is no crime which can more excite and agitate the
passions of men than treason, no charge demands more from
the tribunal before which it is made, a deliberate and
temperate inquiry (Ex parte Bollman, 4 Cranch 75, 125)*

The constitutional and legal foundation for the crime of treason was laid nearly 700 years ago in the English statute of 25 Edward III (A.D. 1350). In order to understand our Constitution's treason provision and its application to Jane Fonda's propaganda broadcasts and her other conduct in North Vietnam, it is necessary to focus on an important part of the Statute of Edward, and to what that part eventually led in the United States of America.

Since fourteenth century England was a monarchy, much of the law of those days was concerned with protecting the monarchical institution and the person who exemplified it — the monarch. Accordingly, among the seven categories of "High Treason" in the Statute of Edward was that of "adhering" to the King's "enemies," giving them "aid and comfort." Although this provision endured throughout the centuries in England, it is with the American colonial experience that its relevance to Fonda begins.

At one point or another, recognition of the crime of treason existed in most of the colonies, either in express legislation or less formally. Whatever form the crime took, it was commonly understood that the colonial version was rooted in the principles and language of the Statute of Edward. However, there is not much legal precedent from the colonial period to illuminate the contours of the "adhering" component of the crime of treason.[1]

For our purposes, the first significant building block in the creation of the modern American crime of treason came shortly before the Declaration of Independence. The Continental Congress had formed an improbably named "Committee on Spies," whose members included John Adams, Thomas Jefferson, Robert Livingston, John Rutledge and James Wilson — all titans of the Revolution.[2] The Committee recommended that the colonies enact treason legislation, and Congress adopted the recommendation, passed it on to the colonies, and, in so doing, utilized the then-familiar language of the Statute of Edward:

Resolved, That all persons abiding within any of the United Colonies, and deriving protection from the laws of the same, owe allegiance to the said laws, and are members of such colony; and that all persons passing through, visiting, or make a temporary stay in any of the said colonies, being entitled to the protection of the laws during the time of such passage, visitation, or temporary stay, owe, during the same time, allegiance thereto:

That all persons, members of, or owing allegiance to any of the United Colonies, as before described, who shall levy war against any of the said colonies within the same, *or be adherent to the King of Great Britain, or others the enemies of the said colonies, or any of them, within the same, giving to him or them aid and comfort,* are guilty of treason against such colony:

That it be recommended to the legislatures of the several United Colonies, to pass laws for punishing, in such manner as to them shall seem fit, such persons before described, as shall be provably attained of open deed, by people of their condition, of any of the treasons before described.[3]

Note the recommendation's reliance on the Statute of Edward's "adherence" prong, its recognition of "enemies," and its explicit "aid and comfort" requirement.

Within a year, most of the former colonies, then members of the "United States," had enacted appropriate legislation using the Committee's and the Congress' recommended language. Thus, at the birth of the Constitution of the United States of America in 1787, there was a 400-year-old acceptance of the idea that it was treason to "adhere" to a government's "enemies" and to give them "aid and comfort." Even though, between Independence in 1776 and adoption of the Constitution in 1787, American courts had not fully fleshed out the meaning of these terms in the context of the newly formed republic. Still, the principle of the crime of treason was well established. That principle would be "codified" in the new Constitution.

The story of dissatisfaction with the Articles of Confederation and the Continental Congress is too well known to be repeated here. Suffice it to say that the absence of an executive power, the chaos of interstate commerce and extreme manifestations of state sovereignty became unacceptable to great numbers of prominent Americans. At first, the idea was simply to strengthen the Articles of Confederation through amendments. One proposal was to give Congress exclusive power to define and punish treason, that power being seen as strictly legislative in nature.[4] The Continental Congress, of course, would in the summer of 1787 be preempted by the Constitutional Convention in Philadelphia. There, the Committee of Detail—which included former Committee on Spies members Rutledge and Wilson—submitted a draft Constitution in August. It contained a treason clause: "treason against the United States shall consist only in levying war against the United States, or any of them; *and in adhering to the enemies of the United States, or any of them.* ...No person shall be convicted of treason, unless on the testimony of two witnesses...."[5]

It is interesting and important for our later purposes to note what this proposal did, and did not, contain. It was the Founders themselves, through their Constitution, who defined the crime of treason, not Congress. The necessity for proof requiring two witnesses was given Constitutional sanction. But the earlier "aid and comfort" requirement was absent. Nor does the draft expressly recognize that the necessary overt act is an element of the offense, and there is no connection made between the overt act and proof of it by two witnesses.

Substantively and procedurally, the draft is quite different from the version that would eventually be proposed and enacted. On August 20, 1787, the entire Convention discussed the proposed treason language.

Mr. Madison thought the definition too narrow. It did not appear to go as far as the Stat. of Edwd. III. He did not see why more latitude might not be left to the Legislature [Congress]. It wd. be as safe as in the hands of State legislatures; and it was inconvenient to bar a discretion which Experience might enlighten, and which might be applied to good purposes as well as be abused.[6]

George Mason had other ideas, rooted in the Statute of Edward. He moved to include the "aid and comfort" language in modification of "adherence." After considerable discussion, the Constitutional Convention formulated Article III, Section 3, which, as we shall see presently, has been held to incorporate four discrete, but related, elements for the crime of treason: (1) an intent to betray, (2) by means of an overt act, (3) testified to by two witnesses, (4) giving aid and comfort to the enemy. Interpreting these essential terms would eventually fall to the post–Constitution judges. Although no treason case would reach the Supreme Court of the United States for a century and a half, two earlier lower court cases are important because they answered a question that has often been asked about the Fonda situation. When discussing Fonda's 1972 trip to North Vietnam — which the United States was not officially at war with — we have often been asked whether one could be convicted of treason absent a declaration of war. The answer is yes.

Historically, neither the text of the Statute of Edward III nor any of the commentary interpreting it, nor, for that matter, the statute's application, suggests that a declared war was a necessary element of the crime of treason. Indeed, the statute's preoccupation was with protection of the monarch from domestic, as well as foreign, enemies and indicates that a declared state of war (whatever that would have been in the Fourteenth Century) was *not* a necessary element.

Additionally, the text of Article III, Section 2, of the Constitution in providing that "[T]reason against the United States shall consist only in *levying war* against them, *or* in adhering to their enemies, giving them aid and comfort,"[7] appears to be saying that the Constitution confines the "war" element to the "levying" prong of the crime, and makes that element inapplicable to the "or adhering" prong.

This interpretation was borne out by two post–Constitution, pre–Supreme Court, cases.

The first was the notorious episode involving one of the most interesting characters of the post-colonial period, Aaron Burr. Thomas Jefferson and Burr were tied for election to the presidency in December 1801. The House of Representatives elected Jefferson, and Burr became Vice President.[8] Though a Republican, Burr not only later made common cause with his party's opponents, the Federalists, but he conspired against the United States. The "Burr Conspiracy," born just at the end of his vice presidency, consisted of a bold plan to "liberate Mexico from Spain, and at the same time make Louisiana an independent republic, which Mississippi Territory would surely decide to join."[9] During preparation of the conspiracy, a confederate betrayed Burr to President Jefferson. Even though the United States was not at war with any other nation at that time, Burr was charged with the "levying war" prong of the treason crime. Thus, if in time of non-declared war, someone like Burr can be charged with that prong of the treason crime, it would seem *a fortiori* that one can be charged with the "adhering" prong during mere hostilities.[10]

The second case occurred in 1863 and arose out of the Civil War.[11]

On the fifteenth day of March, 1863, the schooner J. M. Chapman was seized in the harbor of San Francisco, by the United States revenue officers, while sailing, or about to sail, on a cruise in the service of the Confederate States, against the United States; and the leaders ... [including Greathouse] were indicted ... for engaging in, and giving aid and comfort, to the then existing rebellion against the government of the United States.[12]

Greathouse, like *Burr*, appeared to be a "levying war" case, so the actual legal question before the court was not whether in an "adhering" case a declared war was necessary. However, in dicta, the *Greathouse* Court did have something to say about that issue in Supreme Court Justice Field's discussion of "enemies." According to Field, "The term 'enemies,' as used in the second clause [of the Constitutional treason provision], according to its settled meaning, at the time the constitution was adopted, applies only to the subjects of a foreign power *in a state of open hostility with us.*"[13] Justice Field was a member of the Supreme Court of the United States only 76 years after adoption of the Constitution. He knew his constitutional history, and he chose his words carefully. If, in his discussion of the status of "a foreign power" in relation to the United States, he meant to refer to "war," he certainly would have done so. Instead, he chose the word "hostility," denoting a very different relationship: one not of war.

It is against this background of English, colonial, constitutional and post-constitutional decisional history that we must make our analysis of Jane Fonda's broadcasts and her other conduct in North Vietnam. Accordingly, not only is there no authority for the proposition that before she could be charged with treason the United States had to be in a declared war with the North Vietnamese, but both history and two American cases strongly suggest that a state of hostilities is sufficient.

Cramer v. *United States*[14]

The *Cramer* case is very important because it was the first time in our nation's history that the Supreme Court of the United States accepted a treason case for review. *Cramer* has its roots in an earlier Supreme Court case entitled *Ex parte Quirin* (1942), which was actually seven separate but related cases consolidated by the Court for decision. The others were *Ex parte [Herbert Hans] Haupt, Ex parte Kerling, Ex parte Burger, Ex parte Heinck, Ex parte Thiel* and *Ex parte Neubauer.*

The seven *Quirin* defendants were born in Germany, lived in the United States, and returned to their native country prior to the outbreak of war in 1941. Trained in sabotage, they were landed by German submarines on the U.S. coastline in mid-1942. All wore some German military apparel and carried explosives. Their mission was to destroy war industries and facilities in the United States. Arrested by the FBI before they could do any harm, they were tried and convicted by a military commission appointed by the President, acting in his capacity as President and Commander in Chief. The Supreme Court, asked to rule on the President's power to create the commission, upheld it. For providing assistance to two of the saboteurs (Thiel and Kerling), Anthony Cramer was convicted of treason and sentenced to 45 years imprisonment and a $10,000 fine.[15] His conviction was affirmed by the United States Court of Appeals for the Second Circuit. But then — in a razor-thin 5-4 vote — the Supreme Court of the United States reversed.

As we shall see presently, the majority justices in *Cramer* read the facts adduced at trial in a very narrow fashion, thus allowing them to reach the conclusion that Cramer had not committed a punishable "overt act." Since the fact-intensive overt act component of the treason crime is indispensable for a conviction, and since what separated the majority and the dissent in *Cramer* were their respective views of what Cramer had actually done, it is necessary to examine in considerable detail each side's view of the facts of the *Cramer* case.

According to the majority, which reversed Cramer's conviction by the 5–4 vote,

Cramer owed allegiance to the United States. A German by birth, he had been a resident of the United States since 1925 and was naturalized in 1936. Prosecution resulted from his association with two of the German saboteurs who in June 1942 landed on our shores from enemy submarines to disrupt industry in the United States and whose cases we considered in Ex parte Quirin...

Coming down to the time of the alleged treason, the main facts, as related on the witness stand by Cramer, are not seriously in dispute. He was living in New York and in response to a cryptic note left under his door, which did not mention Thiel, he went to the Grand Central Station. There Thiel appeared. Cramer had supposed that Thiel was in Germany, knowing that he had left the United States shortly before the war to go there. Together they went to public places and had some drinks. Cramer denies that Thiel revealed his mission of sabotage. Cramer said to Thiel that he must have come to America by submarine, but Thiel refused to confirm it, although his attitude increased Cramer's suspicion. Thiel promised to tell later how he came to this country. Thiel asked about a girl who was a mutual acquaintance and whom Thiel had engaged to marry previous to his going to Germany. Cramer knew where she was, and offered to and did write to her to come to New York, without disclosing in the letter that Thiel had arrived. Thiel said that he had in his possession about $3600, but did not disclose that it was provided by the German Government, saying only that one could get money in Germany if he had the right connections. Thiel owed Cramer an old debt of $200. He gave Cramer his money belt containing some $3600, from which Cramer was to be paid. Cramer agreed to and did place the rest in his own safe deposit box, except a sum which he kept in his room in case Thiel should want it quickly.

After the second of these meetings Thiel and Kerling, who was present briefly at one meeting, were arrested. Cramer's expectation of meeting Thiel later and of bringing him and his fiancée together was foiled. Shortly thereafter Cramer was arrested, tried, and found guilty. The trial judge at the time of sentencing said:

> I shall not impose the maximum penalty of death. It does not appear that this defendant Cramer was aware that Thiel and Kerling were in possession of explosives or other means for destroying factories and property in the United States or planned to do that.
>
>   From the evidence it appears that Cramer had no more guilty knowledge of any subversive purposes on the part of Thiel or Kerling than a vague idea that they came here for the purpose of organizing pro-German propaganda and agitation. If there were any proof that they had confided in him what their real purposes were, or that he knew, or believed what they really were, I should not hesitate to impose the death penalty.[16]

In addition to the foregoing recitation of facts, the Court majority added further information, in five extensive footnotes, about Cramer's activities. That information is important both as to Cramer's intent, and as to the overt act requirement for a treason conviction. It is also important, and highly relevant, in assessing Jane Fonda's activities in North Vietnam.

Said the Court:

The testimony of Norma Kopp was probably the most damaging to the prisoner.... She received at Westport, Conn., where she was working as a laundry and kitchen maid, a note from Cramer, asking her to come to New York for an undisclosed reason. She came and Cramer then, she says, told her that Thiel was back, that he came with others, that six of them landed from a submarine in a rubber boat in Florida, that they brought much money "from Germany from the German Government," that Cramer was keeping it for Thiel in his safety deposit box....[17]

When Cramer was arrested by the F.B.I.,

[h]e told the agents that the man he had been with at Thompson's Cafeteria was William Thomas, that Thomas had worked in a factory on the West Coast since March of 1941 and had not been out of the United States. When asked if the true name of William Thomas was not Werner Thiel, he replied that it was, and that Thiel was using an assumed name because of difficulties with his draft board. He stated that the money belt which Thiel had given him contained only $200, which Thiel owed him, and that the $3500 in the safety deposit box belonged to him and had been obtained from the sale of securities. The gravity of the offense with which he might be confronted was intimated to Cramer, and he asked if he might speak with agent Ostholthoff alone. To him he recanted his previous false statements and admitted that he knew Thiel had come from Germany, probably on a mission for the German Government, which he thought was "to stir up unrest among the people and probably spread propaganda." He repeated this in the presence of other agents and stated that he had lied in order to protect Thiel. Cramer authorized the agents to search his room and to open his safe deposit box at the Corn Exchange Bank and remove the contents thereof.[18]

The four dissenters on the Supreme Court — who would have affirmed Cramer's conviction for treason — saw the facts differently. The dissent was written by Justice William O. Douglas.

The opinion of the Court [majority] is written on a hypothetical state of facts, not on the facts presented by the record.... It disregards facts essential to a determination of the question presented for decision. It overlooks the basic issue on which our disposition of the case must turn. In order to reach that issue we must have a more exact appreciation of the facts than can be gleaned from the opinion of the Court.

Cramer is a naturalized citizen of the United States, born in Germany. He served in the German army in the last war, coming to this country in 1925. In 1929 he met Thiel who had come to this country in 1927 from a place in Germany not far from petitioner's birthplace. The two became close friends; they were intimate associates during a twelve-year period. In 1933 Cramer found work in Indiana. Thiel joined him there. Both became members of the Friends of New Germany, predecessor of the German-American Bund. Cramer was an officer of the Indiana local. He resigned in 1935 but Thiel remained a member and was known as a zealous Nazi. In 1936 Cramer visited Germany. On his return he received his final citizenship papers. He and Thiel returned to New York in 1937 and lived either together or in close proximity for about four years. Thiel left for Germany in the spring of 1941, feeling that war between the United States and Germany was imminent. According to Cramer, Thiel was "up to his ears" in Nazi ideology. Cramer corresponded with Thiel in Germany. Prior to our declaration of war, he was sympathetic with the German cause and critical of our attitude. Thus in November, 1941, he wrote Thiel saying he had declined a job in Detroit "as I don't want to dirty my fingers with war material"; that "We sit here in pitiable comfort, when we should be in the battle — as Nietzsche says — I want the man, I want the woman, the one fit for war, the other fit for bearing." In the spring of 1942 he wrote another friend in reference to the possibility of being drafted: "Personally I should not care at all to be misused by the American army as a world conqueror." Cramer listened to short-wave broadcasts of Lord Haw-Haw and other German propagandists. He knew that the theme of German propaganda was that England and the United States were fighting a war of aggression and seeking to conquer the world.

Thiel entered the German army and in 1942 volunteered with seven other German soldiers who had lived in the United States for a special mission to destroy the American aluminum industry. They were brought here by German submarines in two groups. Kerling was the leader and Thiel a member of one group which landed by rubber boat near Jacksonville, Florida on June 17, 1942. They buried their explosives and proceeded to New York City, where on June 21st they registered at the Hotel Commodore under the assumed names of Edward Kelly and William Thomas.

The next morning a strange voice called Cramer's name from the hall of the rooming house where he lived. On his failure to reply an unsigned note was slipped under his door. It read, "Be at the Grand Central station tonight at 8 o'clock, the upper platform near the information booth, Franz from Chicago has come into town and wants to see you; don't fail to be there." Cramer said he knew no Franz from Chicago. But nevertheless he was on hand at the appointed hour and place. Thiel shortly appeared. They went to the Twin Oaks Inn where they talked for two hours. Cramer admitted that he knew Thiel had come from Germany; and of course, he knew that at that time men were not freely entering this country from Germany. He asked Thiel, "Say, how have you come over, have you come by submarine?" Thiel looked startled, smiled, and said, "Some other time I am going to tell you all about this." Thiel told him that he had taken the assumed name of William Thomas and had a forged draft card. Thiel admonished him to remember that he, Thiel, was "anti-Nazi"—a statement Cramer doubted because he knew Thiel was a member of the Nazi party. Thiel indicated he had come from the coast of Florida. Cramer inquired if he had used a rubber boat. When Thiel said that the only time he was "scared to death was when I came over here we got bombed," Cramer replied, "Then you have come over by submarine, haven't you?" Thiel told Cramer that he had "three and a half or four thousand dollars" with him and that "if you have the right kind of connection you can even get dollars in Germany." Cramer offered to keep Thiel's money for him. Thiel agreed but nothing was done about it that evening. Cramer admitted he had a "hunch" that Thiel was here on a mission for the German government. He asked Thiel "whether he had come over here to spread rumors and incite unrest." *Cramer after his arrest told agents of the F.B.I. that he had suspected that Thiel had received the money from the German government, that Thiel in fact had told him that he was on a mission for Germany, and that "whatever his mission was, I thought that he was serious in his undertaking."* Thiel from the beginning clothed his actions with secrecy; was unwilling to be seen at Cramer's room ("because I have too many acquaintances there and I don't want them to see me"); and cautioned Cramer against conversing loudly with him in the public tavern.

So they agreed to meet at the Twin Oaks Inn at 8 P.M. on the following evening, June 23, 1942. At this meeting Kerling joined them. Cramer had met Kerling in this country and knew he had returned to Germany. Kerling and Thiel told Cramer that they had come over together. *Cramer had a "hunch" that Kerling was here for the same purpose as Thiel.* Kerling left Thiel and Cramer after about an hour and a half. Kerling was followed and arrested. Cramer and Thiel stayed on at the tavern for about another hour. After Kerling left, Thiel agreed to entrust his money to Cramer for safekeeping. He told Cramer to take out $200 which Thiel owed him. But he asked Cramer not to put all of the balance in the safe deposit box—that he should keep some of it out "in the event I need it in a hurry." Thiel went to the washroom to remove the money belt. He handed it to Cramer on the street when they left the tavern. From the Twin Oaks Thiel and Cramer went to Thompson's Cafeteria where they conversed for about fifteen minutes. They agreed to meet there at 8 P.M. on June 25th. They parted. Thiel was followed and arrested.

Cramer returned home. He put Thiel's money belt in a shoe box. He put some of the money between the pages of a book. Later he put the balance in his bank, some in a savings account, most of it in his safe deposit box. He and Thiel had talked of Thiel's fiancée, Norma Kopp. At the first meeting Cramer had offered to write her on Thiel's behalf. He did so. He did not mention Thiel's name but asked her to come to his room, saying he had "sensational" news for her. Cramer appeared at Thompson's Cafeteria at 8 P. M. June 25th to keep his appointment with Thiel. He waited about an hour and a half. He returned the next night, June 26th, and definitely suspected Thiel had been arrested. Though he knew Thiel was registered at the Hotel Commodore, he made no attempt to get in touch with him there. When he returned to his room that night, Norma Kopp was waiting for him. *She testified that he told her that Thiel was here; that "they came about six men with a U-boat, in a rubber boat, and landed in Florida"; that they "brought so much money along from Germany, from the German government" he was keeping it in a safe deposit box; and that they "get instructions from the sitz (hideout) in the Bronx what to do, and where to go."* The next morning Cramer left a note for "William Thomas" at the Commodore saying that Norma Kopp had arrived and suggested a rendezvous. Later in the day Cramer was arrested. He told the agents of the F.B.I. that the name of the man who had been with him at Thompson's Cafeteria on the evening of June 23rd was "William Thomas," that "Thomas" had been working in a factory on the West Coast since March, 1941, and had not been out of the United States since then. He was asked if "Thomas" was not Thiel. He then admitted he was, saying that Thiel had used an assumed name, as he was having difficulties with his draft board. He also stated that the money belt Thiel gave him contained only $200 which Thiel owed him and that the $3500 in his safe deposit box belonged to him and were the proceeds from the sale of securities. After about an hour or so of the falsehoods Cramer asked to speak to one of the agents alone. The request was granted. *He then recanted his previous false statements and stated that he felt sure that Thiel had come from Germany by submarine on a mission for the German Government* and that he thought that mission was "to stir up unrest among the people and probably spread propaganda." *He stated he had lied in order to protect Thiel.*

The Court [majority] holds that this evidence is insufficient to sustain the conviction of Cramer under the requirements of the Constitution. We disagree.[19]

Note that in the dissent's recitation of facts that were adduced at Cramer's trial, there was nothing to contradict any of the facts that had been stated by the Court's majority. Indeed, the only difference between them was that the dissent's version of the facts was more fulsome and detailed, and it strongly emphasized Cramer's adherence to his homeland and his anti–American ideas. It was Cramer's connection with Thiel and Kerling that got him indicted for treason. The indictment charged that Cramer's overt acts were that he "did meet with" Thiel, and with Thiel and Kerling, who were "enemies of the United States," and that he "did confer, treat, and counsel with" Thiel and Kerling "for a period of time for the purpose of giving and with intent to give aid and comfort to said enemies."[20] Or, as the dissent understood the indictment, "[t]he charge against Cramer was that of adhering. The essential elements of the crime are that Cramer (1) with treasonable intent (2) gave aid and comfort to the enemy."[21]

Why, then, in light of either version of the facts and the ensuing indictment, and the conviction after trial, did the 5–4 majority of the Supreme Court of the United States reverse Cramer's conviction? Although the majority's opinion is not nearly as clear or unambiguous as it could be, still, it is possible to discern its rationale. To the extent that a single passage in the lengthy opinion captures its reasoning, it is this one:

The Government contends that outside of the overt acts, and by lesser degree of proof, it has shown a treasonable intent on Cramer's part in meeting and talking with Thiel and Kerling. But if it showed him disposed to betray, and showed that he had opportunity to do so, *it still has not proved in the manner required that he did any acts submitted to the jury as a basis for conviction which had the effect of betraying by giving aid and comfort.* To take the intent for the deed would [be unacceptable].[22]

The Court was saying that, in addition to treasonable intent, committing an "overt act" that gives "aid and comfort" to the enemy is an essential — and entirely separate — element of the crime of treason.[23]

What the Supreme Court majority established was an important principle in the law of treason. For a prosecutor to get to a jury, he would have to produce evidence from which that jury could conclude (1) that the defendant had a certain state of mind (the intent to betray), and (2) that the defendant committed an overt act, witnessed by two people, in which he gave aid and comfort to the enemy. In other words, given the gravity of an act of treason — a constitutional crime punishable by death[24] — mere intent without an overt act is insufficient, just as an overt act without the intent to betray is insufficient. The two must join. Daydreaming about intending to betray the United States, without an act, is not treason. Equally, lending money to a spy without knowing he's a spy — and thus with no intent to betray the United States — is not treason.

The majority in *Cramer* went further. The overt act must successfully confer some tangible benefit on the enemy: "[t]he very minimum function that an overt act must perform in a treason prosecution is that it show sufficient action by the accused, in its setting, to sustain a finding that the accused *actually* gave aid and comfort to the enemy."[25]

What did the evidence in the *Cramer* case show?

As to treasonous intent, the majority and dissent did not disagree. Indeed, the majority had no quarrel with the dissent's view of the intent aspect of Cramer's crime:

There was ample evidence for the jury that Cramer had a treasonable intent. The trial court charged the jury that "criminal intent and knowledge, being a mental state, are not susceptible of being proved by direct evidence, and therefore you must infer the nature of the defendant's intent and knowledge from all the circumstances." It charged that proof of criminal intent and knowledge is sufficient if proved beyond a reasonable doubt, and that the two witnesses are not necessary for any of the facts other than the overt acts. On that there apparently is no disagreement. It also charged: "Now gentlemen, motive should not be confused with intent.[26] *If the defendant knowingly gives aid and comfort to one who he knows or believes is an enemy, then he must be taken to intend the consequences of his own voluntary act, and the fact that his motive might not have been to aid the enemy is no defense.* In other words, one cannot do an act which he knows will give aid and comfort to a person he knows to be an enemy of the United States, and then seek to disclaim criminal intent and knowledge by saying that one's motive was not to aid the enemy.[27] So if you believe that the defendant performed acts which by their nature gave aid and comfort to the enemy, knowing or believing him to be an enemy, then you must find that he had criminal intent, since he intended to do the act forbidden by the law. The fact that you may believe that his motive in so doing was, for example, merely to help a friend, or possibly for financial gain, would not change the fact that he had a criminal intent." On that there apparently is no disagreement. A man who voluntarily assists one known or believed to be an enemy agent may not defend on the ground that he betrayed his country for only thirty pieces of silver. See *Hanauer v. Doane....* "The consequences of his acts are too serious and enormous to admit of such a plea. He must be taken to intend the consequences of his own voluntary act" *Hanauer v. Doane....* For the same reasons a man cannot slip through our treason law because his aid to those who would destroy his country was prompted by a desire to "accommodate a friend." Loyalty to country cannot be subordinated to the amenities of personal friendship.

Cramer had a traitorous intent if he knew or believed that Thiel and Kerling were enemies and were working here in the interests of the German Reich. The trial court charged that mere suspicion was not enough; but that it was not necessary for Cramer to have known all their plans. There apparently is no disagreement on that. By that test the evidence against Cramer was overwhelming. *The conclusion is irresistible that Cramer believed, if he did not actually know, that Thiel and Kerling were here on a secret mission for the German Reich with the object of injuring the United States and that the money which Thiel gave him for safekeeping had been supplied by Germany to facilitate the project of the enemy.* The trial court charged that if the jury found that Cramer had no purpose or intention of assisting the German Reich in its prosecution of the war or in hampering the United States in its prosecution of the war but acted solely for the purpose of assisting Kerling and Thiel as individuals, Cramer should be acquitted. *There was ample evidence for the jury's conclusion that the assistance Cramer rendered was assistance to the German Reich, not merely assistance to Kerling and Thiel as individuals.*

The trial judge stated when he sentenced Cramer that it did not appear that Cramer knew that Thiel and Kerling were in possession of explosives or other means for destroying factories in this country or that they planned to do that. He stated that if there had been direct proof of such knowledge he would have sentenced Cramer to death rather than to forty-five years in prison. But however relevant such particular knowledge may have been to fixing the punishment for Cramer's acts of treason, it surely was not essential to proof of his traitorous intent. A defendant who has aided an enemy agent in this country may not escape conviction for treason on the ground that he was not aware of the enemy's precise objectives. Knowing or believing that the agent was here on a mission on behalf of a hostile government, he could not, by simple failure to ask too many questions, assume that this mission was one of charity and benevolence toward the United States. But the present case is much stronger. For Cramer claims he believed the enemy agent's objective was to destroy national morale by propaganda and not to blow up war factories. *Propaganda designed to cause disunity among adversaries is one of the older weapons known to warfare, and upon occasion one of the most effective.*[28]

These very sentiments would later be expressed by O.S.S. and C.I.A. propaganda specialist Edward Hunter in his analysis for the House Committee on Internal Security, quoted in Chapter 5:

What comes from a source on one's own side commands attention.... When the enemy can obtain the assistance of a national of the country, and also to broadcast it personally over the enemy's radio ... it has achieved a form of war propaganda for which as yet there is no professional term — except, perhaps, the old-fashioned word, treason.

Jane Fonda seriously assaulted the stamina of any fighting American listening to her highly dramatic and professional war propaganda....

The dissent in *Cramer* continued:

The defendant Cramer ... is an intelligent, if misguided, man. He has a quick wit sharpened by considerable learning of its kind. He is widely read and a student of history and philosophy, particularly Ranke and Nietzsche. He had been an officer of a pro-German organization, and his closest associate had been a zealous Nazi. He also had listened to German propagandists over the short wave. But, in any event, it is immaterial whether Cramer was acquainted with the efficacy of propaganda in modern warfare. Undoubtedly he knew that the German Government thought it efficacious. When he was shown consciously and voluntarily to have assisted this enemy program his traitorous intent was then and there sufficiently proved.

The Court does not purport to set aside the conviction for lack of sufficient evidence of traitorous intent. It frees Cramer from this treason charge solely on the ground that the overt acts charged are insufficient under the constitutional requirement.[29]

Ultimately, the *Cramer* case turned only on the inadequacy of proof of the "overt act" element of the treason crime. The majority contended that:

The controversy before us has been waged in terms of intentions, but this, we think, is the reflection of a more fundamental issue as to what is the real function of the overt act in convicting of treason.... The very minimum function that an overt act must perform in a treason prosecution is that it show sufficient action by the accused, in its setting, to sustain a finding that the accused actually gave aid and comfort to the enemy. Every act, movement, deed, and word of the defendant charged to constitute treason must be supported by the testimony of two witnesses. The two-witness principle is to interdict imputation of incriminating acts to the accused by circumstantial evidence or by the testimony of a single witness. The prosecution cannot rely on evidence which does not meet the constitutional test for overt acts to create any inference that the accused did other acts or did something more than was shown in the overt act, in order to make a giving of aid and comfort to the enemy. The words of the Constitution were chosen, not to make it hard to prove merely routine and everyday acts, but to make the proof of acts that convict of treason as sure as trial processes may. When the prosecution's case is thus established, the Constitution does not prevent presentation of corroborative or cumulative evidence of any admissible character either to strengthen a direct case or to rebut the testimony or inferences on behalf of defendant. The Government is not prevented from making a strong case; it is denied a conviction on a weak one.[30]

This, then, is what separated the majority and the dissent in *Cramer*, and why the Supreme Court majority believed — erroneously, in our view — that the trial judge had erred in giving the case to the jury. In the majority's view, the prosecution had not submitted enough evidence from which a reasonable jury could conclude that Cramer had committed the constitutionally requisite overt act of giving aid and comfort to the enemy, in the persons of Thiel and Kerling. In the final analysis, the majority and the dissent separated not on whether there *had* to be an overt act actually giving aid and comfort to the enemy (there did), but on whether there was enough evidence from which the jury could have concluded that the testimony of the requisite two witnesses had proved that Cramer's overt act(s) actually gave aid and comfort to the Nazis.

What disturbed the majority was this:

There is no two-witness proof of what they said nor in what language they conversed. There is no showing that Cramer gave them any information whatever of value to their mission or indeed that he had any to give. No effort at secrecy is shown, for they met in public places. *Cramer furnished them no shelter, nothing that can be called sustenance or supplies, and there is no evidence that he gave them encouragement or counsel, or even paid for their drinks.*[31]

To reiterate, the schism between the Court's majority and the dissent was not rooted in disagreement about the law of treason. It was not even about whether courts should, through judicial decisionmaking, extend the scope of that crime and the quantum of evidence needed to prove it. On the contrary, both sides were in agreement as to the law, and as to the need for judicial restraint. They parted company only on what the facts put before the jury actually added up to. As the dissent pointedly observed, the majority had

... conceded that if the two witnesses had testified not only that they saw Cramer conferring with Thiel and Kerling but also heard him agree to keep Thiel's money and saw him take it, the result would be different. But the assumption is that since the two witnesses could not testify as to what happened at the meetings, we must appraise the meetings in isolation from the other facts of the record. Therein lies the fallacy of the argument.[32]

...[T]he requirement of an overt act is designed to preclude punishment for treasonable plans or schemes or hopes which have never moved out of the realm of thought or speech.... The treasonable project is complete as a crime only when the traitorous intent has ripened into a physical and observable act. The act standing alone may appear to be innocent or indifferent, such as joining a person at a table, stepping into a boat, or carrying a parcel of food. That alone is insufficient. *It must be established beyond a reasonable doubt that the act was part of the treasonable project and done in furtherance of it.* Its character and significance are to be judged by its place in the effectuation of the project. That does not mean that where the treasonable scheme involves several treasonable acts, and the overt act which is charged has been proved by two witnesses, that all the other acts which tend to show the treasonable character of the overt act and the treasonable purpose with which it was committed must be proved by two witnesses. The Constitution does not so declare. There is no historical support for saying that the phrase "two Witnesses to the same overt Act" may be or can be read as meaning two witnesses to all the acts involved in the treasonable scheme of the accused. Obviously one overt act proved by two witnesses is enough to sustain a conviction even though the accused has committed many other acts which can be proved by only one witness or by his own admission in open court. Hence, it is enough that the overt act which is charged be proved by two witnesses. As the Court [majority] concedes, its treasonable character need not be manifest upon its face. We say that its true character may be proved by any competent evidence sufficient to sustain the verdict of a jury. Any other conclusion lands to such absurd results as to preclude the supposition that the two witness rule was intended to have the meaning attributed to it.[33]

If this, then, is the true test by which the sufficiency of a treasonable overt act is to be judged, what does applying the test to the facts of the *Cramer* case yield? The dissent was emphatic:

When we apply that test to the facts of this case it is clear to us that the judgment of conviction against Cramer should not be set aside. The historical materials which we have set forth in the Appendix to this opinion establish that *a meeting with the enemy may be adequate as an overt act of treason....* Such a meeting might be innocent on its face. It might also be innocent in its setting ... where, for example, it was accidental. We would have such a case here if Cramer's first meeting with Thiel was charged as an overt act. For, as we have seen, Cramer went to the meeting without knowledge that he would meet and confer with Thiel. *But the subsequent meetings were arranged between them. They were arranged in furtherance of Thiel's designs. Cramer was not only* on notice that Thiel was here on a mission inimical to the interests of this nation. He had agreed at the first meeting to hide Thiel's money. He had agreed to contact Norma Kopp. He knew that Thiel wanted his identity and presence in New York concealed. This was the setting in which the later meetings were held. The meetings take on their true character and significance from that setting. They constitute acts. They demonstrate that Cramer had a liking for Thiel's design to the extent of aiding him in it. They show beyond doubt that Cramer had more than a treasonable intent; that *that intent had moved from the realm of thought into the realm of action.* Since *two witnesses proved that the meetings took place,* their character and significance might be proved by any competent evidence.[34]

A devastating summary of damning facts!

The dissent vigorously disputed the majority's view that Cramer's conduct was ambiguous, or even innocent: "This is not a case where an act innocent on its face is given a sinister aspect and made a part of a treasonous design by circumstantial evidence, by inference, or by the testimony of a single witness for the prosecution. We know from Cramer's own testimony—from his admissions at the trial–exactly what happened. We know the character of the meetings from Cramer's own admissions. We know from his own lips that they were not accidental or casual conferences, or innocent, social meetings. He arranged them with Thiel. When he did so he believed that Thiel was here on a secret mission for the German Reich with the object of injuring this nation. He also knew that Thiel was looking for a place to hide his money. Cramer had offered to keep it for Thiel and Thiel had accepted the offer. Cramer had also offered to write Norma Kopp, Thiel's fiancée, without mentioning Thiel's name. Cramer also knew that Thiel wanted his identity and his presence in New York concealed. Cramer's admissions at the trial gave character and significance to those meetings. Those admissions plus the finding of treasonable intent place beyond a reasonable doubt the conclusion that those meetings were steps in and part and parcel of the treasonable project.... We ... say that *a meeting with the enemy is an act and may in its setting be an overt act of treason*.... Proof of the overt act plus proof of a treasonable intent make clear that *the treasonable design has moved out of the realm of thought into the field of action*."[35]

Justice Douglas, who wrote the dissent in *Cramer*, was with the 8–1 majority in the next treason case to come before the Supreme Court of the United States. In a portion of his concurring opinion in *Haupt*, Douglas refought his losing battle in *Cramer*:

Two witnesses saw Cramer talking with an enemy agent. So far as they knew the conversation may have been wholly innocent, as they did not overhear it. But *Cramer*, by his own testimony at the trial, explained what took place; he knew or had reason to believe that the agent was here on a mission for the enemy and arranged, among other things, to conceal the funds brought here to promote the project. Thus there was the most credible evidence that Cramer was guilty of "adhering" to the enemy, giving him "aid and comfort."[36]

But losing battle or not, Douglas would have acknowledged that the *Cramer* case—the first decision by the Supreme Court of the United States to interpret the constitutional crime of treason—established several important principles:

- "Motive," as compared to "intent" is irrelevant;
- Treasonous intent and an overt act of betrayal are two distinct elements;
- The intent (to aid the enemy and injure the United States) can be proved circumstantially, and a defendant is presumed to expect the natural and probable consequences of his acts;
- The overt act, proved by two witnesses, must provide actual aid and comfort to the enemy. However, *how much* and *what part of* that overt act—testified to by two witnesses—must provide the actual aid and comfort is left somewhat unclear by Cramer, since the five-justice majority believed that not enough evidence had been supplied to the jury concerning the content of Cramer's conversations.[37]

These principles were applied in quite a different fashion, however, in the *Haupt* case.

Haupt v. *United States*

The defendant, Hans Max Haupt — father of one of the saboteurs, Herbert Haupt, convicted in the earlier *Quirin* case — was indicted for treason, tried, convicted and sentenced to life imprisonment and a $10,000 fine.

His son Herbert, after landing by submarine on the United States coast, had obeyed orders "to proceed to Chicago, to procure an automobile for the use of himself and his confederates in their work of sabotage and espionage, to obtain reemployment with the Simpson Optical Company where he was to gather information, particularly as to the vital parts and bottlenecks of the plant, to be communicated to his coconspirators to guide their attack."[38] The son had arrived with specific instructions and equipped with large sums of money.

The father, Hans, was subsequently charged with 12 overt acts in three categories: (1) that Hans had accompanied his son when he sought re-employment in a defense plant that made important military equipment; (2) that Hans had sheltered and harbored his son; and (3) that Hans had accompanied his son to an automobile dealer, then made arrangements to pay for, and purchase, a car for his son. Each of these overt acts was alleged to be in aid of the defendant's son's known purpose of sabotage.

The father's defense was that his acts did not constitute treason because each was "commonplace, insignificant and colorless, and not sufficient even if properly proved to support a conviction."[39]

Eight of the nine Supreme Court justices disagreed:

There can be no question that sheltering, or helping to buy a car, or helping to get employment is helpful to an enemy agent, that they were of aid and comfort to Herbert Haupt in his mission of sabotage. They have the unmistakable quality which was found lacking in the Cramer case of forwarding the saboteur in his mission. We pointed out that Cramer furnished no shelter, sustenance or supplies.... The overt acts charged here, on the contrary, may be generalized as furnishing harbor and shelter for a period of six days, assisting in obtaining employment in the lens plant and helping to buy an automobile. No matter whether young Haupt's mission was benign or traitorous, known or unknown to defendant, *these acts were aid and comfort to him*. In the light of his mission and his instructions, they were more than casually useful; *they were aid in steps essential to his design* for treason. If proof be added that the defendant knew of his son's instructions, preparation and plans, the purpose to aid and comfort the enemy becomes clear. All of this, of course, assumes that the prosecution's evidence properly in the case is credited, as the jury had a right to do. We hold, therefore, that the overt acts laid in the indictment and submitted to the jury do perform the functions assigned to overt acts in treason cases and are sufficient to support the indictment and to sustain the convictions if they were proved with the exactitude required by the Constitution.[40]

Hans Haupt's argument — that the "harboring and sheltering" counts of his indictment lacked proof that son Herbert was actually in the father's apartment and, further, that Hans was in his own apartment at any time his enemy agent-son was there — was a bald attempt to use the *Cramer* majority opinion in his own defense. (One could almost hear Justice Douglas saying, "Not this time you don't!") The *Haupt* Court found there was ample evidence from which the jury could conclude that the evidence on the harboring and sheltering counts was sufficient.

As to the purchase of the automobile, the Court held that testimony of the car salesman and the dealership's sales manager concerning the purchase transaction by Herbert and Hans was enough to take those counts of the indictment to the jury, and that the jury was justified in finding them proved.

As to the "aid and comfort" element of the crime, Hans Haupt had argued his conviction should not be upheld because there was insufficient proof that the supposed acts of "aid and comfort" were anything else but "natural acts of aid for defendant's own son." The Court made short shrift of this argument:

Certainly *that relationship is a fact for the jury to weigh along with others,* and they were correctly instructed that if they found that defendants' intention was not to injure the United States but merely to aid his son "as an individual, as distinguished from assisting him in his purpose, if such existed, of aiding the German Reich, or of injuring the United States, the defendant must be found not guilty." The defendant can complain of no error in such a submission. *It was for the jury to weigh the evidence that the acts proceeded from parental solicitude against the evidence of adherence to the German cause.* It is argued that Haupt merely had the misfortune to sire a traitor and all he did was to act as an indulgent father toward a disloyal son. In view however of the evidence of defendant's own statements that after the war he intended to return to Germany, that the United States was going to be defeated, that he would never permit his boy to join the American Army, that he would kill his son before he would send him to fight Germany, and others to the same effect, *the jury apparently concluded that the son had the misfortune of being a chip off the old block* — a tree inclined as the twig had been bent — metaphors which express the common sense observation that parents are as likely to influence the character of their children as are children to shape that of their parents. *Such arguments are for the jury to decide.*[41]

Accordingly, *Cramer* and *Haupt* together stand for the proposition that in a prosecution for the crime of treason against the United States of America,

- "Motive" is irrelevant;
- Treasonable intent (to aid the enemy and injure the United States) and an overt act of betrayal — two distinct elements of the crime — are required;
- The intent can be proved circumstantially, and the defendant is presumed to intend the natural and probable consequences of his acts;

- The overt act, proved by two witnesses, must provide actual aid and comfort to the enemy;
- *And these questions are to be decided by the jury.* Appellate courts (especially the Supreme Court of the United States) will not reverse a trial judge's submission of a treason case to a jury — or, for that matter, any case — if reasonable jurors

could have disagreed about the evidence. *If reasonable jurors could have disagreed about the evidence, the decision as to intent, act, two-witness proof, and actual aid and comfort, is for the jury to make* — regardless of whether the appellate court would have reached the same conclusion on the same evidence.

In the history of treason jurisprudence in the United States, the Supreme Court would decide only one case after *Haupt*, and that not for several years.[42] It was *Cramer* and *Haupt*, then, that set the decisional stage for five later treason cases in the federal Courts of Appeals. These five cases—*all broadcasting cases*—are discussed in the next chapter. What they, together with *Cramer* and *Haupt*, portend for the case that could have been made against Jane Fonda, is devastating.

---

1. To the extent there are records of colonial treason prosecutions, they deal with the "levying war" prong of the crime, not the "adhering" prong that concerns us here. Since it is the latter prong that could have been the basis of a charge of treason against Fonda, there will be little discussion here of "levying war," as to which there is an abundance of literature.

2. Adams, *Life of John Adams*; 1 *Works of John Adams* (1856) 224–25.

3. 5 *Journals of the Continental Congress* (1906) 475; 6 Force, *American Archives*, 4th ser. (1846) 1720; emphasis added.

4. See 31 *Journals of the Continental Congress* (1934) 497.

5. 2 Farrand, *The Records of the Federal Convention of 1787* (1911) 144, 168, 182; 4 Farrand, *The Records of the Federal Convention of 1787* (rev. ed. 1937) 45; emphasis added.

6. 2 Farrand, *The Records of the Federal Convention of 1787* (1911) 345–50.

7. Emphasis added.

8. It was Alexander Hamilton who cast the crucial vote in the House. Hamilton, an enemy of both Jefferson and Burr, hated the latter more than the former. Burr would later kill Hamilton in a duel.

9. Samuel Eliot Morison, *The Oxford History of the American People*, 369.

10. Burr's trial was presided over by the Chief Justice of the United States, John Marshall. Apparently because of the absence of two-witness proof, among other reasons, the jury acquitted Burr. His acquittal, however, is immaterial to the point made here: that one can be *charged* with treason absent a declaration of war, a state of hostilities being sufficient.

11. *United States* v. *Greathouse*, 26 Federal Cases 18 (1863), was tried in the United States Circuit Court for the Northern District of California. In those days, there were no circuit court judges and the *Greathouse* case was presided over by Justice Field of the United States Supreme Court, sitting as "Circuit Justice," and Judge Hoffman, of the United States District Court. The citation "26 Federal Cases 18" means that the *Greathouse* case can be found at volume 26, page 18, of the Federal Cases reports of decisions by the United States Circuit Courts. If the citation had been to a quotation and read "26 Federal Cases 18, 35," the quotation would have appeared on page 35. See, for example, the *Ex parte Bollman* footnote on the first page of this chapter.

12. 26 Federal Cases, at 18.

13. 26 Federal Cases, at 22; emphasis added.

14. 325 U.S. 1 (1945).

15. Cramer's conviction was for violating Title 18 *United States Code* Section 1, which was derived from the Act of April 30, 1790, chapter 9, section 1, 1 Stat. 112 (1790). This enactment had, in turn, been formulated from Article III, Section 3, of the Constitution of the United States. The current treason statute is Title 18, *United States Code*, Section 2381.

16. 325 U.S. at 3.

17. 325 U.S. at 39, note 46.

18. 325 U.S. at 40, note 47.

19. 325 U.S. at 48; emphasis added.

20. 325 U.S. at 36.

21. 325 U.S. at 54. Implicit in the dissent's characterization of treason's essential elements is that Cramer "gave" aid and comfort by means of an overt act, proved by two witnesses.

22. 325 U.S. at 39; emphasis added.

23. The Court defined "overt act" this way: "An overt act, in criminal law, is an outward act done in pursuance and in manifestation of an intent or design; an overt act in this case means some physical action done for the purpose of carrying out or affecting [*sic*] the treason. *United States* v. *Haupt*,

N.D.Ill.1942, 47 F.Supp. 836, 839, reversed on other grounds, 7 Cir. 1943, 136 F.2d 661. The overt act is the doing of some actual act, looking towards the accomplishment of the crime" (United States v. Stephan, D.C.E.D.Minn. 1943, 50 F. Supp. 738, 742, 743, note).

24. Title 18, *United States Code,* Section 3591.

25. 325 U.S. at 34; emphasis added. It should be noted that the *Cramer* majority failed entirely to provide any historical or precedential authority for its requirement that, for the prosecution to prove an overt act, it must be proven that "actual" aid and comfort have been given to the enemy (whatever that is supposed to mean).

26. This distinction between "motive" and "intent" is discussed at length in the next chapter.

27. As is discussed in Chapter 8, even though Fonda's *motive* in betraying her country was probably connected to her lack of self-esteem and the other related character and personality deficiencies that we have noted in Chapters 1 and 2, still, that would be no defense to a charge of treason if her *intent* was to betray the United States.

28. 325 U.S. at 54, emphasis added.

29. 325 U.S. at 54; emphasis added.

30. 325 U.S. at 34.

31. 325 U.S. at 37; emphasis added.

32. 325 U.S. at 59.

33. 325 U.S. at 61.

34. 325 U.S at 62; emphasis added.

35. 325 U.S. at 63; emphasis added.

36. 330 U.S. at 643; emphasis added.

37. Emphasis added. This question, undecided in *Cramer,* would be answered by the Supreme Court seven years later in another treason case — *Kawakita* v. *United States* — which is examined in the next chapter.

38. 330 U.S. at 633.

39. 330 U.S. at 634.

40. 330 U.S. at 635; emphasis added.

41. 330 U.S. at 641; emphasis added.

42. That case, *Kawakita* v. *United States,* in 1952, clarified the *quantum* aspect of the overt act, but otherwise did not add much substance to the American law of treason. See Chapter 8.

WORLD WAR II
TREASON PROSECUTIONS

*Treason may be predicated upon collaboration as an enemy agent
in the execution of a program of psychological warfare beamed to
the United States over the enemy's short wave radio (Chandler v.
United States, 171 F.2d 921, 940 [1st Cir. 1948])*

Chandler v. United States

Following *Cramer* and *Haupt*, five treason cases—each, like Fonda, involving
Americans who broadcast propaganda for the enemy — were decided by federal Courts
of Appeal. Each case initially went to a jury. Each resulted in a conviction. Each was
appealed.

As in *Haupt*, each conviction was upheld.

In order to understand why Jane Fonda's broadcasts and other conduct in Hanoi
opened her up to indictment and trial, it is essential to have a complete grasp of the
operative facts of the *Chandler* case. They are set forth at length in the opinion of the
United States Court of Appeals for the First Circuit:

Chandler was born in Chicago, Illinois, in 1889, and has always been a citizen of the
United States....

Over the years Chandler had developed an anti–Jewish outlook, and his fierce emotions
on that theme were accentuated by certain personal setbacks which he attributed to
malignant Jewish interference. He came to believe, or to profess to believe, in the existence
of a sinister world-wide Jewish conspiracy. Naturally he found the anti–Jewish climate of
Nazi Germany congenial. While in Germany before the war his interest was cultivated by
one Hoffman, an attaché in the German Press Department, serving as contact man for
foreign journalists. He was favorably impressed with what he saw in Germany and came to
regard the Nazi regime as the bulwark of Western civilization against what he thought to
be the Jewish-Bolshevist menace.

In 1940 he left Yugoslavia and came to Florence. There he conceived the idea of
broadcasting his views to the United States, by way of warning against involvement in the
European war.... Chandler was able to get to Berlin in February, 1941, on a German
Fremdenpass (alien identity card) through the intervention of the German Consul.... He
volunteered his services to the Propaganda Ministry, and arrangements were made for him
to prepare commentaries and record them for broadcast to the United States, on a salaried
basis. His broadcasts commenced in April, 1941. He adopted in his first broadcast, and

retained throughout, the nom de plume "Paul Revere"....[1] ... Other Americans were repatriated from Berlin, but Chandler chose to stay.

Then came the Japanese attack upon Pearl Harbor....

In January, or February, of 1942, he made arrangements for the resumption of his activity as a broadcaster....

Defendant broadcast under these contracts two or three times a week uninterruptedly from February, 1942, to the end of July of that year.... After one of the routine conferences of the commentators, some time [later] he had a conversation with Wagner, the News Editor for the U.S.A. Zone. Wagner expressed his lack of interest in the anti-Semitic theme and his disbelief in the authenticity of the so-called "Protocols of the Elders of Zion." *Chandler reported Wagner to the Gestapo* as one whose loyalty to the Reich was suspect. Later, upon being taxed with this action by Wagner, Chandler said to Wagner: "You have been one of my best friends," but "the interests of the whole, of the Reich, are higher than my personal feelings...."

The objective of the enemy in the operation of its short-wave broadcasts clearly appears in the record, and is indeed a matter of common knowledge. Winkelnkemper, the Director General of the German-Reich-Radio-Corp., testified as follows:

> The German foreign broadcasts were made extensive use of as a means of psychological warfare, as it was done in every country, to support the German war effort by creating disunity in other peoples by undermining the morale, by splitting up the people in different parties, different social and radical parties, political parties, so that the land who is doing this psychological warfare may aim their war objects. And so it was done in Germany, too, and we made an extensive use of these propaganda as a means of psychological warfare.

Chandler with other English-speaking broadcasters regularly attended the daily conferences held by the chief of the U.S.A. Zone, at which the standard propaganda directives as well as the daily directives were relayed and discussed, and instructions were given to the various commentators with reference to particular subjects. The commentators were not left in doubt as to the war mission of the Short Wave Agency. Wagner, the News Editor of the U.S.A. Zone, referring to these U.S.A. Zone conferences, testified:

> We said that German propaganda during the war was to be used chiefly to create disunity among the Allies, England, America, Russia, and also to create disunity within the individual countries. As far as the United States were concerned, in particular to build up racial controversies, to create unrest regarding the economic inequalities in the country, to work on minority problems and similar ideas, with the purpose of ultimately driving a wedge between the people and the Roosevelt Administration, and if possible to get a new election in which a government would be elected in the United States which would be against interference in European affairs, in other words, which would be isolationist in character.

Further, along the same line, he testified:

> The commentators were told to use the threat of inflation, of the collapse of the dollar after the war, as a means of propaganda, all to create unrest along that line. Similar ideas were brought up in connection with defeatist propaganda. Commentators were told to stress themes along the lines that America would never be able to win the war, that it would be much too costly, that the establishment of a Second Front would fail owing to the strength of German armies, that actually America had nothing to do in this European war, that America had no war aims, that the GI did not know what he was fighting for;

and such ideas that were brought up, that we should attempt to create homesickness among the American troops and defeatism in general as to the losses which they might suffer and that these losses would be for nothing.

Twelve recordings of Chandler's Paul Revere broadcasts, made at various dates in 1942, were introduced into the evidence and played back to the jury. Woven through his talks were all the basic themes of the German propaganda line. The recordings made by him were beamed to the United States and frequently picked up at the monitoring station of the Federal Communications Commission in Silver Spring, Maryland. To what extent his broadcasts were heard by other persons in the United States does not appear, though in one of his broadcasts he said: "I am informed that there has been a vast increase in the number of Americans who habitually dial in on the shortwave sending of Berlin Radio."[2]

On the basis of these facts, after the war Chandler was indicted for committing treason. The indictment charged that he was an American citizen owing allegiance to the United States, that between 1941 and 1945, within Germany, in violation of that allegiance, he knowingly, intentionally and traitorously adhered to the enemies of the United States (that is, to the Government of the German Reich and the German Radio Broadcasting Company), giving them aid and comfort. According to the indictment,

... the aforesaid adherence of the defendant and the giving of aid and comfort by him to the aforesaid enemies of the United States "*consisted of working as a radio speaker and commentator* in the U.S. zone of the Short Wave Station of the German Radio Broadcasting Company, a company controlled by the German Government, which work included the preparation and composition of commentaries, speeches, talks and announcements, and the recording thereof for subsequent broadcast by radio from Germany to the United States"; that *these activities of the defendant "were intended to persuade citizens and residents of the United States to decline to support the United States in the conduct of said war, and to weaken and destroy confidence in the administration of the Government of the United States."*[3]

Paragraph 4 of the indictment had set forth some 23 overt acts alleged to have given aid and comfort to the Nazis, which were knowingly and traitorously committed by Chandler with treasonable intent. Thirteen of these overt acts were withdrawn from consideration, some by the prosecution, and others by the district judge. Ten overt acts went to the jury.

Generally described, one of these overt acts was arranging for the making of a recording, two were speaking into a microphone in the actual recording of talks for broadcast, one was participation in a conference for improvement in the operation of the Short Wave Station, two were attendance and participation in conferences of radio commentators at which directives were received from higher authority relative to the content of broadcasts, four were participation in conferences aimed at securing the resumption or continuance of defendant's broadcasting activities.[4]

The jury had to decide (1) whether Chandler intended to betray the United States by injuring it and thus aiding its Nazi enemy, (2) whether he had committed at least one overt act to that end, (3) whether Chandler's commission of that overt act had been proved by the testimony of two witnesses, and (4) whether that act had given aid and comfort to the Nazis.

After a three-week trial — at which Chandler declined to testify on his own behalf (perhaps having learned a lesson from Anthony Cramer's admissions, and from what the *Cramer* dissent made of those admissions) — the jury convicted Chandler, on the ground that the prosecution's evidence proved each of the ten overt acts charged, holding that defendant Chandler had committed "a treasonable act ... with an intent to betray the United States."[5] Chandler was sentenced to life imprisonment and a $10,000 fine.

The Overt Acts

On appeal, Chandler argued that the overt acts charged in the indictment should not have been allowed to go to the jury. In a defense that would reappear in later broadcast treason cases, Chandler maintained that "mere words, the expression of opinions and ideas for the purpose of influencing people, cannot constitute an overt act of treason; that [he] had a right to broadcast, or otherwise disseminate to the American people, the ideas which coincided with the Nazi propaganda line; and that therefore his preliminary steps to that end — his attendance at conferences of commentators, his preparation of commentaries, his speaking into a microphone to make recordings — cannot be treasonable acts."[6]

The First Circuit Court of Appeals rejected this argument:

There are occasional statements to be found in the books to the effect that mere words cannot amount to an overt act of treason.... That is true in the sense that the mere utterance of disloyal sentiments is not treason; aid and comfort must be given to the enemy. *But the communication of an idea, whether by speech or writing, is as much as act as is throwing a brick,* though different muscles are used to achieve different effects. One may commit treason by conveying military intelligence to the enemy, though the only overt act is the speaking of words.... *The significant thing is not so much the character of the act which in fact gives aid and comfort to the enemy, but whether the act is done with an intent to betray.* In *Cramer v. United States* the Court said:

> On the other hand, a citizen may take actions which do aid and comfort the enemy — and making a speech critical of the government or opposing its measures, profiteering, striking in defense plants or essential work, and the hundred other things which impair our cohesion and diminish our strength — but if there is no adherence to the enemy in this, if there is no intent to betray, there is no treason.[7]

The Court of Appeals firmly pointed out that this was not what Chandler was up to in World War II Nazi Germany: "In the present case, however, it cannot be said that what Chandler did was merely exercising his right of free speech in the normal processes of domestic political opposition. He trafficked with the enemy and as their paid agent *collaborated in the execution of a program of psychological warfare designed by the enemy to weaken the power of the United States to wage war successfully.* We have found no indication of a reluctance on the part of the framers of the Constitution to punish as treason any breach of allegiance involving actual dealings with the enemy, provided the case is established by the required two-witnesses proof. *It is preposterous to talk about freedom of speech in this connection;* the case cannot be blown up into a great issue of civil liberties."[8]

The Two-Witness Requirement

Having thus concluded that the ten overt acts proved by the prosecution were sufficient to go to the jury, the court turned to an issue raised by the constitutional requirement of two-witness proof. In stating a principle of treason law that will be applicable when, in Chapter 8, we measure Fonda's broadcasts and her other conduct in Hanoi against that treason law, the First Circuit Court of Appeals noted the following:

Sometimes the overt act charged may be a single isolated act, such as disclosure of battle plans to an enemy agent. In such case the overt act must be proved by the direct testimony of two witnesses who heard the conversation between the accused and the enemy agent. Sometimes, as in [this case], the treason may consist of a course of conduct in a single treasonable enterprise. In Haupt v. United States ... the Court said: "And while two witnesses must testify to the same act, it is not required that their testimony be identical. Most overt acts are not single, separable acts, but are combinations of acts or courses of conduct made up of several elements. It is not easy to set by metes and bounds the permissible latitude between the testimony of the two required witnesses."[9]

In other words, it was not necessary for the prosecution to prove by two-witness proof every aspect of each of the ten overt acts that were submitted to the jury. On the contrary, in words that could have been written about Fonda (as we shall see in Chapter 8), the court entertained *"no doubt that treason may be predicated upon collaboration as an enemy agent in the execution of a program of psychological warfare beamed to the United States over the enemy's short wave radio.* That being so, the case against Chandler has been established by the most satisfactory and overwhelming proof.... The authenticity of the twelve sample Paul Revere recordings introduced into evidence was established by competent testimony, and is not challenged by the defendant. In a statement prepared and signed by Chandler after he was brought back to this country, which statement was received in evidence without objection, he tells the story of his employment as a commentator on the short wave station...."[10] "Two-witness proof of the fragmented elements of Chandler's course of conduct only adds a burden to the prosecution in the nature of an empty technicality." [11]

Aid and Comfort

Remember the Supreme Court's admonition in the *Cramer* case that "[t]he very minimum function that an overt act must perform in a treason prosecution is that it shows sufficient action by the accused, in its setting, to sustain a finding that the accused actually gave aid and comfort to the enemy." [12] So, too, in *Chandler*. The First Circuit Court of Appeals had to decide whether the prosecution had adduced enough evidence from which the jury could reasonably have concluded that Chandler's overt act(s) had indeed provided the constitutionally requisite "aid and comfort" to the Nazi regime. Chandler claimed that not one of the alleged overt acts—in and of themselves—provided aid and comfort to the Nazi's goals.

The Court of Appeals disagreed:

Possibly the overt acts, viewed in rigid isolation and apart from their setting, would not indicate that they afforded aid and comfort to the enemy. But viewed in their setting, which is set forth above ... they certainly take on incriminating significance. They then appear as typical routine activities of Chandler in fulfillment of the purpose of his continuous employment as radio commentator for the German Propaganda Ministry over a period of three years. The enemy's mission which Chandler participated in forwarding— the objective of the German Short Wave radio program beamed to the United States—also appears as part of the setting. *It was an obvious advantage to the enemy in the execution of that program to have the open assistance of a cultivated and widely traveled American citizen like Chandler.*[13] That the enemy deemed Chandler's services to be of aid and comfort is attested by the high salary which they paid him. These services consisted not merely of the culminating act of making a recording, but also of the necessary preliminary acts directed to that end. They were all part and parcel of the totality of aid and comfort given by the course of conduct as a whole. Attending a conference of commentators, at the summons of the Chief of the U.S.A. Zone, in order that directives as to the current propaganda line might be relayed and discussed and individual assignments made, could reasonably be found to have been of aid and comfort to the enemy. The proof under overt acts 4 and 5 established Chandler's participation in two such conferences. And certainly the making of recordings by Chandler, on the occasions proved under overt acts 17 and 18, warranted findings that Chandler gave aid and comfort to the enemy. The evidence under overt act 17 showed two recordings by Chandler on the same occasion: one a recording for his regular Paul Revere broadcasts, and another a recording of a special mixed program of poetry and music. The evidence under overt act 18 showed the making of a dialogue recording by Chandler and one Sittler, who was employed as a translator in the U.S.A. Zone.[14]

Intent to Betray

The *Chandler* case is as good place as any to address, and dispose of, the issue we raised in the Introduction to this book: "motive." In that chapter and the following one, we established that Jane Fonda was, in her own eyes, a person of little or no worth, lacking, by her own admission, self-esteem and a sense of her own identity. Her personal identity crisis drove her to seek what might be called pseudo self-esteem through the approval of others and by attaching herself to a series of causes. One need only recall from those early chapters Fonda's upbringing; her drifting from one meaningless activity to another; her expatriate days with Vadim and his clique of intellectual French Marxist friends and associates; her militant New Left escapades with Indians, feminists, farm workers and the Black Panthers; and her hitching her star to Tom

Hayden and his pro–Communist, anti–American "revolutionary" movement. In Chapter 2, we noted that, in large measure, Fonda's own pro–Communist and anti–American sentiments were motivated by that lack of identity.

We are not here addressing her *intent*— to injure the United States and help the North Vietnamese — nor the *means* she employed to achieve that end: traveling to Hanoi, making pro–Communist, anti–American broadcasts and engaging in related conduct. We are focusing, for the moment, exclusively on Fonda's *motive*. In Chandler's case, it was anti–Semitism. In Fonda's, it appears to have been that driving need to "find herself." In the context of a treason prosecution, what, then, is the relevance of "motive"?

Chandler appealed his conviction, in part, on the ground that the trial judge had erred in his charge to the jury concerning "intent" and "motive" by making the following distinction between the two:

In the law of treason, like the law of lesser crimes, *every person is assumed to intend the natural consequences that he himself knows will result from his acts.* And, in this case, if you find the defendant Chandler committed a voluntary act or acts which actually gave aid and comfort to the enemy and at that time and in his circumstances he knew, or with his knowledge had reason to know that the natural consequence of his act would be that aid and comfort would result to the enemy in the conduct of its war against the United States, *you would be warranted in finding from the commission of the acts themselves that he intended to give aid and comfort to Germany,* that he intended to adhere to the enemy, that he intended to strike at his own country and betray it and the fact that his motive might not have been to aid the enemy is no defense. In other words a person cannot do an act which he knows will give aid and comfort to the enemy and then attempt to disclaim criminal intent and knowledge by saying that one's motive was not to aid the enemy.

Motive cannot negate an intent to betray, if you find the defendant had such an intent. *Where a person has an intent to bring about a result which the law seeks to prevent, his motive is immaterial.*[15]

Was the trial judge correct in drawing this important distinction between motive and intent in a treason prosecution — a distinction that would allow a prosecutor to negate whatever psychological and/or other problems that may have accounted for Fonda's actions?

Said the United States Court of Appeals for the First Circuit: "We think the above charge stated the law with sufficient accuracy. The argument is made that treason is a crime dependent upon the actor's motives; that the jury should have been told that the defendant could not be found to have had an 'intent to betray' if he believed that he acted from patriotic motives upon the sincere conviction that what he did was for the best interests of the United States. Appellant is surely wrong in that contention."[16]

It could be no other way.

[I]n the first place, consider the subtle task which would be imposed upon the jury by an inquiry of that kind. [Chandler] had become ... "fanatically anti–Semitic". What part did this factor play in his motivation? ... Did Chandler carefully inquire into the supposed facts upon which his intense views and opinions were based? In weighing the evidence, did he make a conscious effort to discount the distorting influence of his prejudices, before arriving at his conclusions? *Whether Chandler was "sincere" in what he did, whether he had the heart of a patriot, is a matter that may be sifted out at the last Great Judgment Seat; but the law of treason is concerned with matters more immediate.*

Furthermore, if [Chandler's] argument in this connection were sound, it would of course be applicable whatever might be the character of the overt acts of aid and comfort to the enemy. Suppose Chandler had obtained advance information of the Anglo-American plans for the invasion of North Africa and had passed the information on to the enemy. Would a treason prosecution fail if he could convince the jury that, in his fanatical and perhaps misguided way, he sincerely believed his country was on the wrong side of the war; that he sincerely believed his country's ultimate good would be served by an early withdrawal from the war; that he sincerely believed that the best, perhaps the only, way to accomplish this good end was to bring it about that the first major military operation of the United States should be a resounding fiasco, thereby stimulating such a revulsion among the American people that the perfidious administration would be forced to negotiate a peace? It is hardly necessary to state the answer to that question.[17]

As the court implies, human motives are virtually without limit, and ascertaining them is a matter for psychologists and theologians, rather than jurors in a treason case.

The court concluded: "When war breaks out, a citizen's obligation of allegiance puts definite limits upon his freedom to act on his private judgment. *If he traffics with enemy agents, knowing them to be such, and being aware of their hostile mission intentionally gives them aid in steps essential to the execution of that mission, he has adhered to the enemies of his country, giving them aid and comfort, within our definition of treason. He is guilty of treason, whatever his motive.*"[18]

Gillars v. United States

Mildred Elizabeth Gillars, known to countless GIs of World War II as the infamous "Axis Sally," was notorious for broadcasting Nazi propaganda. As the United States Court of Appeals for the District of Columbia Circuit put it, *Gillars took "part in psychological warfare against [the] United States by participating in recording of radio drama."*[19] More specifically,

There was before the jury evidence from which they could find the following: Appellant was a native born citizen of the United States and therefore owed allegiance to the United States ... she left the United States in 1933, and took up residence in Berlin in 1934 ... in 1941 she took part ... in an overseas service program broadcast to the United States; the United States declared war on Germany December 11, 1941; the German Radio Broadcasting Company was a tax-supported agency of the German Government ... *the purpose of the broadcasts by the Foreign Branch was to disseminate to the Armed Forces and civilians of the United States and her allies propaganda along lines laid down by the German Propaganda Ministry and the Foreign Office to aid Germany and to weaken the war effort of the nations at war with her....*

Further, the evidence enumerates the large number of programs which appellant recorded, *evidencing active participation in the propaganda activities;* that this included, in 1943, *participation in the recordings of messages of prisoners in camps and prison hospitals* transmitted to the United States beginning in December 1943; that in making these recordings appellant was accompanied to the camps and hospitals by radio and sound technicians from the German Radio Broadcasting Company; that a high official of the company and of the Foreign Office made arrangements for interviews at camps and hospitals but the actual interviews were conducted by appellant herself....

As to the overt act No. 10, on the basis of which she was convicted, three witnesses, Schnell, Haupt and von Richter, testified to her participation in the recording of Vision of Invasion and *she admits doing so....*

Witnesses who participated in the broadcast testified that the purpose was to prevent the invasion of Europe by telling the American people and soldiers that an attempted invasion would be risky with respect to the lives of the soldiers. It was to show "Americans that an invasion would be a very costly and daring undertaking."[20]

On the basis of these facts, Gillars was indicted for treason. The indictment alleged that "within the German Reich ... in violation of her duty of allegiance [to the United States] she knowingly and intentionally adhered to the enemies of the United States, to wit, the Government of the German Reich, its agents, instrumentalities, representatives and subject with which the United States was at war, and gave to said enemies aid and comfort ... *by participating in the psychological warfare of the German Government against the Untied States. This participation is alleged to have consisted of radio broadcasts and the making of phonographic records with the intent that they would be used in broadcasts to the United States and to American Expeditionary Forces in French North Africa, Italy, France and England.*"[21]

To satisfy the overt act requirement, the indictment charged the commission of ten overt acts, one of which (number 10) charged "[t]hat on a day between January 1, 1944 and June 6, 1944, the exact date to the Grand Jurors being unknown, said defendant, at Berlin, Germany, did *speak into a microphone in a recording studio* of the German Radio Broadcasting Company, and thereby did participate in a phonographic recording and cause to be phonographically recorded a radio drama entitled 'Vision of Invasion,' said defendant then and there well knowing that said recorded radio drama was to be subsequently broadcast by the German Radio Broadcasting Company to the United States and to its citizens and soldiers at home and abroad as an element of German propaganda and an instrument of psychological warfare."[22]

Gillars was convicted on overt act Number 10. On appeal, in addition to several technical arguments that were rejected by the court, she made two main substantive arguments. The first, given short shrift by the court, was in the nature of a general defense. All Gillars was engaged in, she claimed, was an exercise of free speech. Citing and quoting from *Cramer*, where, as we have seen, the Supreme Court of the United States had laid to rest such a defense, the Court of Appeals (relying also on the First Circuit's decision in *Chandler*) stated categorically:

While the crime [of treason] is not committed by mere expressions of opinion or criticism, *words spoken as part of a program of propaganda warfare,* in the course of employment by the enemy in its conduct of war against the United States, to which the accused owes allegiance, *may be an integral part of the crime.* There is evidence in this case of a course of conduct on behalf of the enemy in the prosecution of its war against the United States. The use of speech to this end, as the evidence permitted the jury to believe, made acts of words.... *words which reasonably viewed constitute acts in furtherance of a program of an enemy to which the speaker adheres and to which he gives aid with intent to betray his own country, are not rid of criminal character merely because they are words.*[23]

Gillars' second main argument was that the prosecution had not adduced enough evidence on any of the four requisite elements of the crime of treason sufficient to take the case to the jury. The United States Court of Appeals for the District of Columbia Circuit rejected this argument, too:

In the light of the uncontradicted evidence of her participation in the recording of Vision of Invasion, testified to by more than two witnesses, as a part of her employment by an agency of the German Government, and the evidence as to the nature and purpose of this employment, of the intended use of the recordings and programs, the evidence of her citizenship, and the fact of war between the United States and Germany, we hold that the evidence furnished an adequate basis for the jury to find that appellant, while owing allegiance to the United States, adhered to the enemy, giving such enemy aid and comfort, and that this was done knowingly and with the intention of aiding the enemy in the war in which it was then engaged with the United States.[24]

Thus, Axis Sally went the way of Douglas Chandler.

Best v. *United States*[25]

A mere six weeks later, the same Court of Appeals that had decided *Chandler* was presented with a similar treason case. The following parallel between the actions of Jane Fonda and Robert H. Best is so striking that a lengthy recitation of facts from the *Best* case is warranted.

Best was born in Sumter, South Carolina, on April 16, 1896, the son of an itinerant Methodist preacher. He was, then, an American citizen from birth, and he has remained such throughout....

After the Nazis came to power in Germany, Best found much to admire in the Hitler regime. He became more and more fanatically anti-Jewish and anti-Communist. In the summer of 1941 he made overtures to be allowed to broadcast to America over the German radio, to warn against certain tendencies in the foreign policy of the Government of the United States; but no such arrangement was consummated at that time.

In April, 1942, Best commenced his radio activities in Berlin. At the outset he served in a dual capacity, as a news editor and as a radio commentator.

Over the whole period, Best made as many as 300 broadcasts. These broadcasts were monitored and recorded at the monitoring station of the Federal Communications Commission in Silver Hill, Maryland; and numerous witnesses testified to having picked up Best's broadcasts on their short wave receiving sets at scattered points throughout the United States.

On the issue of appellant's treasonable intent, seven authenticated recordings of appellant's broadcasts were played back at the trial, and manuscripts of ten of the "BBB" broadcasts were read to the jury. In these exhibits may be found all the main Nazi propaganda themes, with particular emphasis upon the alleged menace of a Jewish world-wide conspiracy and Jewish infiltration into controlling positions in the Government of the United States, and also upon the depicting of Hitler's Germany as a great bulwark of Christianity and civilization against Bolshevism.

Appellant was thoroughly aware of the objective of the psychological warfare being waged over the German short wave radio, including the U.S.A. Zone. *It was to foster a spirit of defeatism, of hopelessness in the face of vaunted German might; to induce an overwhelming war-weariness among the members of the U.S. armed forces and the civilian population; to insinuate into the minds of the American people a conviction that they had been betrayed and tricked into an unholy war by faithless leaders who were responsive to the machinations of the Jewish-Bolshevist conspirators; to sow the seeds of disunity at home and distrust of the countries allied with the United States in the war.* To the extent that this elaborate radio propaganda should succeed in undermining the moral and spiritual stamina of the American people, so much the easier, it was anticipated by the Propaganda Ministry, would be the triumph of the German arms.

In this effort Best was willing, even eager, to play the Nazi game.... In one of his broadcasts he sneered at American women, who were expressing in letters to their loved ones in the armed forces their confidence that the warrior boys would return safely home "and when you do come back you will find, just as you left them, everything your letters tell me that you hold dear"....[26]

Based on these facts, Best was indicted on a charge of treason. Twelve overt acts went to the jury, which found that every one of them constituted "a treasonable act committed by the defendant Best with an intent to betray the United States."[27] Accordingly, Best was convicted of treason.

Like Chandler before him, on appeal Best asserted that whatever he may have done, his *motive* was not to betray the United States. This argument did Best no more good than it had done Chandler:

Appellant's contention on this branch of the case is that the trial judge erred in making a distinction between 'motive' and 'intent' in the charge to the jury, and in failing to instruct the jury, in effect, that the defendant could not be found to have had an "intent to betray" the United States, if the motive for his acts was good and was to advance what he thought were the best interests of the United States. In this respect Judge Ford charged the jury in substantially the same terms he used in the Chandler case.... "When war breaks out, a citizen's obligation of allegiance puts definite limits upon his freedom to act on his private judgment. If he traffics with enemy agents, knowing them to be such, and being aware of their hostile mission intentionally gives them aid in steps essential to the execution of that mission, he has adhered to the enemies of his country, giving them aid and comfort, within our definition of treason. He is guilty of treason, whatever his motive." A country fights its wars one at a time, and takes its allies where it finds them. Best having knowingly aided agents of the enemy in their efforts to bring about the military defeat of the United States, it is of no consequence that he may have thought it was for the ultimate good of the United States to lose World War II, in order that Hitler might accomplish the destruction of an ally of the United States whom Best regarded as a potential enemy. So far as the legal issues of the present case are concerned, it is entirely irrelevant to speculate whether the present position and prospects of the United States in world affairs are better or worse, as compared with what would probably have been the alternative prospect of facing the final life-and-death struggle with a triumphant Hitler, master of most of the world outside the Americas.[28]

With the "motive/intent" distinction out of the way, once again, the Court of Appeals turned to the treason elements that we've seen so far in *Cramer, Haupt, Chandler* and *Gillars*: intent, overt act, two-witness proof, and aid and comfort.

As to intent, "[t]he evidence in this case of intent to betray was quite as strong as that presented in the Chandler case.... Best certainly knew that he was dealing with enemy agents. He knew the hostile mission of the German Short Wave Station, which was to facilitate a German military triumph by disintegrating the fighting morale of the American armed forces and the civilian population. He voluntarily hired himself to the German Radio Broadcasting Company, with the intention of contributing to the execution of that hostile mission. Not only did he so contribute, but he was constantly alert to suggest improvements of method whereby the German psychological warfare might be made more effective."[29]

Best's argument as to the lack of overt acts fared no better:

As to the sufficiency of the overt acts alleged in the indictment and established by two-witness proof as specially found by the jury, we refer to what we said in the Chandler case.... The overt acts, like those submitted to the jury in the Chandler case, related for the most part to typical routine activities of Best, on identified occasions, in fulfillment of the purpose of his continuous employment as radio commentator and news editor for the German Propaganda Ministry. For instance, one of the overt acts related to Best's participation in a particular round-table conference of commentators, whose unrehearsed discussion and colloquy were recorded by a microphone and subsequently broadcast to the United States. Another overt act established by two-witness proof was Best's making of a live broadcast of a special program prepared by him, in conjunction with a German Luftwaffe officer who had accompanied the German paratroopers participating in the "liberation" of Mussolini. In this broadcast, Best played up the episode as a daring feat of German arms, which did "the world a great favor by rescuing Benito Mussolini from the hands of his would-be murderers in Downing Street and the White House." The overt acts, viewed in their setting above summarized, were "part and parcel of the totality of aid and comfort given by the course of conduct as a whole."[30]

The *Best* prosecution having adduced proof of the four requisite elements (intent, overt act, two-witness proof, and aid and comfort), the case went to the jury, the jury finding that all four elements had been proved beyond a reasonable doubt. The broadcaster's conviction was upheld on appeal.

Burgman v. United States[31]

Herbert John Burgman was another United States citizen who contributed to the Nazi propaganda effort, making records in Berlin for broadcasts "addressed to the armed forces of the United States, allegedly seeking to impair the morale of those forces and to dissuade them from support of this country."[32] Indicted for treason on some 69 overt acts, Burgman was convicted by a jury.

On appeal to the same United States Court of Appeals that had decided the *Gillars* case, Burgman raised the now-familiar "free speech" defense that "broadcasting is merely a passive, verbal description of thoughts and so falls within the rule that no mere thought is a criminal act."[33] The Court of Appeals responded with an equally familiar answer: "This contention was examined in the Gillars case, and we adhere to the view there taken upon that point."[34]

D'Aquino v. United States[35]

Iva Ikuko Toguri, the wife of a Portuguese citizen named D'Aquino, was a United States citizen educated in America. Shortly prior to the outbreak of war with Japan, she traveled there to study medicine. Once war began, she was unable to return to the United States. During 1942 and early 1943, D'Aquino held various jobs in Tokyo, and in the fall of 1943 went to work as a typist at the Broadcasting Corporation of Japan — an entity under the control of the Japanese Government. Soon after, Mrs. D'Aquino began her broadcasting.

According to the United States Court of Appeals for the Ninth Circuit, the prosecution produced evidence that when D'Aquino

... took her voice test and accepted employment as an announcer and broadcaster for Radio Tokyo she knew that her work was to be concerned with a program known as "Zero Hour" which was to be beamed and directed specially to Allied soldiers in the Pacific. She was told and understood that the program would consist of music and entertainment designed to procure a listening audience among Allied soldiers, *and that there was to be interspersed news and commentaries containing propaganda which was to be used as an instrument of psychological warfare. Their object was to cause the Allied troops to become homesick, tired and disgusted with the war.*

[D'Aquino] participated in some 340 programs on the Zero Hour. She announced herself as "Ann" or "Orphan Ann." From time to time she attended meetings of the participants in the Zero Hour program where the Japanese Army officers in command of the enterprise advised the persons present of the strategic importance of the program and urged continued efforts by the participants.

The overt act No. 6 was testified to by the requisite number of witnesses who observed *and listened to* the broadcast in question. One of them was a participant in the same Zero Hour program. He told [D'Aquino] of a release from Japanese General Headquarters giving the American ship losses in one of the Leyte Gulf battles and requested [her] to allude to those losses. She proceeded, as this witness and another testified, to type a script about the loss of ships. That evening, when [D'Aquino] was present in the studio, the news announcer broadcast that the Americans had lost many ships in the battle of Leyte Gulf. Thereupon [D'Aquino] was introduced on the radio and proceeded to say in substance: "Now you fellows have lost all your ships. You really are orphans of the Pacific. Now how do you think you will ever get home?"

It is true that [D'Aquino's] version of her role as a broadcaster was substantially different from that which we have here summarized from the testimony of the Government witnesses. According to [her] version of the matter, the programs were exclusively entertainment and for that purpose only, she having been informed by the officer in command that the time for propaganda would not arrive until the Japanese were having more military and naval successes. Some of [D'Aquino's] witnesses testified that they were responsible for having her brought into the Zero Hour program. These persons were American prisoners of war who testified that they had been coerced into participation in this program. They testified that what they were up to was a sabotaging of the program insofar as it was designed to be propaganda to American soldiers, that they managed to inject in the program many reports of American prisoners of war and messages from them, and [D'Aquino] co-operated with them in their efforts to frustrate the purposes of the Japanese military operating through the broadcasting corporation to destroy the morale of the American soldiers.[36]

In order to provide additional facts about the broadcasting activities of Mrs. D'Aquino—known to GIs in the Pacific Theater as Tokyo Rose—the Court of Appeals appended a lengthy footnote to the foregoing quotation. It follows, verbatim.

Witnesses who identified [D'Aquino's] voice testified to sundry broadcasts by her which would fall in the psychological warfare pattern claimed by the Government.... Included were broadcasts that "Joe Brown was out with Sally Smith. He is a rejectee who is getting the cream of the crop while you Joes are out there knocking yourselves out"; "What are your wives and sweethearts doing?" and "Wouldn't it be nice to be home now, driving down to the park and parking and listening to the radio a while"; "Why don't you kick in now? There's no hope. You can be treated right by the Japanese people. When the Japanese finally take over they are not going to be hard on you"; "The Japanese were kicking hell out of the American troops in Tacloban, and that by New Year's Day the Japanese would be in Palau"; "There is no sense in being out there in those mosquito infested islands, perhaps getting yourselves killed"; "The Island of Saipan was mined with high explosives, and that the Americans would be given forty-eight hours to clear off the island, and that if they did not, the island would be blown sky high"; "I wonder who your wives and girl friends are out with tonight? Maybe a 4F. Maybe someone working in a war plant making big money, while you are out here fighting, knowing you can't succeed"; "Wake up you boneheads. Why don't you see your commanding officer and demand to be sent home? Don't stay out in that stinking mosquito infested jungle and let someone else run off with your girl friend"; "You boneheads—if you boneheads want to go home, you had better leave soon. Haven't you heard? Your fleet is practically sunk"; "You know the boys at home are making the big money and they can well afford to take your girl friends out and show them a good time."[37]

Based on these facts, and many more like them, D'Aquino was indicted for committing treason against the United States. "The indictment charged that she adhered to the enemies of the United States giving them aid and comfort by working as a radio speaker, announcer, script writer and broadcaster for the Imperial Japanese Government and the Broadcasting Corporation of Japan, between November 1, 1943, and August 13, 1945; that such activities were in connection with the broadcasting of programs specially beamed and directed to the American Armed Forces in the Pacific Ocean area; and, that [D'Aquino's] activities were *intended to destroy the confidence of the members of the Armed Forces of the United States and their allies* in the war effort, *to undermine and lower American and military morale, to create nostalgia in their minds, to create war weariness among the members of such armed forces, to discourage them,* and to impair the capacity of the United States to wage war against its enemies."[38]

Of the eight overt acts charged in the indictment, Tokyo Rose was convicted of Number 6 by the jury: "That on a day during October, 1944, the exact date being to the Grand Jurors unknown, said defendant, at Tokyo, Japan, did speak into a microphone concerning the loss of ships."[39]

On appeal, in addition to a large number of technical defenses (all of which were rejected), D'Aquino argued that the jury wrongly convicted her because a reasonable doubt existed as to her guilt. Her counsel contended that "other activities of [D'Aquino's] concerning which witnesses on both sides testified, were such as to require a conclusion that there existed reasonable doubt of appellant's intention to adhere to the enemy and reasonable doubt of her treasonable intent. These activities were certain acts of kindness and assistance which [D'Aquino] tendered to Allied prisoners of war, some of whom were working with her on Radio Tokyo, and some of whom were imprisoned at Camp Bunka. The testimony was that she brought food, cigarettes, medicine, a blanket and short wave news of Allied successes to these prisoners, and that she did this frequently at substantial risk to herself."[40]

D'Aquino's defense team had made a tactical choice. Since her role in the broadcasts, and the actual broadcasts, spoke for themselves, since there was two-witness proof, and since it would not be (and, as it turned out, was not) difficult for the jury to conclude that D'Aquino had thus rendered aid and comfort to our Japanese enemies, her best defense seemed to be lack of intent. While that may have been a good tactic with the jury, once that jury had weighed the evidence of what D'Aquino had done and drawn whatever inferences it did from her conduct, and had then resolved the intent issue against her, it was a foregone conclusion that the appellate court would not tamper with the jury's decision. Said the Court of Appeals: "We are unable to perceive the force of [D'Aquino's] argument in this respect. A general treasonable intent to betray the United States through the impairing of its war effort in the Pacific, might well accompany a particular feeling of compassion toward individual prisoners and sympathy for the plight in which they found themselves. If it were psychologically impossible for a person engaged in a treasonable enterprise simultaneously to furnish cigarettes and food to individual prisoners, [D'Aquino's] argument upon this point might have some weight. We think that the question of the effect of these acts of kindness upon [D'Aquino's] intent was one for the jury. Certainly, under the circumstances here, the court cannot declare that there must be a reasonable doubt in a reasonable mind and hence direct a verdict. *The question of the existence of a reasonable doubt was for the jury.*"[41]

Kawakita v. *United States*[42]

Tomoya Kawakita, a national of both the United States and Japan, found himself in Japan when the war began. He became an interpreter in a civilian-owned war plant run by the Japanese army and utilizing American prisoner of war labor. There, he abused the POWs through extremely cruel acts, which included torture. After the war, Kawakita was indicted for treason, the overt acts charged relating to his treatment of the American prisoners. The jury convicted him —finding the requisite intent, overt acts, two-witness proof, and aid and comfort to the enemy. Kawakita was sentenced to death. The United States Court of Appeals for the Ninth Circuit affirmed the conviction and the sentence. Kawakita appealed to the Supreme Court of the United States. There, he made the usual arguments, which the Supreme Court easily disposed of: The prosecution had presented sufficient evidence from which the jury could conclude that: (1) Kawakita had an intent to betray the United States, (2) he committed eight overt acts pursuant to that intent, (3) his acts provided aid and comfort to our Japanese enemies. But it was the fourth element — two-witness proof — that attracted the Court's attention and was probably the reason it accepted Kawakita's case for review.

Kawakita contended on appeal that the overt acts had not been sufficiently proved by two witnesses. The Court ruled otherwise.

Each witness who testified [against Kawakita] to an overt act was, however, an eye-witness to the commission of that act. They were present and saw or heard that to which they testified. In some instances there was a variance as to details. Thus overt act (b) was testified to by thirteen witnesses. They did not all agree as to the exact date when the overt act occurred, whether in April, May, or June, 1945. But they all agreed that it did take place, that Grant was the victim, and that it happened between 3 and 6 o'clock in the afternoon; and most of them agreed that [Kawakita] struck Grant. The Court of Appeals concluded, and we agree, *that the disagreement among the witnesses was not on what took place but on collateral details.* "While two witnesses must testify to the same act, it is not required that their testimony be identical." There is no doubt that as respects each of the eight overt acts the witnesses were all talking about the same incident and were describing the same conduct on [Kawakita's] part.[43]

With the Supreme Court's decision in *Kawakita*, the law of treason had been settled. It is now clear exactly what constitutes treason. The only remaining question is whether one has committed the crime, and that depends on clearly established criteria: whether a jury decides that an American citizen had the intent to betray his or her country, had committed an overt act of betrayal testified to by two witnesses, and in so doing had provided aid and comfort to his or her nation's enemy. This remains the test today. Only one question now remains: How does the test apply to Jane Fonda's broadcasts and her other related conduct in wartime North Vietnam?

1. Footnote 1 to the court's opinion reads as follows: "In one of his broadcasts, in 1942, he referred to this non de plume as his 'nom de guerre.'"

2. 171 F. 2d at 925; emphasis added.
3. 171 F. 2d at 928; emphasis added.
4. 171 F. 2d at 928.
5. 171 F.2d at 928.

6. 171 F. 2d at 937.

7. 171 F. 2d at 937; emphasis added.

8. 171 F.2d at 939; emphasis added.

9. 171 F.2d at 939.

10. 171 F.2d at 940; emphasis added.

11. 171 F. 2d at 940.

12. 325 U.S. at 34.

13. Footnote 5 of the court's *Chandler* opinion stated: "Compare the remark of the Lord Chancellor in Joyce v. Director of Public Prosecutions ... [in the British treason prosecution of the so-called Lord Haw Haw] that 'the special value to the enemy of appellant's services as a broadcaster was that he should be represented as speaking as a British subject'" (171 F.2d at 945).

14. 171 F. 2d at 941

15. 171 F.2d at 942; emphasis added.

16. 171 F. 2d at 943.

17. 171 F.2d at 943; emphasis added.

18. 171 F.2d at 944; emphasis added.

19. *Gillars* v. *United States*, 182 F.2d 962 (1950); emphasis added. As we have seen in Chapter 4, not only did Fonda make live broadcasts from North Vietnam, but tape recordings of her broadcasts were made as well.

20. 182 F.2d at 967; emphasis added.

21. 182 F.2d at 966; emphasis added.

22. 182 F.2d at 966; emphasis added.

23. 182 F.2d at 971; emphasis added.

24. 182 F.2d at 968.

25. 184 F.2d 131 (1st Cir. 1950).

26. 184 F.2d at 133; emphasis added.

27. 184 F.2d at 136.

28. 184 F.2d at 137.

29. 184 F.2d at 137.

30. 184 F.2d at 136.

31. 188 F.2d 637 (D.C. Cir. 1951).

32. 188 F.2d at 186.

33. 188 F.2d at 186.

34. 188 F.2d at 186. Burgman made other, technical, objections to his conviction, all of which were considered and rejected by the court.

35. 192 F.2d 338 (9th Cir. 1951).

36. 192 F.2d at 352; emphasis added.

37. 192 F.2d at 376; emphasis added. The trial record naturally contained considerably more facts about D'Aquino's conduct in Tokyo than did the Court of Appeals opinion, and the Court of Appeals drew on some of them in response to other of D'Aquino's arguments. For example, certain of her "broadcasts, after proceeding for most of the hour with musical entertainment, wound up with the kind of propaganda which many of the witnesses for the Government described from their recollections. Thus the conclusion of exhibit 75 was as follows: "This is still the 'Zero Hour' calling in the Pacific on the nineteen and twenty-five meter bands. (Voice — with dramatic background music) There's something mighty funny about all these navy bigshots resigning. First, there are all these admirals of the different fleets who got relieved of duty. Then there's a hell of a big shift in high positions. I didn't think much about it at the time. I thought it was only routine changes, but now the Secretary of the Navy Forrestal and the Undersecretary of Navy Ralph (Powers) have sent in their resignations. Now the whole navy is trying to get away from (this war?). Although President Truman has accepted (Powers'?) resignation, he says he ain't got no intention of accepting Forrestal's quittin' papers. He said that Forrestal's resignation was submitted as routine after the death of President Roosevelt, but I'm thinkin' that there's more to it than that. Now why should they change horses in the middle of the stream when everything is going smoothly? Or is everything going along smoothly? Maybe that's why Forrestal wants to quit. He don't want to take the responsibility of the big naval losses in this Okinawa campaign. Now the Secretary of the Navy is supposed to be the top man in the navy next to the president, and so he should stick to his guns 'til the last shot is fired or the last ship is sunk or somethin' like that. But what I mean is that he should see the thing through to the very end. He ain't got no more right to send in a resignation than the next one, or maybe he can't take it. Maybe the beatin' the navy took in the Okinawa campaign was too much for him; the blood of too many men and officers and the destruction of too many ships was on his hands, and so he wanted to quit. But after all, he's a civilian and he's got a perfect right to quit. He ain't like you or me, buddy. We try somethin' like that and it's court (martial) for us. According to Nimitz, there was only twenty-five ships sunk during the Okinawa campaign and if that's so, I say that that was pretty darned good because you gotta expect casualties in any kind of fight and for large scale fightin' like the Okinawa blowout, I say that twenty-five ships sunk is not so bad. But then you know Nimitz. He don't like big figures. By taking what he says, you multiply it by ten and get closer to the right figure. But in the case of the Okinawa navy casualties, it seems that you gotta multiply it by fifty to get the right figure. Now according to the announcement made by the Japanese side, more than five hundred and fifty ships were done for and even if they like to talk in big figures there's too much difference between their figure and the one Nimitz gives. Now I got it figured out that that's the answer to all the changes among the big shots and the resignation of the navy cabinet members. I think that the navy took a bigger

beatin' than Nimitz cares to admit. That's the only way I can figure it out. In the first place, you (and me?) who's been around the Pacific all this time have a pretty fair sample of how the Japanese fight, and you can't tell me that there's only twenty-five ships sunk during that campaign. And so the Japanese figures that there's over five hundred and fifty ships done for would be closer to the truth. But that's all right for the big shots. They can quit or be replaced when things get tough, but as I have said, you just try it and see

what happens.' While this conclusion was not read by [D'Aquino], the evidence shows she did participate in the same broadcast at an earlier stage" (192 F.2d at 376).

38. 192 F.2d at 348; emphasis added.
39. 192 F. 2d at 34
40. 192 F.2d at 353.
41. 192 F.2d at 353; emphasis added.
42. 343 U.S. 717 (1952).
43. 343 U.S. at 742; emphasis added.

JANE FONDA AND
THE LAW OF TREASON

Whether Chandler was "sincere" in what he did, whether he
had a heart of a patriot, is a matter that may be sifted out at
the last Great Judgment Seat; but the law of treason is concerned
*with matters more immediate (*United States v. Chandler,
171 U.S. 921 [1st Cir. 1948])

The genesis of Jane Fonda's broadcasts and other conduct in wartime Hanoi is found in the history of Communist efforts to take over Vietnam.[1] In the 1930s, anti-colonial sentiment in Vietnam was in disarray. Into the vacuum stepped a young Marxist, later to be called Ho Chi Minh. In the 1930s and early '40s, Ho led under-ground activities against the French and Japanese. After the war, Ho and his military commander Vo Nguyen Giap openly fought the French, whose northern fortress, Dien Bien Phu, fell to the Viet Minh in 1954. The French pulled out and Vietnam was partitioned, the United States stepping in as a patron of the South. By mid-1965, America was embroiled in a war with the Viet Cong in the South, and the North Viet-namese in both South and North.

From the beginning of Ho's war against the South and his effort to solidify his hold on the North — doubtless under the tutelage of his Soviet, Chinese, and North Korean Communist colleagues—"Ho and his cadres installed a propaganda network throughout the North Vietnamese countryside — broadcasting official statements over village loudspeakers, holding indoctrination and 'reeducation' classes for dissidents, and wringing 'confessions' from those suspected of plotting against the regime — a system of mind manipulation and control that the Viet Minh had used effectively with French PWs ... and that American PWs would experience firsthand in the years to come."[2]

As early as 1954, five American enlisted men, assigned to support the French mil-itary, were captured by Viet Minh guerrillas near Da Nang. Though released a few months later, they were obliged during their detention to complete lengthy personal history forms (nearly identical to those that had been extracted from UN prisoners in Korea by the Chinese and North Koreans). After being interrogated for military information and drawn into political discussions, the Americans were treated to a his-tory of Vietnam's centuries-old exploitation by foreign powers.

That the Americans were favorably impressed if not converted was attested by their comments following repatriation. Upon their release, the Viet Minh broadcast on the radio a prepared statement, attributed to the five Americans and circulated in the world press, that suggested how successful the Communists had been in conveying their point of view: "Since our capture we slowly came to realize American intervention in the Indochina war was against peoples fighting resolutely for independence. Had we realized the truth beforehand, we would not have agreed to come to this country."[3]

Sound familiar? It should. In the years following 1954, much of the Communist propaganda emanating from North Vietnam — *including the broadcasts of Jane Fonda from Hanoi in 1972* — was of the same flavor.

The essential point here is that virtually from the first day of Ho Chi Minh's bid to take over the country, he viewed indoctrination and propaganda as important weapons on a par with military hardware. The following — one of hundreds of similar stories — makes this point eloquently:

[A prisoner of the Viet Cong] later recounted his amazement at the VC's extraordinary effort to obtain what seemed to him so trivial — a mild propagandistic statement. They had constructed a camp in a remote jungle area, staffed it with trained interrogators and guards, and spent more than two months — not to learn vital military information, but to force him to say merely that they were treating him well, that the Viet Cong were good people, and that the United States was interfering in their just struggle. It would be years … before he would realize the importance the Communists attached to such statements. Then he would learn about the antiwar movement in the United States, *Hanoi's international propaganda campaign*, and the lengths to which the Viet Cong and North Vietnamese would go to present their case.[4]

It was on behalf of Hanoi's "international propaganda campaign" that Jane Fonda would be recruited, and would serve so well.

A Question for the Jury

With few exceptions, defendants in federal criminal trials are tried, not by a judge, but by a jury. In each of the treason cases discussed in the last two chapters, the jury, as trier of fact, had the burden of deciding whether the four requisite elements of the crime of treason — intent, overt act, two-witness proof, aid and comfort — had been proved beyond a reasonable doubt. Before measuring these four elements against Jane Fonda's activities in North Vietnam, let us stress that the question we are addressing *is not whether a jury necessarily would have convicted Fonda* — remember the verdict in O. J. Simpson's criminal case — *but only whether there was sufficient evidence of her intent, her overt acts, two-witness proof, and aid and comfort to the North Vietnamese, to submit to a jury.*

Intent[5]

Let us revisit legal precedents on the essential element of intent:

There was ample evidence for the jury that Cramer had a treasonable intent. The trial court charged the jury that "criminal intent and knowledge, being a mental state, are not susceptible of being proved by direct evidence, and therefore you must infer the nature of the defendant's intent and knowledge from all the circumstances." ... It also charged ... *If the defendant knowingly gives aid and comfort to one who he knows or believes is an enemy, then he must be taken to intend the consequences of his own voluntary act....* ... So if you believe that the defendant performed acts which by their nature gave aid and comfort to the enemy, knowing or believing him to be an enemy, then you must find that he had criminal intent, since he intended to do the act forbidden by the law....

Cramer had a traitorous intent if he knew or believed that Thiel and Kerling were enemies.... ... *The conclusion is irresistible that Cramer believed, if he did not actually know, that Thiel and Kerling were here on a secret mission for the German Reich with the object of injuring the United States and that the money which Thiel gave him for safekeeping had been supplied by Germany to facilitate the project of the enemy.* The trial court charged that if the jury found that Cramer had no purpose or intention of assisting the German Reich in its prosecution of the war or in hampering the United States in its prosecution of the war but acted solely for the purpose of assisting Kerling and Thiel as individuals, Cramer should be acquitted. *There was ample evidence for the jury's conclusion that the assistance Cramer rendered was assistance to the German Reich, not merely assistance to Kerling and Thiel as individuals.*

The trial judge stated when he sentenced Cramer that it did not appear that Cramer knew that Thiel and Kerling were in possession of explosives or other means for destroying factories in this country or that they planned to do that. He stated that if there had been direct proof of such knowledge he would have sentenced Cramer to death rather than to forty-five years in prison. But however relevant such particular knowledge may have been to fixing the *punishment* for Cramer's acts of treason.... But the present case is much stronger. For, it surely was not essential to proof of his traitorous intent. A defendant who has aided an enemy agent in this country may not escape conviction for treason on the ground that he was not aware of the enemy's precise objectives. Cramer claims he believed the enemy agent's objective was to destroy national morale by propaganda and not to blow up war factories. Propaganda designed to cause disunity among adversaries is one of the older weapons known to warfare, and upon occasion one of the most effective. No one can read this record without concluding that the defendant Cramer knew this. ...*When he was shown consciously and voluntarily to have assisted this enemy program his traitorous intent was then and there sufficiently proved....*[6]

And *Cramer* v. *United States* was not even a propaganda case.

Best v. *United States* was:

The evidence in this case of intent to betray was quite as strong as that presented in the Chandler case. ...Best certainly knew that he was dealing with enemy agents. *He knew the hostile mission of the German Short Wave Station, which was to facilitate a German military triumph by disintegrating the fighting morale of the American armed forces....* He voluntarily hired himself to the execution of that hostile mission.[7]

In paraphrase of the Supreme Court's words in *Cramer*: Was there "ample evidence for the jury" that Jane Fonda had "a treasonable intent"? Must Fonda "be taken to intend the consequences" of her "voluntary" acts?

If Cramer's intent was deemed "traitorous" because he knew or believed that Thiel and Kerling were enemies working in the interests of the German Reich, could a jury have deemed Fonda's intent similarly because she knew or believed that North Vietnamese propaganda experts were working in the interests of North Vietnam?

If Cramer's "traitorous intent" was "sufficiently proved" by his knowing participation in "propaganda designed to cause disunity among adversaries"— and if Best's "intent to betray" grew out of broadcasts designed to "facilitate a German military triumph by disintegrating the fighting morale of the American armed forces"—could a jury have fairly concluded that Fonda's knowing participation in North Vietnamese propaganda, unabashedly aimed at undermining the morale of embattled POWs and American troops in the field, sufficiently proved the necessary intent?

The question presented is whether these Supreme Court findings of "ample" evidence and "irresistible" conclusions as to treasonous intent could reasonably have been applied by a jury to the following acts by Jane Fonda:

- Touring the so-called "War Crimes" museum in the company of North Vietnamese Communist civilian and military officials and members of the international press, and there making pro–Communist and anti–American propaganda statements, as set forth in Chapter 4 above and in the Appendix.
- Touring a North Vietnamese hospital in the company of North Vietnamese Communist civilian and military officials and members of the international press, and there making pro–Communist and anti–American propaganda statements.
- Touring dikes and populated areas in the company of North Vietnamese Communist civilian and military officials and members of the international press, and there making pro–Communist and anti–American propaganda statements.
- Touring the North Vietnamese countryside in the company of North Vietnamese Communist civilian and military officials and members of the international press, and there making pro–Communist and anti–American propaganda statements.
- Making a live broadcast, through the radio facilities of the North Vietnamese regime, containing pro–Communist, anti–American propaganda, which broadcast was taped for later replay.
- Touring a textile center in the company of North Vietnamese Communist civilian and military officials and members of the international press, and there making pro–Communist and anti–American propaganda statements.
- Making a second live broadcast, through the radio facilities of the North Vietnamese regime, containing pro–Communist, anti–American propaganda, which broadcast was taped for later replay.
- Meeting with seven captured American airmen and haranguing them with pro–Communist, anti–American propaganda.
- Being interviewed by a French journalist and continuing to make her pro–Communist, anti–American propaganda statements.
- Making a third live broadcast, through the radio facilities of the North Vietnamese regime, containing pro–Communist, anti–American propaganda, which broadcast was taped for later replay.
- Holding a press conference in Hanoi, where she described her activities since arriving in North Vietnam, and continuing to make her pro–Communist, anti–American propaganda statements.
- Making a third live broadcast, through the radio facilities of the North Vietnamese regime, containing

pro–Communist, anti–American propaganda, which broadcast was taped for later replay.

- Making two more live broadcasts on one day, through the radio facilities of the North Vietnamese regime, containing pro–Communist, anti–American propaganda, which broadcasts were taped for later replay.
- Meeting with North Vietnamese Vice Premier Nguyen Duy Trinh and continuing to make her pro–Communist, anti–American propaganda statements.
- In the company of Communist civilian and military officials and members of the international press, posing in the control seat of a North Vietnamese anti-aircraft gun, feigning taking sight on an imaginary American aircraft, and, by her conduct and words, continuing to make her pro–Communist, anti–American propaganda statements.

When one compares what the courts have deemed sufficient evidence of intent in the eight treason cases discussed in Chapters 6 and 7, it is our opinion that the above evidence would have been more than sufficient to submit to a Fonda jury, and that the jury could have found Fonda intended to betray her country — based on any *one* of the foregoing episodes.

Overt Act

To get to a jury on this essential element, a treason prosecutor needs only one overt act. As the Court said in *Kawakita*, "One overt act alone, properly proved, would be sufficient to sustain the conviction, all other elements of the crime of treason being established."[8] And as the Court of Appeals said in *Chandler*, "It is enough if any one of the overt acts, in its setting, warranted a finding [by the jury] that the accused actually gave aid and comfort to the enemy."[9]

How have the treason cases defined an "overt act"? You may recall that one of Chandler's defenses was "freedom of speech" and that, in rejecting the defense, the Court forcefully observed the following on the subject of overt acts: "It cannot be said that what Chandler did was merely exercising his right of free speech in the normal processes of domestic political expression. *He trafficked with the enemy and ... collaborated in the execution of a program of psychological warfare designed by the enemy to weaken the power of the United States to wage war successfully.*"[10]

The actions in collaborating with the enemy by Cramer, Haupt, Chandler, Axis Sally, Best, Burgman and D'Aquino — one after another — were characterized as sufficient treasonable "overt acts." Those acts included

- Cramer's meeting with Nazi saboteurs Thiel and Kerling, arranging for Thiel's girlfriend to come to New York, safeguarding Thiel's money, and lying to the F.B.I. to protect Thiel;
- Haupt's facilitating his Nazi saboteur son's attempt to obtain employment in a sensitive defense plant, sheltering and harboring his son, and purchasing a car for him;
- Chandler's broadcasting Nazi propaganda and otherwise consorting with Nazi propagandists;
- Gillars' (Axis Sally) broadcasting Nazi

propaganda and otherwise consorting with Nazi propagandists;

- Best's broadcasting Nazi propaganda and otherwise consorting with Nazi propagandists;
- Burgman's broadcasting Nazi propa-

ganda and otherwise consorting with Nazi propagandists.

- D'Aquino's (Tokyo Rose) broadcasting Japanese propaganda and otherwise consorting with Japanese propagandists.

What actions of Fonda's could properly have been submitted to a jury as "overt acts"? The catalogue is extensive:

- Touring the so-called "War Crimes" museum in the company of North Vietnamese Communist civilian and military officials and members of the international press, and there making pro–Communist, anti–American propaganda statements (as set forth in Chapter 4 above and in the Appendix).
- Touring a North Vietnamese hospital in the company of North Vietnamese Communist civilian and military officials and members of the international press, and there making pro–Communist, anti–American propaganda statements.
- Touring dikes and populated areas in the company of North Vietnamese Communist civilian and military officials and members of the international press, and there making pro–Communist, anti–American propaganda statements.
- Touring the North Vietnamese countryside in the company of North Vietnamese Communist civilian and military officials and members of the international press, and there making pro–Communist, anti–American propaganda statements.
- Making a live broadcast, through the radio facilities of the North Vietnamese regime, containing pro–Communist, anti–American propaganda, which broadcast was taped for later replay.
- Touring a textile center in the company of North Vietnamese Communist civilian and military officials and members of the international press, and there

making pro–Communist, anti–American propaganda statements.

- Making a second live broadcast, through the radio facilities of the North Vietnamese regime, containing pro–Communist, anti–American propaganda, which broadcast was taped for later replay.
- Meeting with seven captured American airmen and haranguing them with pro–Communist, anti–American propaganda.
- Being interviewed by a French journalist and continuing to make her pro–Communist, anti–American propaganda statements.
- Making a third live broadcast, through the radio facilities of the North Vietnamese regime, containing pro–Communist, anti–American propaganda, which broadcast was taped for later replay.
- Holding a press conference in Hanoi, where she described her activities since arriving in North Vietnam, and continuing to make her pro–Communist, anti–American propaganda statements.
- Making a third live broadcast, through the radio facilities of the North Vietnamese regime, containing pro–Communist, anti–American propaganda, which broadcast was taped for later replay.
- Making two more live broadcasts on one day, through the radio facilities of the North Vietnamese regime, containing pro–Communist, anti–American propaganda, which broadcasts were taped for later replay.

- Meeting with North Vietnamese Vice Premier Nguyen Duy Trinh and continuing to make her pro–Communist, anti–American propaganda statements.
- In the company of Communist civilian and military officials and members of the international press, posing in the control seat of a North Vietnamese anti-aircraft gun, feigning taking sight on an imaginary American aircraft, and, by her conduct and words, continuing to make her pro–Communist, anti–American propaganda statements.

Two-Witness Proof

The Constitution, the federal treason statute, and the treason cases we've examined in the last two chapters, all make clear that in a treason prosecution, the overt act must be proved by the testimony of two witnesses. It was in *Kawakita* that the Supreme Court had the last word on this third essential element:

Each witness who testified [against Kawakita] to an overt Act was, however, an eye-witness to the commission of that act. They were present and sought or heard that to which they testified. In some instances there was a variance as to details. Thus overt act (b) was testified to by thirteen witnesses. They did not all agree as to the exact date when the overt act occurred, whether in April, May, or June, 1945. But they all agreed that it did take place, ... and most of them agreed that [Kawakita] struck Grant. The Court of Appeals concluded, and we agree, *that the disagreement among the witnesses was not on what took place but on collateral details.* "While two witnesses must testify to the same act, it is not required that their testimony be identical." [citing *Haupt*]. There is no doubt that as respects each of the eight overt acts the witnesses were all talking about the same incident and were describing the same conduct on [Kawakita's] part.[11]

Without a doubt, a prosecutor could have adduced the requisite two-witness proof sufficient to go to a jury on at least one of the nearly score of Jane Fonda's overt acts. On every one of her tours, and at all four of her press conferences, she was surrounded not only by North Vietnamese Communist civilian and military officials, but by members of the international press. Many of the journalists filed text and photographic stories about her conduct. There is motion picture evidence of her tours; of Fonda posing on the North Vietnamese antiaircraft gun; of Fonda cavorting with her Communist hosts. Moreover, scores of journalists interviewed her at formal press conferences held in at least four major cities. Countless American POWs, as well as soldiers, sailors, airmen and marines still in the field, heard her broadcasts. *Seven American prisoners of war — not merely the required two —* met with Fonda in Hanoi and suffered her propaganda harangue.

Perhaps most significantly, Jane Fonda admitted publicly — with seeming pride — all that she had done.

Aid and Comfort

Could a Fonda jury have concluded that her overt acts, as described above — tours, broadcasts, meetings and other conduct — constituted giving aid and comfort to the North Vietnamese enemy?

In *Haupt*, the father was deemed to have provided aid and comfort to his saboteur son. If "facilitation of the [son's] mission"— trying to get his son a job at a sensitive defense plant, sheltering and harboring the son, getting him a car — remains
the criterion by which the requisite element of "aid and comfort" is to be judged, certainly a jury could have concluded that Fonda's broadcasts and other conduct in
Hanoi "facilitated" the North Vietnamese enemy's international propaganda mission. In *Chandler*, the court emphasized those aspects of the defendant's credentials
that made his broadcasting all the more effective. "It was an obvious advantage to the
enemy in the execution of that [broadcast propaganda] program to have the open assistance of a cultivated and widely traveled American citizen like Chandler."[12]

Fonda, of course, was an international celebrity, and a jury could have concluded that her status, by itself, was sufficient to provide aid and comfort to the North
Vietnamese. As the court stated categorically: "Certainly the making of recordings
by Chandler, on the occasions proved under overt acts 17 and 18 warranted findings
[by the jury] that Chandler gave aid and comfort to the enemy."[13] So, too, in *Best*,
Burgman, *Gillars* and *D'Aquino*.

In *Kawakita*, the Supreme Court characterized the defendant's overt acts as
"more than sympathy with the enemy, more than a lack of zeal in the American cause,
more than a breaking of allegiance to the United States. They showed conduct which
actually promoted the cause of the enemy. They were acts which tended to strengthen
the enemy and advance its interests. These acts in their setting would help make ...
prisoners fearful, docile, and subservient. ...These acts would tend to give the enemy
the 'heart and courage to go on with the war.' ...*All of the overt acts tended to strengthen
Japan's war efforts; all of them encouraged the enemy and advanced its interests.*"[14]

A Fonda jury could have concluded that her conduct in North Vietnam also
went beyond mere sympathy with the enemy, beyond severing allegiance to her country. It could be argued that she crossed the line and "actually promoted" Hanoi's
cause because her broadcasting and other conduct, in *their* setting, had a devastating
impact on morale:

- POWs tormented by endless replays of her broadcasts;
- POWs punished for not listening to her anti–American harangues;
- POWs distraught and horrified that a prominent American movie star — Henry Fonda's daughter, no less! — would propagandize for their captors;
- POWs being coerced into meeting with her;
- POWs, and American troops still in the field, undermined by the knowledge that her propaganda efforts were buoy-ing up the enemy's spirits and keeping them in the fight.[15]

A Fonda jury also would have been apprised of the international publicity her
propaganda trip to North Vietnam garnered, as well as the extensive media coverage
her Hanoi, Paris, New York and Los Angeles press conferences generated.

As for giving the enemy "the heart and courage to go on," what would the jury have made of this revealing statement by a high-ranking North Vietnamese functionary at the conclusion of Fonda's trip: "That visit and the support it showed had great impact on the Vietnamese people…. We realized that there were two Americas—one who dropped bombs on us, and the other who had sympathy."[16]

Finally, given the theme and content of Jane Fonda's broadcasts and other statements (as discussed in Chapter 4), it is reasonable to assume that testimony by the following three experts on psychological warfare on the issue of "aid and comfort" would have had a profound impact on a Fonda jury.

Said Edward Hunter:

- When the American citizen, especially one with the glamour and the prestige value of a Jane Fonda can travel back and forth between the United States and the enemy capital without interference or arrest by the American authorities, the effect on military morale is devastating.
- What comes from a source on one's own side commands attention, under any circumstance. When the enemy can obtain the assistance of a national of the country it is fighting, to propagate its material in his or her own country, and also to broadcast it personally over the enemy's radio, going to its capital city to do so, it has achieved a form of war propaganda for which there is no professional term — except, perhaps, the old fashioned word, treason.
- Fonda has taken this technique a big step forward, proportionate to the new "psywar" dimension in modern warfare, by being able to operate both on her own soil and in Communist areas. Once we entered World War II, neither Germany or Japan had this advantage.
- Jane Fonda seriously assaulted the stamina of any fighting American listening to her highly dramatic and professional war propaganda. An incalculable number of Americans must have been more or less shaken. The impact of war propaganda is frequently a delayed reaction, that rises to the surface during a period of fatigue, frustration or personal danger. Jane Fonda's emotional outpourings were particularly attuned to this characteristic.
- Jane Fonda's broadcasts and declarations parallel in the points she stressed and in what she did not mention, precisely what the enemy was insisting upon or ignoring.
- Two of the most forceful tactics in a propaganda warfare assault on troops require precisely the contribution made by Fonda.
- Jane Fonda's broadcasts and other declarations made in North Vietnam fit neatly into the up-to-the-minute, Communist party line, and were tactically adapted to the most recent developments in the fighting and "peace" sectors. They were visibly the product of communist psychological warfare planning. Their wording was highly professional in structure and aims. Her varied talks and statements dovetailed, with her arguments adapted to different audiences. Her operations were those of a team member in the enemy's "psywar" organization.
- Any soldier who listened, or read her crisp, dramatic presentations, could not help but be at least subtly affected, in present or future attitudes.
- Her broadcasts and statements at Hanoi reinforced and coordinated major issues that the Communists are propagandizing in the United States and elsewhere.
- She supported the Communist claims by clever use of calculating selected material such as the Pentagon Papers.

- Rarely did even Goebbels go to greater extremes of calculated distortion and propaganda lying against the United States than Fonda did during her brief month of North Vietnamese vituperation against her native land.
- She supported, in this contest, Hanoi's insistence on American submission to each of its demands.
- Subtly, she supported the build-up ... of an Orwellian basis for the concocted charge of genocide against the United States....
- Her accusations against us [the United States government] actually surpassed those of Tokyo Rose.
- An up-to-the-minute propaganda service was rendered to the enemy by Fonda.
- These lies by an American citizen whom every movie goer knew, whose prestige had only just been shockingly enhanced by receipt of a top Hollywood award, were translated into Vietnamese. They could not be without impact on those who heard her in the South.
- [One] broadcast declared that the American people were demanding acceptance of Hanoi's demands, and that "we identify with the struggle of your people," referring to the Communist side. The Vietnamese who hear this— and many Americans too—knowing that she passed freely between the United States and enemy territory, implementing her self appointed task, could only be confused, certain that for her to be able to do this, there must be powerful influences in the American government—wittingly or unwittingly –supporting this. Vietnamese must remember that treason inside the French government facilitated France's defeat in Indo-China, and cannot help but equate the situation today. Too many parallels exist. Americans hearing her preach this way can only have their doubts and frustrations increased.

- *What I have found in her work was irrefutable evidence of intent to assault the morale and stamina of the American fighting man and the South Vietnamese soldier.*
- *This appeal to GIs encouraged them to disobey orders, turn their weapons against their officers, desert, and generally take the side of the enemy.*
- Jane Fonda's July 30 broadcast to the GIs was in unabashed support of the campaign to destroy the American forces, particularly the U.S. Army, from within.
- The patent objective, too, was to encourage treason in faculties and student bodies, a prime target of worldwide communism. The age of the American troops made them particularly vulnerable to this approach.
- When Jane Fonda can come out and say over the air, as she did that July 26, from Hanoi, describing the United States as a country where "people have no reason for living," it is a particular propaganda gain for the Reds. Those inside Communist quarters who are thinking of resistance can be discouraged from undertaking it, and in frustration, may even turn their hatred against America, which they then see as letting them down. This is a longtime Red propaganda operation to which Jane Fonda contributed her prestige and dramatic skill.
- Her report on American prisoners of war followed the long established routine by which a few were trotted out for abject interviews, obviously cowed and rehearsed. The Hanoi regime, in support of this P.O.W. operation, extracts weeks of favorable nation-wide publicity in the United States by releasing, at long intervals, three American prisoners—always three.
- *This must have been a cruel ordeal for the P.O.W.s. The questioning by an American actress who was taking the enemy's position on all things*

assaulted whatever stamina they had been able to maintain, and to have seemed to confirm the communist propaganda that their country was letting them down, and of invincible Red victory.

- The deteriorating effect on morale and stamina of the Fonda broadcasts should not be underestimated, nor the delayed impact of her tactically chosen subject matter, and its relationship to the major issues with which the Marxist network was concerned.
- She went farther, in her assaults on her own country in this Vietnam warfare than Tokyo Rose or even Lord Haw Haw in World War II. The prestige value to the enemy of her as a movie star gave her activities an added impact that none of her predecessors in wartime broadcasting from enemy capitals possessed.[17]

Said Francis M. Watson, Jr.:

- Her techniques, phraseology, and themes are more comparable to combat propaganda operations, designed to encourage misbehavior on the part of troops, than anything else I can think of.
- Finally, there are some distinct advantages to Jane Fonda, American movie star, and frequent personality around Army posts, as a speaker. She is immediately known. She is glamorous. She has all the trappings of self-sacrifice, and she has rapport. She knows youth and she knows the Army. In this respect she is better than any Tokyo Rose history has ever known — she is a walking encyclopedia of current, cultural and technical intelligence on the U.S. military and the young people who occupy so many of its ranks. She is even an expert on the anti-military movement. She mentions that and thus provides a readily available philosophy and group-association for her listeners.[18]

Said Brigadier General S.L.A. Marshall:

- There is no question about the intent of the Fonda broadcasts. The evidence prima facie is that the purpose is to demoralize and discourage, stir dissent and stimulate desertion.
- Would it have any one or all of these effects provided the words of the broadcaster were heard by a vulnerable individual? Here I speak of the Fonda production as a whole. There is no reason to doubt that it would.
- I would stand on the general proposition that in the occurring circumstances, when any fellow citizen is permitted with impunity to go to such extremes, men and women in the serving forces feel resentful, and in the overwhelming majority, to the degree that they believe they have been let down by government because it does not act, their own feelings of loyalty become taxed. The hurt here is long-term and indirect.[19]

From the beginning, propaganda was an integral part of Ho Chi Minh's strategy. Clearly, the North Vietnamese, like their Communist brethren elsewhere in Asia, understood the crucial importance of orchestrating political and military propaganda on a worldwide scale. Among their most effective weapons was Jane Fonda. Indeed, "many a torture was accomplished just to force a POW to say or agree to the same things that were attributed to fellow Americans [like Jane Fonda]...."[20] In other words, tortured American POWs refused to give up the propaganda that Fonda gave the North Vietnamese voluntarily. Did Fonda's activities in wartime North Vietnam make for a jury question? Undoubtedly, the answer is *yes*. And that answer necessarily gives rise to yet another question: *Then why wasn't Jane Fonda prosecuted?*

1. Rochester and Kiley, *Honor Bound*, in Chapter 1, contains a succinct overview of Vietnamese history.

2. Rochester and Kiley, *Honor Bound*, 6.

3. Rochester and Kiley, *Honor Bound*, 27.

4. Rochester and Kiley, *Honor Bound*, 8; emphasis added.

5. Since the Supreme Court of the United States and at least two of the Courts of Appeal have definitively distinguished between "motive" and "intent" in the context of a treason case, and conclusively held that the former is quite different from the latter and no defense to a charge of treason, we shall not address the concept of motive here.

6. 325 U.S. at 54; emphasis added [*Cramer*].

7. 184 F.2d at 137; emphasis added.

8. 343 U.S. at 736.

9. 171 F.2d at 942.

10. 171 F.2d at 939; emphasis added.

11. 343 U.S. at 742; emphasis added.

12. 171 F.2d at 941.

13. 171 F.2d at 941.

14. 343 U.S. at 965; emphasis added.

15. See, generally, Chapters 4 and 5.

16. *Hearing Report*, 7670.

17. See Mr. Hunter's remarks in Chapter 4. His testimony to the House Internal Security Committee is quoted verbatim, and the emphasis has been added.

18. See Mr. Watson's remarks in Chapter 4. His testimony to the House Internal Security Committee is quoted verbatim.

19. See General Marshall's remarks in Chapter 4. His testimony to the House Internal Security Committee is quoted here verbatim.

20. Day, *Return with Honor*, 131.

Part IV

CLOSURE

THE GOVERNMENT'S CAPITULATION

Treason doth never prosper: what's the reason? For if it prosper, none
dare call it treason (Sir John Harington [1561–1612] Epigrams of Treason)

Fonda had not been back from Hanoi very long, nor from her inflammatory press conferences in Paris, New York and Los Angeles, when "an unprecedented influx of mail demanding action against her"[1] began to arrive in Washington. Given Fonda's notorious activities in Hanoi, the impact that they had, the high-profile publicity they attracted, and the resultant outcry that followed in the United States, certain Members of Congress demanded that something be done. Indeed, "[s]oon after learning of [Fonda's] initial broadcasts ... Congressman Fletcher Thompson [of Georgia] asked that the Committee on Internal Security [of the House of Representatives] conduct an investigation of the matter, giving consideration to the issuance of a subpoena to Miss Fonda."[2]

According to a UPI press release:

Rep. Fletcher Thompson, R-Ga., accused actress Jane Fonda today of giving aid and comfort to the enemy and asked the Justice Department to charge her with treason.

Thompson ... quoted Miss Fonda as urging U.S. troops in Vietnam to "desert and turn themselves in to the North Vietnamese."

"Declared war or undeclared war," Thompson said, "this is treason. It is time this government took some action against such people as Jane Fonda giving aid and comfort to an enemy."

Thompson said he was writing Attorney General Richard G. Kleindienst "urging him to investigate fully and to bring charges of treason against Jane Fonda."

Miss Fonda has been in Hanoi and among other statements, according to Radio Hanoi, has called on U.S. pilots to quit bombing North Vietnam.

Later Thompson told a reporter he was asking the Attorney General to determine the facts and, if Miss Fonda has been quoted accurately, to bring treason charges against her.[3]

Accordingly, the Chief Investigator for the House's Internal Security Committee tried to contact Fonda to arrange an interview. It is noteworthy that even though the Committee, from the outset, handled Fonda with kid gloves, still, she stonewalled:

On August 7, 1972, after determining that Fonda was at her home in North Hollywood, California, Chief Investigator Robert M. Horner[4] made three attempts to reach her by telephone for the purpose of arranging a personal interview, speaking on each occasion to Ruby Ellen, self-described as Fonda's "assistant". At 5:00 p.m. the same day Horner received a telephone call: from Leonard Weinglass[5] who described himself as Fonda's attorney "for this purpose" and said he practices from offices at 208 Washington Street, Newark, N. J. Horner explained to Weinglass the Committee's interest in Fonda's trip to Hanoi, particularly her broadcasts from Hanoi, and said the purpose in attempting to contact her was to determine if she would be agreeable to a staff interview; that no subpoena was involved; that the interview would be strictly voluntary on her part and would be scheduled at her convenience but preferably within the next several days. Weinglass said he would discuss the matter with Fonda and furnish her decision the following day. On August 8th Weinglass informed Horner that Fonda would not agree to an interview. Weinglass asked what she might expect next and was told that as the purpose of Horner's contact was to arrange for a voluntary interview, which Fonda would not agree to, it appeared that the matter was concluded [and] that Weinglass would have to confer with the Committee's Chief Counsel as far as any other Committee action was concerned. The Committee staff has received no subsequent communication from Fonda or her attorney.[6]

So a mere two weeks after Fonda had returned from Hanoi, the House Internal Security Committee — even after an avalanche of complaints, some from highly reputable sources — was pussyfooting around: repeated attempts to reach her by phone, a "strictly voluntary" interview, if that was "agreeable," possible scheduling at Fonda's convenience, reassurance that no subpoena was involved. Despite this delicate approach, Fonda's lawyer put off the Committee. Nothing in the Reports of the Hearings even suggests that the Committee ever again sought to interview Fonda, let alone subpoena her.

What is not commonly known is that, in fact, the Committee considered issuing a subpoena.

The committee met on August 10 [1972] to take the request of Mr. Thompson [for an investigation and a subpoena] under advisement. By a vote of 8 to 1[7] the committee agreed to ask the Department of Justice for a report on the case.[8]

In a press release of the same day, after the Committee had concluded its "executive session" — a euphemism for a meeting closed to outsiders — it issued a surprising announcement:

Members of the House Committee on Internal Security, meeting in executive session, agreed that a subpoena of actress Jane Fonda for testimony about her recent trip to North Vietnam would not be appropriate at this time.

What follows is the press release's somewhat labored explanation:

A Committee Member, Rep. Fletcher Thompson, R-Ga., had advocated issuance of such a subpoena at a news conference [suggesting] that she would be an appropriate subject for a Committee hearing.

After lengthy discussion at today's Committee meeting, [Internal Security Committee] Chairman Richard H. Ichord, D-Mo., said "there are several reasons why it would be improper to subpoena Miss Fonda.

"One is that her actions are already well known to the public and the Congress and little, if any, value would be gained through further airing of them, particularly before a Congressional forum. The Justice Department is studying tapes of her broadcasts to determine whether she was in violation of the 1940 Sedition Act. I think that is a course that should be pursued vigorously by the Department of Justice. Should Justice decide to prosecute Miss Fonda, hearings before our Committee prior to prosecution might serve only to cloud the legal issue."

Ichord said that "the Committee's overriding interest is not in what additional information might be secured from Fonda, but rather any deficiency in the law or any dereliction on the part of the Department of Justice." Ichord added that "It is the responsibility of the Congress, and each Committee within its own jurisdiction, to insure that the Executive Branch is enforcing the law enacted by the Congress, and if not, to effect remedies."

He said, "it is the duty and obligation of the Department of Justice to determine whether the broadcasts in question did indeed cause or attempt to cause disloyalty or refusal of duty."

In other words, it is not our job — at least, not at this time.

On Ichord's motion ... [it was] resolved that "the Committee continue the staff investigation of Fonda's activities and in the event the Justice Department determines that the broadcasts of Jan [*sic*] Fonda from Hanoi during July 1972 do not constitute treason or sedition, or that her conduct cannot be reached by existing statute for any other reason, then the Department should render a full explanation to the Committee by September 14 with recommendations for legislation which would be effective to impose criminal sanctions. In the event the report is not submitted on or before September 14, a representative of the Department of Justice will be expected to appear before the Committee on September 14, to furnish explanation."

"Whatever the outcome of this matter," Ichord said, "Miss Fonda is indeed fortunate to have the protection of U.S. citizenship. Personally I believe that her disgraceful and shameful activities speak for themselves. She is being and should be tried at the bar of public opinion.

"I also feel that Congressman Thompson should be complimented for his action in highlighting this matter. Her actions and statements were at the most treasonable. At the very least they revealed her to be a woman with an extremely distorted sense of values who has apparently allowed herself to be used by communist propaganda experts."

The press release concluded:

Miss Fonda has long been a militant opponent to American involvement in Southeast Asia. Broadcasts she made while in Hanoi aimed at U.S. servicemen in South Vietnam apparently sought to raise doubts in their minds about the morality of performing their duties.[9]

On the same day, August 10, 1972 — only three days after Chief Investigator Horner's abortive attempt to talk to Fonda — Chairman Ichord wrote to the Attorney General of the United States:

Dear Mr. Attorney General: The Committee on Internal Security met this morning in executive session to consider a request that a subpoena be issued to require Jane Fonda to appear before the Committee in regard to her travel to North Vietnam and radio broadcasts to U.S. military forces during July 1972. During the meeting a number of reasons were expressed as a basis for opposition to the issuance of a subpoena. Important factors in the ultimate determination of the Committee were that the facts seemed to be already rather well-known, that the matter was under study by the Department of Justice and Fonda would be entitled to the full protection of the Fifth Amendment, that any such hearing might work to the prejudice of the Government in the event prosecution is undertaken and that the Committee's overriding interest is not in what additional information might be secured from Fonda, but rather in any insufficiency in the terms of the law or in its enforcement.

Translation: In a closed session, some Committee members, whose identities will never be known, voiced objections to issuing a subpoena that would have forced Fonda to appear before the Committee (and, doubtless, before television cameras).

Why? Let's look at the professed reasons Ichord advanced to the Attorney General.

"[T]he facts seemed to be already rather well-known."

Why, then, did Chief Investigator Horner want to "interview" Fonda only a few days earlier? What facts were "already rather well known"? As the material in Chapter 4 shows, all the Committee knew was where Fonda went, the text of her broadcasts, and some of the people she met with. There was much more that the Committee apparently did *not* know. Who sponsored her trip? Who accompanied her? Was she in touch with North Vietnamese, Viet Cong, Soviet, Chinese, North Korean or other Communist intelligence agents? Which American POWs did she meet with, under what circumstances, and what was their condition? Did any of the POWs give her messages? What were her instructions from those who sent her, and from the Communists in Hanoi? Who did she report to when she returned? What did she tell them? And so much more.

"[T]he matter was under study by the Department of Justice."

So what? The Department of Justice is part of the Executive Branch of our government. Its constitutional responsibility under our separation of powers system is to enforce the laws. Equally, Congress' constitutional duty is to make those laws. Incident to that legislative duty is the power to investigate. Congressional investigations—including hearings as part of those investigations—are an everyday occurrence, as, for example, the Truman Committee Hearings during World War II, the Army-McCarthy Hearings of the 1950s, and the Iran-Contra Hearings in the 1980s. For the Internal Security Committee to have demurred about subpoenaing Fonda because "the matter was under study by the Department of Justice" was a cop-out.

"Fonda would be entitled to the full protection of the Fifth Amendment."

This excuse strains credulity. In the first place, it presumes to know that had Fonda been subpoenaed to testify before the Committee, she would have "taken the

Fifth." There is no way the Committee could have known what Fonda would or would not have done — particularly since, as a prominent celebrity, she would have had to weigh the cost of taking the Fifth very carefully.

Secondly, if the Committee actually anticipated Fonda's taking the Fifth, that alone might have been sufficient reason to subpoena her. Let's not forget — as Ichord apparently did — that this important constitutional right can be invoked only if an answer would "tend to incriminate."

"[A]ny such hearing might work to the prejudice of the government."

This platitude has no meaning whatsoever — which is probably why Ichord made no effort to explain it. Apparently, he thought it sufficient merely to drop two buzz-words — "prejudice" and "government" — and all discussion, let alone inquiry, would end. To the contrary, not only would a hearing *not* have prejudiced the government, but it would have benefited the government in at least three ways and at a very opportune time.

First, even as the government sought to cope with the unbridled attacks by the virulent anti-war movement, it was trying to extricate the country from a war that had occupied four administrations, from Eisenhower through Nixon. Fonda's conduct in North Vietnam, had it been exposed for all Americans to see, could have triggered patriotic sentiment and, ironically, helped the government to end that war.

Second, a hearing could have had the effect of reassuring the American people that their government would not tolerate pro–Communist, anti–American, free-lancers who had no inhibitions about junketing to the bosom of our enemy. An enemy, it should be stressed, that had tortured and killed American servicemen (and some civilians, for good measure) even while hosting the likes of Hayden, Lynd, Aptheker, Dellinger and other anti-war zealots.

Third, hearings would have demonstrated that our North Vietnamese enemies were — with great success — orchestrating morale-breaking propaganda in an effort to undermine our military efforts.

Chairman Ichord's letter to Attorney General Kleindienst continued:

I am sure that you recognize the pernicious nature of Miss Fonda's statements to our servicemen, and the seriousness with which nearly all Members of Congress view her conduct. Although it might be fairly said that public support for American involvement in the Vietnam conflict is steadily declining, such *aid and comfort* to a nation with which we are engaged in hostilities is nevertheless condemned by the public. But whatever political or public reaction might obtain under the circumstances, I am sure you agree that the Department of Justice has a most solemn obligation to engage the full weight of the law against conduct which the Congress has made criminally punishable.[10]

You can be sure that Ichord's letter did not go out to Kleindienst until it had been carefully reviewed, if not actually written, by Internal Security Committee lawyers. The dead giveaway is reflected in the words italicized: "aid and comfort." The Committee Chairman, in characterizing Fonda's conduct in Hanoi, refrained from using the actual word *treasonous.* Clearly under no illusions about the political aspects of the Fonda case — "whatever political or public reaction might obtain under the circumstances" — still, he reminded the Attorney General of the Department of Justice's "solemn obligation to engage the full weight of the law against conduct which the Congress has made criminally punishable." In other words, Ichord was saying, Fonda may have committed treason, and no matter what the political fallout, the Department of Justice (not the Internal Security Committee) had a duty to enforce the treason laws.

Ichord didn't stop there:

The Committee has reviewed the treason, sedition and other relevant statutes. It has also been informed of Fonda's travel itinerary, and has studied the transcripts of her broadcasts while recently in Hanoi. It is not difficult to perceive why a cry of treason has been raised. But if the burden of proof is too great for treason, would not a prima facie case exist under Section 2387 of Title 18, United States Code or even Section 2388, notwithstanding the jurisdictional limitation?

At this stage of the proceedings, it had become obvious that the House Internal Security Committee was of two minds. On the one hand, Ichord wanted to avoid getting too deeply involved in the Fonda affair. On the other, he seemed genuinely concerned about whether Jane Fonda had committed treason in Hanoi and, to that end, he pressed the Attorney General into service:

In discharging its responsibility to the Congress to insure that statutes within its oversight jurisdiction are being duly enforced by the Executive Branch, the Committee resolved that the staff investigation of Fonda's activities will continue, and in the event the Justice Department determines that the broadcasts of Jane Fonda from Hanoi during July 1972 do not constitute treason or sedition, or that her conduct cannot be reached by existing statute for any other reason, then the Department is requested to furnish a report to the Committee with recommendations for legislation which would be effective to impose criminal sanctions under similar circumstances in the future. Desiring to resolve the questions at an early date, but hoping to avoid an unreasonable burden upon the Department, the Committee voted to request that the report be submitted by September 14, or in the alternative, that a representative of the Department appear before the Committee on that date.

In other words, Congress had a right to know that the laws it passed were being enforced, and to that end, the Committee's own staff investigation of Fonda's activities would continue, with the Department of Justice keeping the Committee in the picture.

Five days later, on August 15, 1972, Chairman Ichord stood in the well of the House of Representatives and made the following statement:

Mr. Speaker, last week the Committee on Internal Security discussed, at some length, the question of whether or not to issue a subpoena to the actress, Jane Fonda, with respect to broadcast statements she made over the Communist Radio Hanoi to our troops in Vietnam.

It was agreed by the committee that it would be best, at this time, to give the Justice

Department time to complete its announced inquiry into the Fonda affair before considering any further course by the committee.

At the request of my colleagues on the committee, I addressed a letter which was hand-delivered Friday afternoon to Attorney General Kleindienst setting forth the committee's concern with this matter and our desire to have a report from the Justice Department by September 14 or an explanation on that date regarding what can be done with respect to Miss Fonda's activities in the capital of our enemy.[11]

Ichord got a response nearly two weeks later.

As you know, the Department is currently reviewing the texts of statements allegedly made by Miss Fonda and broadcast over Radio Hanoi. We are still receiving such statements. However, in the event our review of this material is completed on or before September 14, 1972, we will be pleased to furnish you with a report at that time.

> Sincerely,
> A. William Olson[12]
> *Assistant Attorney General*

The day before the deadline, Olson wrote again to Ichord:

Dear Mr. Chairman: In my letter of August 22, 1972, regarding Jane Fonda you were advised that in the event our review of this matter is completed before September 14, 1972, we would be pleased to furnish you with a report by that date.

We have since received, and are continuing to receive, material and information which is pertinent to our review of the activities of Miss Fonda. Since this matter is still under active consideration in the Department, I know you will appreciate that it would be inappropriate, and contrary to long standing Department policy, to comment upon a pending matter.

I regret, therefore, that in these circumstances, I cannot furnish you *the report* at this time. However, I shall contact you further when our review is completed and a decision is reached in this matter.

> Sincerely,
> A. William Olson
> Assistant Attorney General[13]

Ichord was not pleased:

Dear Mr. Attorney General: I have received the letter of Assistant Attorney General A. William Olson dated September 13, 1972 in regard to Jane Fonda. It was with regret that I read of the declination of the Department of Justice to furnish a report to the Committee on Internal Security at this time.

While it is gratifying to learn that the Department of Justice is considering the ramifications of the activities of Miss Fonda, it is at the same time disappointing that your review cannot be completed more promptly. Certainly there are understandable difficulties of proof but the views of the Department would be helpful to the Committee in evaluating whether there is a necessity for new legislation, and if so in formulating its terms.

In my letter to you of August 10 I related the Committee's desire for a report by September 14, or in the alternative that a representative of the Department appear before the Committee on that date. Inasmuch as no report has been furnished[14] the Committee would be pleased to receive your oral views, or your official representative, in an executive meeting which I am scheduling for 10:00 a.m. on Tuesday, September 19, 1972 in Room 311 of the Cannon House Office Building.

I hope this will be convenient, and I am looking forward to a discussion Tuesday which will produce a solution to the problems resulting from activities such as those engaged in by Miss Fonda.

> Sincerely,
> RICHARD H. ICHORD,
> *Chairman*

It was clear that Ichord was going nowhere with his correspondence. A face-to-face confrontation would produce no better results. It quickly became apparent that the Department of Justice was not interested in pursuing the issues that the Internal Security Committee had raised about Fonda's conduct. And, clearly, some members of the committee knew it, as would become obvious at the hearing.

HEARINGS REGARDING H.R. 16742:
RESTRAINTS ON TRAVEL TO HOSTILE AREAS[15]

TUESDAY, SEPTEMBER 19, 1972

U.S. House of Representatives
Committee on Internal Security
Washington, D.C.
Executive Session

The Committee on Internal Security met, pursuant to call, at 10:05 a.m., in room 311, Cannon House Office Building, Washington, D.C., Richard H. Ichord, chairman, presiding.

Committee members present: Representatives Richard H. Ichord of Missouri, Richardson Preyer of North Carolina, Robert F. Drinan of Massachusetts, Roger H. Zion of Indiana, and Fletcher Thompson of Georgia.

Staff members present: Donald G. Sanders, chief counsel; Alfred M. Nittle; legislative counsel; Daniel R. Ferry, assistant counsel; and DeWitt White, minority legal counsel.

The Chairman. The committee will come to order.

Without objection, the meeting will be held in executive session.

As ordered by the committee on August 10, the Chair directed a letter to Attorney General Kleindienst, asking that, in the event that the Attorney General determines that the travel of Jane Fonda did not constitute sedition or treason, the Department of Justice furnish a report to the committee on the matter, together with recommendations of action that the Congress should take or, in the alternative, a representative of the Department appear before the committee.

This letter was acknowledged on August 22.

On September 13 Mr. William Olson advised the Chair that the Fonda matter was still under consideration and that it would be inappropriate under the circumstances for the Department to comment upon a pending matter and therefore a report could not be furnished.

On September 14, by letter to Mr. Kleindienst, the Chair asked that a representative meet at this executive meeting today.

Without objection, I would direct that the correspondence referred to be placed in the record at this point.[16]

The Chairman. Mr. William Olson, Assistant Attorney General in charge of internal security, is with us today in response to my letter of September 10.

Mr. Olson, it is a pleasure to welcome you to the committee. You are accompanied by Mr. Maroney. Do you have a prepared statement, Sir?

Mr. Olson. Yes, I do, Mr. Chairman.

The Chairman. Without objection, then, the gentleman will be recognized to proceed with his statement.

Testimony of A. William Olson, Assistant Attorney General, Internal Security Division, Department of Justice, Accompanied by Kevin T. Maroney, Deputy Assistant Attorney General, Department of Justice

Mr. Olson. Mr. Chairman, I am appearing today in response to your request that the Attorney General or his official representative appear before the committee for the purpose of discussing matters relating to the treason and sedition statutes. The Logan Act is also relevant to a consideration of this matter.

As I informed the committee in my letter of September 13, 1972, it would be inappropriate for me to comment on the reported activities of Jane Fonda in North Vietnam since that is a matter presently under active consideration in the Department. I would like again to make that point clear.

The Federal Bureau of Investigation has been requested to conduct an investigation regarding Miss Fonda's activities, and, of necessity, we cannot complete our review or come to a prosecutive determination until all investigation is concluded. To comment on this matter at this time would not only be contrary to longstanding policy of the Department, but could very well prejudice any possible prosecution, if such should eventuate. (See *Delaney v. United States, 199 F. 2d* 107 (1st Cir. 1952) .)

I regret therefore that *I cannot testify concerning any of the facts regarding Miss Fonda's activities in North Vietnam, nor can I answer any hypothetical questions which might in any way relate to that subject matter.*

Mr. Sanders, of your staff, has been furnished with a written report discussing the law of treason and sedition. I think it might at this time be appropriate to review the provisions of these statutes and briefly discuss their application.[17]

Interestingly, the Department of Justice's "written report" was entitled "Memorandum of Law," and its significance rests not so much in what it contains, but in what was left out.

Memorandum of Law Concerning Treason (18 U.S.C. 2381)

Title 18, United States Code, Section 2381, provides that:
Whoever, owing allegiance to the United States, levies war against them or

adheres to their enemies, giving them aid and comfort within the United States or elsewhere, is guilty of treason....

Treason is a breach of allegiance to the government, and as an offense against the state, it has always been regarded as the most serious and heinous of all crimes. In early English law, "treason" was given a very broad scope and became an instrument of oppressing anyone who opposed the will of the King. However, to avoid such evils, the framers of our Federal Constitution, although resorting to some of the terms of the old English Statute of Edward III, commonly known as the "Statute of Treason," made great effort to carefully define the offense of treason, specifically limiting its scope. Significantly, the principal discussion in connection with the drafting of the treason clause of the Federal constitution centered around three aspects; namely, the two-witness requirement: the concept of an overt act, and the concept of "aiding and comforting the enemy."

The basic law of treason was not written into the constitution by accident. It was framed and put there by men who had been taught by experience and by history to fear the abuse of the treason charge almost as much as they feared treason itself. Treason under English law had became so broad and loose as to make treason consist not only of a breach of allegiance to the crown by adherence to its enemies, but to include the mere utterance of opinions. Many of our colonies had enacted similar broad treason statutes. None of the framers intended to withdraw the treason offense from use as an effective instrument against treachery that would aid external enemies nor did they appear reluctant to punish as treason any genuine breach of allegiance to one's government. But the thing they did want to prevent was legislation in later years becoming so broad as to make treason consist of the mere utterance of an opinion.

The proceedings of the Constitutional Convention of 1787 reflect that Charles Pinckney proposed that Congress be given the power to declare what should be treason against the United States; however, the "Committee on Detail" reported a draft constitution which left no latitude to create new treasons and after thorough and able discussion, this was the provision adopted. The framers combined all known protection against the extension of treason and wrote into the organic act a prohibition of legislative or judicial creations of treason. In doing so they seemed to have been concerned by two kinds of dangers: (1) the suppression by lawful: authority of peaceful political opposition; and (2) the conviction of the innocent as a result of perjury, passion or inadequate evidence. To correct the first they limited treason to levying war or adhering to the enemies of the United States, giving them aid and comfort, thus making it impossible for lesser offenses to become treason. To correct the second and safeguard the procedures incident to the trial of those persons charged with treason, they provided that no one should be convicted except upon the testimony of two witnesses to the same overt act or upon confession in open court.

The Constitution of the United States (Art. III, Sec. 3, cl. 1), as well as the statutory provision relating to treason (Title 18, United States Code, Section 2381), specifically provide that treason shall: consist only (1) in levying war against the United States or, (2) in adhering to enemies of the United States, giving them aid and comfort. Unless the activities in question constitute making war against the United States or the giving of aid and comfort to an "enemy," that is, a foreign power with whom we are in a state *of at least open hostilities if not war*[18], the crime of treason is not applicable. Thus, the Constitution has placed specific limitations on the crime of treason and such provisions were inserted to prevent the possibility of extension of treason to offenses of minor importance. The crime of treason, moreover, was never to be extended by construction to doubtful cases....

The crime of treason is unique among criminal statutes as regards the stringent requirements of proof which it places upon the prosecution of such cases. The Government is required to allege specific overt acts of treason upon the part of the accused and to prove each of these acts *by* the testimony of two eyewitnesses to the particular act. In the Supreme Court's decision in *Cramer* v. *United States* ... Justice Jackson presented an exhaustive treatise on the history of the treason statute....

This three-and-one-half-page Memorandum of Law, containing a bit of history and a brief quote from the *Cramer* case, did not even mention, let alone discuss, the two other Supreme Court treason cases (*Haupt* and *Kawakita*), nor the five Courts of Appeal broadcast treason cases (*Chandler, Burgman, Gillars, Best,* and *D'Aquino*)— all of them crucially important and highly relevant, as I demonstrated in Chapters 6 and 7. Choosing to ignore the cases placed the Justice Department in the "judicious" position of not having to deal with them in its glaringly deficient Memorandum of Law.

And this, in turn, resulted in a Memorandum that could not — and thus did not — compare the facts and the precedential holdings of those eight cases to the facts involving Fonda. Significantly, the Memorandum does not even mention Jane Fonda's name.

Olson's two-and-a-half page oral testimony on the subject of treason was similarly without substance and suffered from significant omissions. Again, he delved briefly into history. Again, he steered clear of mentioning Fonda by name. Again, he made no attempt to connect the facts and holdings of the treason cases to the Fonda facts. On the contrary, Olson, albeit implicitly, tried to uncouple the relevant precedent cases from Fonda and to undermine their applicability to her. Here is what he said:

There are some important factors in these World War II cases bearing on intent to adhere to the enemy. In each of the cases the defendants were voluntary, *paid employees* [emphasis is Olson's] of the "enemy" who were *hired* [emphasis is Olson's] for the purpose of dispensing (i.e., broadcasting) anti-U.S. propaganda to the military and who remained at their jobs for most, or a considerable part, of the war. Their adherence to the enemy, their intent to betray, was knowing, willful, and clear. It is "made clear" [quotation marks are ours] in the cited World War II cases that when broadcasting is charged as the overt act, the two-witness rule means two witnesses who saw the act of broadcasting and heard the words spoken by the defendant. Circumstantial evidence is not admissible to prove this point.[19]

Olson's oral testimony is thus evasive and misleading in several ways. He does not recognize, let alone address, the truism that intent (as with the other three requisite elements necessary to prove treason) is ultimately a question for the jury — so long as there is *some* evidence of that intent. He avoids actually saying that the World War II broadcast treason cases militate against a prosecution of Fonda, though that is what he means. In fact, as we showed in Chapter 8, they do not. He hedges what those cases say about intent by stating that "important factors" have a "bearing." But what all of the Chapter 7 broadcast cases hold about intent is that *the defendant's state of mind is a question for the jury.*

Let's take a closer look at those "important factors" which Olson identifies. He emphasizes that the defendants were "paid employees" who were "hired" to propagandize, and who worked at their tasks for all or most of the war. Yet, not one of those cases turned on the defendants' employee status or on the duration of their propagandizing — nor did any of the cases hold that these two criteria were necessary for a treason indictment or conviction. Indeed, for at least two reasons, the cases could not have turned on those grounds. For one thing, pay and duration, even if relevant, would only be *indicia* of intent to betray, which, as we have seen time and again, is a question for the jury. For another, while Olson did not discuss *Cramer* or *Haupt*, it is noteworthy that there was no evidence in either case that the defendants were in the pay of the Nazis (indeed, the evidence was to the contrary), or that their traitorous conduct lasted for all or most of the war.

Finally, Olson (or, more likely, the Justice Department law clerk who wrote the Memorandum of Law) could not have really believed that the prosecutors who indicted Chandler, Gillars, Best, Burgman and D'Aquino would not have done so if they had made only a few propaganda broadcasts within a few days. If Tokyo Rose, without pay, had broadcast the most vile Japanese propaganda on December 8, 1941, and again during the Bataan Death March, and then retired, it is hard to believe that Olson would have advised the Attorney General of the United States that there was insufficient evidence of her intent to send to a jury.

Perhaps most misleading of all is Olson's glib reference to what the "World War Two" treason cases presumably "made clear." Every lawyer knows — as Olson knew — that appellate courts don't make "clear," they make "holdings." They establish legal principles. Olson's interpretation of the two-witness rule is specious. *Not one of those five cases even stated, let alone held, that "the two-witness rule means two witnesses who saw the act of broadcasting... ."* In *Chandler*, "[t]he authenticity of the twelve sample Paul Revere recordings introduced into evidence was established by competent testimony, *and is not challenged by the defendant.*"[20] In *Gillars*, while there was testimony by those who saw Axis Sally make the recordings, *she admitted doing so.* Accordingly, the Court did not have to rule on, and therefore did not rule on, whether the proof had to show independently that two people saw her speak into the microphone. In *Best*, the Court repeated what it had said about overt acts in *Chandler*: "[t]he overt acts, *viewed in their setting* ... were part and parcel of the totality of aid and comfort given by the *course of conduct as a whole.*"[21] In *Burgman*, propaganda broadcast records made by the defendant were presented as evidence at the trial. Significantly, in

D'Aquino, the Court of Appeals noted that overt act Number 6 was testified to by witnesses who not only observed the broadcast, but *also listened to it* — thus making it unnecessary for the court to rule on whether two-witness proof required that, for a broadcast overt act to be sufficient, the speaker had to be observed by two witnesses while actually speaking. In addition, even before these five cases were decided by the Courts of Appeals, the Supreme Court had held in *Haupt:*

The Constitution requires testimony to the alleged overt act and is not satisfied by testimony to some separate act from which it can be inferred that the charged act took place. And while two witnesses must testify to the same act, *it is not required that their testimony be identical. Most overt acts are not single, separable acts, but are combinations of acts or courses of conduct made up of several elements. It is not possible to set by metes and bounds the permissible latitude between the testimony of the two required witnesses....* One witness might hear a report, see a smoking gun in the hand of defendant and see the victim fall. Another might be deaf, but see the defendant raise and point the gun, and see a puff of smoke from it. The testimony of both would certainly be "to the same overt act," *although to different aspects.* And each would be to the overt act of shooting, although neither saw the movement of a bullet from the gun to the victim. It would still be a remote possibility that the gun contained only a blank cartridge and the victim fell of heart failure. *But it is not required that* [two-witness] *testimony be so minute as to exclude every fantastic hypothesis that can be suggested.*[22]

Olson surely had to know that in *Kawakita,* which he also failed to mention, the Supreme Court had expressly ruled with regard to the two-witness rule, albeit not in a broadcast case, that "[w]hile two witnesses must testify to the same act, it is not required that their testimony be identical. There is no doubt that as respects each of the eight overt acts the witnesses were all talking about the same incident and were describing the same conduct on [Kawakita's] part."[23]

Lastly, it needs to be emphasized that Olson knew Fonda had done much more in North Vietnam than merely broadcast. He said nothing about whether her other conduct — tours, consorting with Communists, "interviewing" American POWs — was potentially grounds for a treason prosecution. Seven American military witnesses — who would eventually be repatriated — were, as Fonda readily admitted, "interviewed" by her. Why didn't Olson regard even *that* as an overt act? Yet, Mr. Olson had nothing to say about any of Fonda's non-broadcast conduct.

A. William Olson, the Justice Department's witness before the House Committee on Internal Security, did not try very hard to convince the Committee that there were grounds for a possible treason case against Jane Fonda. It appears that he was trying to do just the opposite.[24]

Olson concluded his formal remarks. Questions and answers followed.

The Chairman. Thank you, Mr. Olson. I can fairly well understand the evidential difficulties in the Fonda case and I also well understand the reluctance of the Department of Justice to testify in regard to the matter because of the possibility that it would prejudice any eventual prosecution. That, in fact, was one of the reasons why the Chair did not favor a subpoena for Miss Jane Fonda to testify before this committee. But it has been over 2 months since Miss Fonda made her first broadcast from North Vietnam; it has been over a month since the committee asked for the Department's opinion. I wonder if you can be more specific.

You have gone over the statutes involved which obviously have applicability to the matter. I wonder if you can be more specific in apprising the committee of why the Department requires so much time to reach a conclusion when the statements are readily available to the Department of Justice and to the public and to this committee.

Mr. Olson. Miss Fonda's statements were made, I believe, during a period from July 12 to July 25 approximately. We were receiving in our division transcripts of broadcasts that were made and continue to be made after she left. The last such transcription that we received was on August 29. We feel now that we have probably received all of them. Up until that time we had not looked at all of the broadcasts, all of the transcriptions.

I would like to read a little quote regarding the amount of time that has been taken and may still have to be taken before this matter is resolved, from Justice Marshall in the *Ex parte Bollman* case many years ago: "As there is no crime which can more excite and agitate the passions of men than treason, no charge demands more from the tribunal before which it is made a deliberate and temperate inquiry."

The Chairman. Is the delay brought about by the belief that the Department may not be successful in a prosecution, or *is it brought about by fear of making a martyr of Miss Fonda ?*

Mr. Olson. I don't know that we have reached that particular situation right now where we are weighing these factors. The first inquiry was trying to get all of the statements that were made and, once we had what we thought were all of them, analyzing them for content. Necessarily next comes an investigation of the evidentiary problems that you have, of securing the necessary evidence if it is available, et cetera.

Mr. Thompson. Mr. Olson, is this a proper statement, then: The reason for your reluctance to discuss fully and completely Jane Fonda's involvement as it is viewed by the Justice Department is because of your concern for prejudicing any of her rights or jeopardizing a possible prosecution should you in the future decide that the evidence warrants a prosecution?

Mr. Olson. That is the primary reason for my reluctance. It is a matter of policy, but that is the reason behind the policy.

Mr. Thompson. So this matter is still under active investigation; a decision has not yet been made whether or not there should or should not be prosecution, and until such time as a decision is reached, you would prefer not to make statements which would tend to jeopardize your case or possibly prejudice the rights of a person who may be charged with a crime?

Mr. Olson. That is very true and that is better than I could have said it.

Mr. Thompson. I would like to refer to your statement and try to ask you some general questions relating to treason, sedition, and the Logan Act.

I have a question concerning adherence to the enemy, rendering him aid *and* comfort. Do the cases in this area require that adherence to the enemy or [25] rendering him aid and comfort be only an overt act of aid or may it also be psychological aid, such as a series of statements which have a psychological impact and which, it may be argued, does have the effect of aid and comfort? If there should be a finding by the court that a psychological statement would have in fact aided the enemy, would that suffice to meet the requirements of the second part of the definition of treason? Adherence has been established as the first part, and aid and comfort to the enemy as being the second part of the definition. In short, could a psychological type broadcast render aid and comfort to the enemy within the meaning of the treason statute?

Mr. Olson. I believe that it could. I believe that type of broadcast we are speaking of was present in the Axis Sally and Tokyo Rose cases. I think the overt act is the fact of making the broadcast itself.

Mr. Thompson. Concerning the requirement of two witnesses, does this require that there be two witnesses present to the act of broadcasting or may there be two persons who have heard a live or recorded broadcast who are familiar enough with the voice of the person broadcasting to testify that "I heard this," or does it require an actual visual sighting of two witnesses of the person charged with treason actually speaking the words into a microphone or recording device?

Mr. Olson. It is my understanding of the law that it is the former. There must be two perceptive witnesses to the act of broadcasting, if you will, in the studio where the broadcast is made. I believe that is the enunciated factor in the Axis Sally and Tokyo Rose cases.

Mr. Thompson. You say there must be two in the studio. There must be two persons in the studio at the time that the broadcast is made, who actually viewed the broadcast rather than hearing it over the air?

Mr. Olson. That's right.

We must interrupt the Thompson-Olson colloquy at this point. As I said above, Olson is at least mistaken and, at worst, attempting to mislead. Whatever he meant by "the enunciated factor in the Axis Sally [Gillars] and Tokyo Rose [D'Aquino] cases," *in neither of those cases was the question presented to the Court as to whether the two witnesses had to have actually seen the broadcasts. Why? Because two witnesses had seen Sally and Rose at the microphone.* Accordingly, the Court did not decide the question. Nor has any other court, anywhere, ever explicitly decided the question As We suggested above, if the question were to be decided, reason, logic and precedent dictate what the courts would hold: *that two-witness proof would be sufficient if it showed the defendant made the broadcast — however that was demonstrated.* It is apparent from Mr. Thompson's next question to Assistant Attorney General Olson that the Congressman was not satisfied with the answers he was getting:

Mr. Thompson. What if an individual secrets himself in a room with a tape recorder and records a message and then takes it and hands it to the radio who then play it over the air? Would it be impossible even if they advocated killing the President, advocated the troops rebelling, killing their commanders, and so forth, to ever prove treason?

Mr. Olson. I think possibly that you could, if you could show witnesses to the recording.

Mr. Thompson. I am saying there is no witness to a recording; in other words, a person closes himself off into a room with a tape recorder and speaks into this tape recorder calling on the troops to mutiny, to kill their officers and so forth, and then that is, in turn, broadcast. Are we in a position by which there can be no treason under such circumstances?

A very good question. One which removes from the equation actual witnesses to the broadcaster's physical act of facing a microphone and speaking words. In other words, what if there's no question that the alleged traitor made the broadcast, proved by two witnesses who heard, or by the speaker's own admission, but no one actually saw a microphone, and saw the speaker's lips move, and saw words come out? A direct answer — up or down, yea or nay — was called for. And Olson's response?

Mr. Olson. It would seem to offer problems.

Problems, indeed. Olson was telling an important Congressional Committee, *without a shred of precedential authority to back him up,* that in a treason prosecution evidence of an overt act of broadcasting would be insufficient to go to a jury unless there were two witnesses to the act of speaking words. This equivocation by a ranking member of the United States Department of Justice is as shocking today as it must have been some 30 years ago.[26]

Mr. Thompson. The *New York Times* on August 15 carried a small item date-lined San Francisco, August 14: "Mr. Kleindienst said at a news conference here that the Justice Department had found no evidence of criminal violations by Miss Fonda."

That is the complete full statement of the *New York Times.* It is about three-quarters of an inch. Has there been a finding by the Justice Department, is this an accurate reporting by the *New York Times* that Mr. Kleindienst says there has been no finding of criminal violation by Miss Fonda, or what is the status?

Mr. Olson. I am aware of that news release. I discussed that with the Attorney General and that was not the intent of what he said. He did not mean to say we conducted a full investigation and it had been completed and as a result thereof we found no violations. That was not the intent. I believe he meant when he was asked a question regarding Miss Fonda that as of this instance, as far as an inquiry has progressed, we have no statements to make.

Mr. Thompson. You had no statement to make back on August 14.

Now on September 16 there is an item, this happens to be from the *Pittsburgh Press,* but also there is an item in The *Evening Star:* "Antiwar activist Jane Fonda in a brief visit here said the U.S. Justice Department has dropped its investigation of her Hanoi radio broadcasts."

Have you dropped your investigation?

Mr. Olson. Certainly not. I don't know where she got her information. I don't believe her sources are very good.

Mr. Thompson. So the matter is still under active investigation. A determination has not yet been made whether or not there should be prosecution or no prosecution.

Mr. Olson. That is correct.

Mr. Thompson. Is there any political reason as to why the Department of

Justice would delay any action on the Jane Fonda matters until after the election for the President of the United States in November?

Mr. Olson. I don't think it is the Department of Justice's role to engage in judging prosecutions based upon political expediency. That is my personal opinion.

Mr. Thompson. Does the Department of Justice from time to time try to time the request for indictments before a grand jury dependent upon external events that are occurring in the United States, such as elections or possibly emotional events that are taking place, or do you operate strictly upon the facts of the case and, once your investigation is complete, then present it to a grand jury independent of external events which are occurring in other branches of Government?

Mr. Olson. When we have matters under investigation and come to the point where we recommend prosecution, we usually prepare a prosecution memorandum, and many times it has to go higher up to be approved. Sometimes it is approved, sometimes it isn't approved. I don't know what goes into all of the decisionmaking process of those decisions.

Mr. Thompson. The decision-making process, would this reach the President's desk in some instances as to whether or not a prosecution would be brought? Is he ever consulted in a matter such as this?

Mr. Olson. I don't have any knowledge about that. I am not quite high enough up in the echelon.

Mr. Thompson. Do you have an estimate of the time interval that we should expect before a decision is made in the Jane Fonda matter, concerning whether or not there would be prosecution or no prosecution? Would this occur before the November elections?

Mr. Olson. Congressman, I could not make an estimate on that. We have requested certain investigation to be completed, to be looked into, certain evidentiary matters. When we will receive the necessary information to put into the whole picture I could not say. It could be before and it could be after.

Mr. Thompson. Here is something you can answer. Would you in your Department be governed to any extent by the political factors of a request for prosecution occurring before the election? *Would that cause you to either delay or to prevent it before the election?* In other words, would your Department, I am talking of yourself, would you be motivated by political factors in this?

Mr. Olson. As far as I am concerned, you are asking me subjectively would I and I would say "No."

Mr. Thompson. Mr. Chairman, may I ask one more question, make one more observation?

The Chairman. Mr. Thompson.

Mr. Thompson. Concerning specifically the Jane Fonda matter and the time frame, I take what you are saying is that there is no deliberate procrastination within the Department for political reasons in pursuing the Jane Fonda matter, that you are pursuing it with all deliberate speed, whatever that may be, and that when your investigation is full and complete a determination will be made. If possible, this will be before the election; it is possible it will be after the election but that you want to be very careful and certain that when you do make a recommendation that it is substantiated by a complete, thorough investigation whether this takes 1 month or 4 months or whatever it may be, and that at that time it would be released without regard to political impact?

Mr. Olson. That is correct.[27]

What was going on here? After some back and forth, the head of the Justice Department's Internal Security Division finally deigns to appear before the House of Representatives Committee on Internal Security. The grave matter before the Committee is Jane Fonda's trip to Hanoi, which could have exposed her to extremely serious criminal liability. But Olson cannot discuss the subject. His proffered excuse of an ongoing investigation, and the Justice Department's wish to protect Fonda's rights in the meantime, sounds embarrassingly lame. Then Olson produces a written "report," one that fails to mention any of the three Supreme Court treason cases or any of the five lower court treason cases (*every one of them "broadcast" cases*). Fonda's name is omitted. No attempt is made to connect the legal precedents to her broadcasts and other conduct in Hanoi.

Olson's oral testimony is cut from the same cloth. He goes a step further in a transparent attempt to undermine valid, and controlling, legal precedents on three specious grounds: hire and money; duration of the treason; and the need for the two requisite witnesses to actually see (and actually hear?) the broadcast(s). The tenacious Congressman Thompson, refusing to be sidetracked or blindsided, has the guts to ask Olson whether the Justice Department has succumbed to political expediency by throwing in the towel — and gets what he probably expects: a quick, forceful denial. Nor is Olson about to respond to Chairman Ichord's musings about whether Fonda, and her seven radical friends from Chicago, were too hot to handle.

Following the September 19, 1972 hearing, and remarks by Chairman Ichord in the House on September 20,[28] and yet another hearing on September 25, 1972, which again didn't deal with the question of whether Fonda may have committed treason in Hanoi, nothing was ever again heard on that subject from Congress. Nor, not surprisingly, from the Department of Justice.

We now know why. As the result of public outcry to Members of Congress, the House Committee on Internal Security had contacted the Department of Justice's Internal Security Division. They, in turn, had asked the Federal Bureau of Investigation to obtain the Fonda Hanoi broadcasts, to transcribe them and to acquire other information about her conduct in North Vietnam. The FBI did so, and forwarded the material to the Criminal Section of the Internal Security Division of the United States Department of Justice. The Criminal Section did its own analysis of the FBI–generated data, and recommended to the Assistant Attorney General in charge of the Internal Security Division — the same Mr. A. William Olson who was later to testify before Ichord's committee — that Fonda not be prosecuted for treason. Olson and his people in this division of the Justice Department agreed, virtually unanimously. The next step was to have the Assistant Attorney General recommend non-prosecution to the Attorney General. This was done. The chief law enforcement officer of the United States concurred, and Jane Fonda was never prosecuted for her reprehensible conduct in wartime North Vietnam.

If this was not a political decision, then that term has no meaning. What both Chairman Ichord and Committee Member Thompson feared would happen had come to pass. Although persons who were close to the decision not to prosecute Fonda have offered, as part of the reason, that there were some legal problems with a treason case, that was by no means the primary reason, and, more likely, a handy excuse.

Ironically, the very reason that argued in favor of Fonda *being* indicted for treason — that her celebrity was what made her invaluable to the North Vietnamese propaganda efforts— is what in the chaotic fall of 1972 *saved* her. *Fonda was a famous, even admired, actress, protesting an unpopular war. The United States Department of Justice feared that Fonda, aided and abetted by savvy militant left-wing counsel, would "make a monkey out of us,"* and, consequently, government lawyers worried about being able to convict.[29]

Was the government really doubtful about being unable to obtain an indictment? About getting a case against Fonda to a jury? That was not what kept the Justice Department from moving forward. What our government feared was being made to look stupid by the likes of Jane Fonda and the rabble-rousing counsel whom she doubtless would have employed. The government of the United States feared losing the case before a jury. This strongly implies— nay, virtually admits— that there was a case that could have been brought against Jane Fonda. It must be said that even if the Justice Department's pessimistic assessment had been correct, still, there was a case to be made.

It would have been easy to draw an indictment against "Hanoi Jane."

---

1. Editorial, *Tallahassee Democrat*, August 10, 1972.

2. Statement of Richard H. Ichord, Chairman, House Committee on Internal Security, Hearings, at 7634.

3. United Press International release, July 18, 1972, via Washington Capital News Service. (In the possession of the authors.) Indeed, some newspapers had already editorialized that an inquiry was warranted. See, for example, the *Tallahassee Democrat* of August 10, 1972: "The law is perfectly clear. What is not clear is exactly what Miss Fonda said to American troops during her broadcasts. Inevitably, Miss Fonda and her supporters will decry the Justice Department investigation as political persecution. We doubt many Americans will agree, however, for if there is any foundation to press accounts of Miss Fonda's broadcasts from Hanoi, they are certainly a proper subject of inquiry."

4. Horner had been an F.B.I. investigator.

5. Weinglass was a lawyer whose career was laced with the representation of left-wing figures.

6. *Hearing Report*, at 7681.

7. It is noteworthy that one Member of the Committee was Father Robert F. Drinan (D.–Mass.), a well known anti-war activist.

8. *Hearing Report*, at 7634.

9. News Release, House Committee on Internal Security, August 10, 1972.

10. Emphasis added.

11. *Hearing Report*, at 7633.

12. Mr. Olson, a World War II veteran (1943–1946) who had served in the South Pacific, was a staff sergeant in a rifle company. He received his law degree from the University of Southern California in 1950, during 1971–1972 was Deputy Assistant Attorney General, and during 1971–1972 was Assistant Attorney General in the Internal Security Division of the Department of Justice.

13. *Hearing Report*, at 7541. Emphasis added.

14. In fact, the Committee's Chief Counsel-Staff Director, Donald G. Sanders, a former F.B.I. agent from Chairman Ichord's State of Missouri, had tasked a Committee lawyer to produce a written Opinion as to whether Fonda had committed treason. The legal staffer's Opinion reached the conclusion that while it was a close question, on the basis of six precedents (the treason cases analyzed in Chapter 7) there had been no treason committed. (Interview with confidential informant.) The staffer was confusing two issues, putting himself in the position of a jury. As we

have seen, whether the government could have gotten an indictment, and then gotten Fonda's case to the jury, was a far different question from whether the jury, after hearing the evidence, would have convicted. The staffer was asked the *former* question; there is no way he could have been asked — or answered — the *latter* one.

15. The following material from the Hearings — including the testimony of Mr. Olson, the Department of Justice Memorandum and the questions and answers between the committee members and Mr. Olson — are reproduced here verbatim, except for material indicated as having been omitted an added. In order that this material be presented exactly as it appears in the *Hearing Report,* no effort has been made to correct typographical and other errors.

16. The correspondence to which Chairman Ichord referred is set forth above.

17. *Hearing Report,* 7543–7546; emphasis added.

18. Here, Olson's Memorandum of Law inserted a footnote quoting from the *Greathouse* case: "It would appear that the treason statute would be applicable when the United States is engaged in open *hostilities,* even in the absence of a declaration of war" (*Hearing Report,* 7626; emphasis added). The significance of the text and footnote is that in their Memorandum of Law Olson and the Department of Justice recognized, as we argued in Chapter 6, that treason *can* be committed in the absence of a formal declaration of war.

19. *Hearing Report,* 7545.

20. 171 F2d at 940; emphasis added.

21. 171 F.2d at 941; emphasis added.

22. 330 U.S. at 640.

23. 343 U.S at 742. The quotation is from *Haupt.*

24. *Hearing Report,* 7543–7546, 7626–7632.

25. This was a misstatement. The Constitutional provision is not in the disjunctive, but rather the conjunctive: adhering *and* giving aid and comfort. Emphasis added.

26. Olson's position is also absurd. Would he have contended, for example, that there was no overt act if one witness to the actual broadcast were deaf but saw the microphone, and saw the speaker mouth the words? Or if the other witness were blind and did not see the microphone, but did hear the words? Could Olson have really believed, especially in light of *Kawakita,* that each witness had to perceive exactly the same thing at the same time?

27. *Hearing Report,* 7539–7560. It is noteworthy that virtually the last statement of substance made by Chairman Ichord at this hearing was to raise the question of whether "the Department of Justice fears making a martyr out of the individuals or at least fears that the trials would enter the political arena, such as the Conspiracy Seven [Ichord meant the infamous "Chicago Seven"] ..." (*Hearing Report,* 7560). All emphasis in the Committee's colloquy with Olson has been added.

28. Basically, Ichord stated what Fonda had done, and the Committee's response.

29. Indeed, this was the same sort of reasoning that accounts for Fonda's never being subpoenaed by the House Internal Security Committee: strong anti-war sentiment in the country, and fear that providing Fonda with a forum in an appearance before the Committee would create "turmoil." (The sources for the information in note 14 and this note are confidential informants whom we interviewed, whose comments were imparted to us with the understanding that the sources remain anonymous. We can say, however, that there is no doubt whatsoever that the information is correct.)

It is worth noting that the craven attitude of the United States Department of Justice and the House of Representatives regarding Fonda was shared by the Pentagon in the matter of the so-called "Peace Committee" in an Hanoi prison called the Plantation. Among enlisted men POWs in Hanoi, there was a small group of collaborators who became known as the Peace Committee (PC), some of whom actually petitioned the North Vietnamese to join their army rather than be repatriated. After repatriation, Lt. Col. Ted Guy, now deceased, "charged the PCs with aiding and abetting the enemy, accepting gratuities, and taking part in a conspiracy against the U.S. government.... I was walking the corridors of the Pentagon, beating on the doors, asking that a complete investigation be conducted. The U.S. Army didn't want to press charged against the PCs.... The army's argument was that we should forgive and forget.... The army and navy later conceded that they had not conducted an investigation" (Grant, *Survivors,* 334–343). In addition, there were at least two officer collaborators in Hanoi who met with Fonda, and soon after repatriation Admiral Stockdale pressed charges against them. Again, as with the Peace Committee members, the Navy and Marines declined to prosecute (Rochester and Kiley, *Honor Bound,* 568).

UNITED STATES OF AMERICA *v.* JANE FONDA

*Whoever, owing allegiance to the United States ... adheres
to their enemies, giving them aid and comfort within the
United States or elsewhere, is guilty of treason and shall
suffer death, or shall be imprisoned not less than five years
and fined under this title but not less than $10,000; and shall
be incapable of holding any office under the United States
(Title 18, United States Code, Section 2381)*

Jane Fonda will never be prosecuted for her broadcasts and other conduct in Hanoi, North Vietnam, in July 1972. If she had been, this is what the indictment might have looked like.

**IN THE UNITED STATES DISTRICT COURT
FOR THE EASTERN DISTRICT OF NEW YORK[1]**

UNITED STATES OF AMERICA,)	
)	CRIMINAL NO. 72 -
)	Constitution—Article III,
)	Section 3, and
)	18 United States Code,
vs.)	Section 2381 (Treason).
)	
)	
)	
JANE FONDA,)	
)	
Defendant.)	

INDICTMENT

The Grand Jury charges:

INTRODUCTORY ALLEGATIONS

1. Jane Fonda, also known as Jane Plemiannikov (hereafter "Fonda"), was born in the City of New York, State of New York, United States of America.

2. At birth, Fonda was a citizen of the United States of America.

3. Fonda has never repudiated or relinquished her American citizenship.

4. At all times hereafter mentioned, Fonda was a citizen of the United States.

5. At all times hereafter mentioned, Fonda owed allegiance to the United States.

6. At the end of World War II, Japanese occupation forces were expelled from Vietnam.

7. In an effort to regain its former colony, France went to war with indigenous Communist forces in Vietnam.

8. From the beginning of those hostilities, the Communists used propaganda as a major weapon in their warfare.

9. Following the 1954 French defeat, in July of that year an agreement in Geneva partitioned Vietnam along a north-south axis with the Communists holding power in the north and anti–Communists controlling the south.

10. The next year, nearly one million North Vietnamese refugees fled the Communist regime in the north, where pro–Communist, anti–South Vietnamese propaganda was pervasive and dissidents were fanatically "reeducated."

11. By 1960, with the United States having been training the South Vietnamese army by then for five years, there were hundreds of American advisors in South Vietnam.

12. As soon as he took office in 1961, President Kennedy expanded the role of the United States military in South Vietnam, in an effort to combat North Vietnam's orchestration of the Viet Cong's guerrilla war in the south. North Vietnam continued to utilize propaganda as a weapon of control against its own people in the north, and as an adjunct to its surrogate's war in the south.

13. In 1963, President Johnson declared that the United States would not allow South Vietnam to fall to the Communists.

14. In August 1964, Congress passed the Gulf of Tonkin Resolution, authorizing President Johnson to use American forces to defeat the North Vietnamese.

15. Thereafter, President Johnson committed American forces to the Vietnam conflict until, by 1968, approximately a half million troops were engaged there.

16. During the entire time American forces were fighting in Vietnam, the

North Vietnamese government (Democratic Republic of Vietnam) orchestrated an international pro–Communist, anti–American propaganda campaign aimed, *inter alia*, at legitimizing North Vietnam's attempt to subjugate South Vietnam, and at countering the United States' effort to militarily defend South Vietnam.

17. The aforesaid propaganda campaign was directed at American citizens in the United States, at soldiers, airmen, sailors and marines in the field and in captivity in South and North Vietnam, and at other persons throughout the world.

18. The aforesaid propaganda was detrimental to the entire United States military effort, both in the United States and in Vietnam.

19. The aforesaid propaganda was beneficial to the North Vietnamese themselves, and to their Viet Cong surrogates in the South.

20. In the year 1972, the United States—through air, ground and naval forces—was engaged in hostile military action against the government of North Vietnam (Democratic Republic of Vietnam) in both North and South Vietnam, and against the National Liberation Front (Viet Cong) in South Vietnam.

21. On or about July 8, 1972, the exact date being unknown to the grand jurors, Fonda arrived in Hanoi, the capital of North Vietnam.

22. Fonda remained in North Vietnam for approximately three weeks, departing on or about July 22, 1972, the exact date being unknown to the grand jurors.

OVERT ACTS

23. While in North Vietnam, Fonda, in violation of her duty of allegiance to the United States, intentionally adhered to the enemies of the United States, to wit, to the government of North Vietnam and the National Liberation Front, their agents, instrumentalities, representatives and subjects, with whom the United States was engaged in hostile military action, and gave to said enemies aid and comfort in the following manner:

A. On or about July 9–11, the exact dates being unknown to the grand jurors, in Hanoi, Fonda, in the company of North Vietnamese Communist civilian and military officials and members of the international press, toured a so-called "War Crimes" museum and there made pro–Communist and anti–American propaganda statements.

B. On or about July 9–11, the exact dates being unknown to the grand jurors, in Hanoi, Fonda, in the company of North Vietnamese Communist civilian and military officials and members of the international press, toured a North Vietnamese hospital and there made pro–Communist and anti–American propaganda statements.

C. On or about July 12, the exact date being unknown to the grand jurors, outside of Hanoi, Fonda, in the company of North Vietnamese Communist civilian and military officials and members of the international press, toured dikes and populated areas and there made pro–Communist and anti–American propaganda statements.

D. On or about July 13–16, the exact dates being unknown to the grand jurors, outside of Hanoi, Fonda, in the company of North Vietnamese Communist civilian and military officials and members of the international press, toured the countryside and there made pro–Communist and anti–American propaganda statements.

E. On or about July 14, 1972, the exact date being unknown to the grand jurors, in Hanoi, Fonda made a live broadcast, through the radio facilities of the North Vietnamese government, containing pro–Communist, anti–American propaganda, which broadcast was taped for later replay.

F. On or about July 17–18, the exact date being unknown to the grand jurors, in Hanoi, Fonda, in the company of North Vietnamese Communist civilian and military officials and members of the international press, toured a textile center and there made pro–Communist and anti–American propaganda statements.

G. On or about July 17, 1972, the exact date being unknown to the grand jurors, in Hanoi, Fonda made a live broadcast, through the radio facilities of the North Vietnamese government, containing pro–Communist, anti–American propaganda, which broadcast was taped for later replay.

H. On or about July 18, 1972, the exact date being unknown to the grand jurors, in Hanoi, Fonda met with seven captured American airmen, one of whom was visibly injured, and harangued them with pro–Communist, anti–American propaganda.

I. On or about July 19, 1972, the exact date being unknown to the grand jurors, in Hanoi, Fonda was interviewed by a French journalist and continued making her pro–Communist, anti–American propaganda statements.

J. On or about July 19, 1972, the exact date being unknown to the grand jurors, in Hanoi, Fonda made a live broadcast, through the radio facilities of the North Vietnamese government, containing pro–Communist, anti–American propaganda, which broadcast was taped for later replay.

K. On or about July 20, 1972, in Hanoi, Fonda held a press conference, described her activities since arriving in North Vietnam, and continued making her pro–Communist, anti–American propaganda statements.

L. On or about July 20, 1972, the exact date being unknown to the grand jurors, in Hanoi, Fonda made a live broadcast, through the radio facilities of the North Vietnamese government, containing pro–Communist, anti–American propaganda, which broadcast was taped for later replay.

M. On or about July 21, 1972, the exact date being unknown to the grand jurors, in Hanoi, Fonda made two live broadcasts, through the radio facilities of the North Vietnamese government, containing pro–Communist, anti–American propaganda, which broadcasts were taped for later replay.

N. On or about July 21, 1972, the exact date being unknown to the grand jurors, in Hanoi, Fonda met with North Vietnamese Vice Premier Nguyen Duy Trinh and continued making her pro–Communist, anti–American propaganda statements.

O. Between July 8 and July 22, 1972, the exact date being unknown to the grand jurors, in Hanoi, Fonda, in the company of Communist civilian and military officials and members of the international press, posed in the control seat of a North Vietnamese anti-aircraft gun, feigned sighting on an imaginary American aircraft, and by her conduct and words continued making her pro–Communist, anti–American propaganda statements.

In violation of Article III, Section 3,
Constitution of the United States of America
and 18 United States Code, Section 2381.

A TRUE BILL:

_____

FOREPERSON OF THE GRAND JURY[2]

United States Attorney[3]
July 8, 1973[4]

---

1. Fonda would have been indictable in the first federal district into which she came upon her return from North Vietnam. She landed at Kennedy Airport in Long Island, which is located in the federal Eastern District of New York.

2. It is here, above the title, that the grand jury foreperson would sign the indictment.

3. It is here, above the title, that the United States Attorney for the Eastern District of New York would sign the indictment.

4. We chose this date for the indictment because it is the one-year anniversary of Fonda's arrival in Hanoi, and would have been long enough after the POWs' repatriation to have allowed for the readjustment of those who would have been witnesses against her.

CONCLUSION

No matter how ill-advised America's misadventure in Vietnam may have been, the errors of our leaders cannot be allowed to mitigate Fonda's activities in Hanoi.[1] For better or worse, the United States *was* committed in South Vietnam, and in a manner approved by each of the three branches of our federal government: by the president, as Commander-in-Chief who ran the war; by Congress, as the war-declaring (or, as in the Gulf of Tonkin Resolution, war-authorizing) and funding branch; and by the courts, which consistently turned back constitutional challenges to the war's legitimacy. While America's commitment in South Vietnam may have been ill-advised — even immoral — *it was legal.* That being so, the only appropriate and democratic way to oppose the war was *politically* — which is precisely what happened when anti-war sentiment forced Lyndon Johnson to stand down in the 1968 presidential election.

It was *unfair* to vent one's frustration with the war on those who — some voluntarily, others involuntarily — sought to serve their country honorably in what was, at root, a no-win situation, both for them and for the United States.

It was *unpatriotic* to defame American servicemen and women.

It was *defamatory* to paint them as the killers of innocent men, women and children.

It was *beneath contempt* to exploit American prisoners of war.

It was *unconscionable* — perhaps even *criminal* — for American citizens to assist the international propaganda machine of the Communist North Vietnamese.

It was *immoral* for Americans to exploit a freedom they took for granted, to further the cause of the enemy.

And it would not have been unreasonable for a jury to have concluded that Jane Fonda intentionally betrayed the United States of America in North Vietnam by committing at least one overt act giving aid and comfort to our Nation's enemy.

Although there is no legal statute of limitations for the crime of treason — "An indictment for any offense punishable by death [that is, treason] *may be found at any time without limitation*"[2] — no legal indictment will ever be laid against Jane Fonda.

But there is another kind of indictment: a moral one. And that one, too, has no statute of limitations. Nor should it.

Benedict Arnold and Aaron Burr escaped legal punishment as contemptible traitors, yet their names were, appropriately, sullied for all time. The names Axis Sally and Tokyo Rose remain synonymous with betrayal of their country. Apart from legal guilt, these four names have become generic descriptions of persons whose conduct was morally reprehensible at times when their country was at risk. So, too, with Jane Fonda.

It is a moral imperative to treat Fonda with the same contempt — if one understands the meaning of morality. "Moral" is conventionally defined as "relating to, dealing with, or capable of making the distinction between, right and wrong in conduct."[3]

"Right and wrong." That says it all.

It was right for the democratic process to elect leaders who made choices about Vietnam, even if those choices were mistaken. It was right for people to repudiate those leaders when their policies became discredited. It was right for America to care about her fighting men, and to work to repatriate our prisoners of war. It was right for those POWs to resist, usually at risk of life and limb.

And, so, it was wrong for Jane Fonda to journey to hostile North Vietnam and there make her pro–Communist, anti–American broadcasts, go on her tours, fraternize with the enemy, and engage in all the other activities from which our foes benefited.

When we pass this moral judgment on Jane Fonda, we recognize that moral values are a transcendent, indispensable, concern to civilized people — and in possessing, defending, and living by those values, we rise above those who betray them.

---

1. Although Fonda's perfidy is known, it is not well known that other Americans preceded Fonda to Hanoi, eager to feed the Communists' propaganda machine. Their conduct set the stage for Jane Fonda's July 1972 pilgrimage. They, like Fonda after them, would give the North Vietnamese what they needed: propaganda aimed at legitimizing the North's attack on the South and undermining U.S. military attempts to defend South Vietnam. Each wave of these activists who journeyed to Hanoi and did their propaganda work on behalf of the North, and then returned with impunity to the United States, unpunished, made it easier for the next wave — and ultimately for Fonda, herself.

2. Title 18, *United States Code*, Section 3281.

3. *Webster's New American Dictionary of the American Language*, 925.

APPENDIX*: TEXTS OF FONDA'S HANOI BROADCASTS TO U.S. SERVICEMEN

7644

REPORT ON JANE FONDA'S ACTIVITIES, STATEMENT ON BOMBED DIKES

Hanoi VNA in English to Havana [XX]

[for Nguyen Duy Phuc, correspondent of *Voice of Vietnam*]

[Text] Hanoi — Visiting American actress *Jane Fonda* July 12 went to see the dikes bombed by American planes the day before in Nam Sach district, Hai Hung Province. She noted that in the area she visited, it was easy to see that there are no military targets ,there is no important highway, there is no communication network and there is no heavy industry. In her assessment, the U. S. has made deliberate attacks on dikes to jeopardize life and terrorise the people.

Later she visited Hong Phong village, remote locality far from major communication lines and industrial centres. On July 11, at daybreak when the villagers were about to begin farm work, U. S. war planes raced in and wantonly bombed a hamlet in the village. Many houses were blasted, fruit trees mangled and household furniture was seriously damaged. Two old persons were killed and many others wounded.

Jane Fonda felt great indignation at this U. S. attack on civilian populations. In the past few days, she had contacts with many workers, peasants and intellectuals to gather information. She called on the special representation of the RSV in Hanoi, had conversations with a number of fighters, artists and victimized people coming from South Vietnam. She was cordially received by Nguyen Phu Soai, acting head of the special representation.

Statement by Jane Fonda, After Visiting Dikes and Dams at Nam Sach Hit by U. S. Aircraft

Yesterday morning on [XX], I went to the district of Nam Sach to see the damage that has been done to the dikes in that district. And I wondered what has been going on with the hands of those who were pulling the lever and dropping the bombs on the fields and on the dikes of the Red River Delta. Do you know, for example, that for centuries since the Middle

The pages in this Appendix are reproduced and numbered exactly as they appear in the Hearing Report. *In that Report, certain material has been blocked out. In the pages that follow, the blocked out material is represented by: [XX]. The typographical errors and misspellings are as they appear in the original*

Ages, the Vietnamese peasants have built, built up, and reinforced a great complex network of dikes which hold back the torrential water of the rivers flowing down from the mountains in summer during the monsoon season.

7645

Without these dikes 15 million people's lives would be endangered, and would die by drowning and by starvation. Anthony Lewis from the *New York Times* wrote an article just before I left the U. S. in which he said that successive U. S. administrations had rejected the ideas of bombing the dikes in the Red River Delta, because they all felt the dikes aren't entirely military targets. This was the type of terrorist tactic that is unworthy of American people and of American flags. But today, American Phantom jets are bombing the strategic points in the dike networks in this area.

In the area where I went yesterday it was easy to see that there are no military targets. There is no important highway, there is no communication network, there is no heavy industry. These are peasants. They grow rice and they rear pigs. They are similar to the farmers in the midwest many years ago in the U. S. They are happy people, peace-loving people. When I went by walking on the way to the dikes to see the damage, would it be made enough I was an American and I was afraid of the reaction would be taken by the local people. [Sentence as received] But they looked at me curiously and I saw no hostility in their eyes. I looked very carefully. I thought curiously. I am the woman. They seemed to be asking themselves: What kind of people can Americans be, those who would drop all kinds of bombs, so carelessly on their innocent heads, destroying their villages and endangering the lives of these millions of people.

Fuller Version of Statement

Hanoi VNA International Service in English [XX]

[Text] Hanoi VNA July 14 — Contrary to the statement of U. S. Assistant Secretary of Defense Daniel Henkin who claimed that U. S. planes on July 12 only hit military targets in Nam Sach district, about 60 kilometers east of Hanoi, actress Jane Fonda now on a visit to North Vietnam asserted that "there was no military target" in the bombed area.

She went to the place shortly after the raid took place and made this comment over *Voice of Vietnam Radio*, addressing *all the U. S. servicemen involved in the bombing of North Vietnam:*

Yesterday morning, [XX], I went to the district of Nam Sach to see the damage that has been done to the dikes in that district, and I wondered what has been going on with the hands of those who are pulling the lever and dropping the bombs on the fields and on the dikes of the Red River Delta. Do you know, for example, that for centuries since the middle ages, the Vietnamese peasants have built up and reinforced a great complex network of dikes which hold back the torrential water of the rivers flowing down from the mountains in summer during the monsoon seasons? Without these dikes 15 million people's lives would be endangered, and would die by drowning and by starvation. Anthony Lewis from the *New York Times* wrote an article just before I left the U. S. in which he said that successive U. S. administrations had rejected the idea of bombing the dikes in the Red River Delta, because they all felt the dikes are not entirely military targets and that this was the type of terrorist tactic that is unworthy of American people and American flags. But today, as you know better than I, American Phantom jets are bombing strategic points in the dike networks in this area.

I (?implore) you, I beg you to consider what you are doing. In the area where I went yesterday it was easy to see that there are no military targets, there is no important highway, there is no communication network, there is no heavy industry. These are peasants. They grow rice and they rear pigs.

7646

They are similar to the farmers in the midwest many years ago in the U.S. Perhaps your grand-mothers and grandfathers would not be so different from these peasants. They are happy peo-ple, peace-loving people. When I went by walking on the way to the dikes to see the damage, would it be made enough I was an American and I was afraid of the reaction would be taken by the local people. [Sentence as received] But they looked at me curiously and I saw no hos-tility in their eyes. I looked very carefully. I thought curiously. I saw the women. They seemed to be asking themselves: What kind of people can Americans be, those who would drop all kinds of bombs, so carelessly on their innocent heads, destroying their villages and endan-gering the lives of these millions of people.

All of you in the cockpits of your planes, on the aircraft carriers, those who are loading the bombs, those who are repairing the planes, those who are working on the 7th Fleet, please think what you are doing.

Are these people your enemy? What will you say to your children years from now who may ask you why you fought the war? What words will you be able to say to them?

7647

Hanoi in English to American Servicemen Involved in the Indochina War [XX]

[Text] Last week, actress *Jane Fonda* visited Hanoi's Bach Mai hospital which was seriously damaged by U.S. bombs during a recent air raid. After the visit she had this to *talk to Amer-ican servicemen* still involved in the Vietnam war. [Follows recorded female voice with Amer-ican accent]

This is Jane Fonda speaking from Hanoi, and I'm speaking particularly to the U.S. service-men who are stationed on the aircraft carriers in the Gulf of Tonkin, in the 7th Fleet, in the Anglico Corps in the south of Vietnam.

You are very far away, perhaps, and removed from the country that you're being ordered to shoot shells at and bomb. And so it's perhaps very hard for you to to understand in concrete human terms what the effects of, of these bombs and these shells are having.

I'm sure if you knew what was inside the shells that you're dropping, you would ask yourself as, as I have been doing for the last few days since I have seen the victims: What do the men who work for Honeywell and the other companies in the United States that invent and, and, and make these weapons—what do they think in the morning at breakfast? What do they dream about when they sleep at night?

Yesterday, I went through the war museum in Hanoi, where there is a display of all the different kinds of antipersonnel weapons the different kinds of bombs, the guava bomb, the pineapple bomb, the spider bomb, different kinds of shells that contain toxic chemicals, the new kinds of napalm, combinations of napalm and phosphorus and thermite. The list is endless as are the, the victims from these weapons. And, it absolutely amazed me, the length to which man's mind — or at least some men in the United States— their minds have gone to create new ways of killing people. They must want to die very much themselves to think this much about new ways of killing people.

7648

I don't know what your officers tell you that you are dropping on this country. I don't know what your officers tell you, you are loading, those of you who load the bombs on the planes. But, one thing that you should know is that these weapons are illegal and that's not, that's not just rhetoric. They are outlawed, these kind of weapons, by several conventions of which the United States was a signatory — two Hague Weapons And the use of these bombs or the condoning the use of these bombs makes one a war criminal.

The men who are ordering you to use these weapons are war criminals according to international law, and in, in the past, in Germany and in Japan, men who were guilty of these kind of crimes were tried and executed.

Now I know that you are not told these kind of things, but, you know, history changes. We've witnessed incredible changes for example in the United States in the last 5 years. The astounding victory that has just been won by George McGovern, for example, who, who was nominated by the Democratic Party, is an example of the kind of changes that are going on — an example of the overwhelming, overwhelming feeling in the United States among people to end the war. McGovern represents all that is good to these people. He represents an end to the war, an end to the bombing.

The women and the mothers in the United States are weeping for the damage and death and destruction that is being caused to the mothers of Vietnam. Very soon, very soon even the people in the United States who have not yet spoken out will be admitting that this war is the most terrible crime that has ever been created against humanity.

It may be very difficult for you who have been asked to fight it to, to think about the war in a new kind of way, to not think about it in an abstract way, to not think about it as some, sole land down there underneath your planes or beyond the sight of your guns, that is just sand or rubble or trees with a lot of gooks or Charlies or whatever you've been taught to call the people who live here.

This is a country that is 4,000 years old. It is a very rich country, it has a rich culture, it has a rich, a rich growth. The trees are lush, the flowers are beautiful. I've been in many countries around the world, I have traveled widely, I've been very fortunate. Never in my life have I been in a country of people that are so loving, and so nonalienated. They are truly at peace with their land and with each other. What do you see in the streets? You see people holding hands, arms around each other, helping each other, talking to each other, hugging each other, working together in the fields. These are peasants. These are people who are used to being part of their land. Their clothes are stained with the land, their houses are made with land.

There's an expression which is used to describe Vietnamese women, which says: Feet in the dust and hands in the mud. And you see all these beautiful Vietnamese women leaning over in the rice fields, with their hands in the mud planting the rice. Their pagodas are made of mud.

And their land is being destroyed. Why? Certainly not for anything that is in your interests, the soldiers of the United States, or in the interests of any of the people in the United States except the very few people who are determined to prevent the nation of Vietnam from achieving freedom and independence.

7649

How this came about is an astonishing thing. How it is that a country like the United States of America, which fought for its own freedom and independence, has become a nation which will deprive another nation of freedom and independence is something that we will all have to answer one day. We'll all have to find out how this came about. But right now, we must, we must stop, we must stop dropping these bombs on the people of Vietnam.

I visited a hospital today, the Bach Mai hospital. I saw a huge bomb crater in the center of the hospital. It was obviously dropped there on purpose. With the kind of bombs, the kind of techniques that have been developed now, you know, particularly you pilots know, that accidents like that don't happen. This was no accident. It destroyed wards filled with patients. It destroyed hospital equipment. It killed some doctors. It is a terrible thing to see what has been done.

Why? Why do you do this? Why do you follow orders telling you to destroy a hospital or bomb the schools. Do you know what happens to the women when the napalm that you're dropping lands on them? You have no idea. Deformed hands, necks twisted out of shape, women with five children who were working women who are used to working with their hands, who were lovely and alive and graceful — the way Vietnamese women are with the long black hair — twisted out of shape, not dead, not spared the pain and the misery of living as a mutilated person, forever in physical pain.

Why, why is this being done? The victims in the hospitals with thousands of holes in their body, from the steel pellets that are being dropped, and even worse now the Nixon administration has gone one step further from the Johnson administration — the steel pellets have been perfected, they're now plastic, rough-edged plastic. Why? Because plastic doesn't show up on X-rays, which means that these people spend the rest of their lives with their bodies filled with plastic pellets and every time they move, it causes excruciating agony.

The women that I have talked to who were not even under your bombs but came to help *victims of the chemical bombs, and the chemical toxic gasses* were so strong that even after the bomb, long after the bomb had exploded when these women came to save the other people, they got sick. And, and weeks and months later they still — they pass out, they have headaches, they are losing their memory. Women who, who were pregnant are, are, are giving birth to deformed babies.

How can it be that the people of the United States have caused this kind of terrible, terrible suffering on a nation so far away? On a nation that has caused us no harm? I mean, what do you think? That the Vietnamese people are going to row across the Pacific in canoes? *So I ask you and I will continue to ask you as long as I am here and I ask you as an American and I ask you because I cry every night when I think of, of what these people are having to go through, and I cry every night, when I think of the danger that is being* done to them because *of the bombing of their dikes. And I say why? And I say that the time has come for us to stop it.* [recording ends]

That was American movie actress Jane Fonda addressing U.S. servicemen involved in the Indochina War.

K 22

FURTHER REPORTS ON JANE FONDA'S ACTIVITIES IN DRV

Report on Nam Dinh Visit

Hanoi in English to Europe, Africa and the Middle East 2000 GMT 19 Jul 72 B

[Text] U. S. warplanes have conducted savage airstrikes on Nam Dinh, North Vietnam's third largest city. The effects bear an extermination character.

7650

American actress *Jane Fonda*, now in North Vietnam, on [XX] visited the bombed city. Follows her address to American servicemen involved in the Vietnam war after visiting Nam Dinh: [follows recorded female voice with American accent]

I was taken to all parts of the city. I saw with my own eyes that in this city which is the textile capital of Vietnam, there are no military targets.

I saw for example, on Hang Tien Street, bombed on the 23d of June, huge bomb craters which had destroyed houses in this very populated residential section of town. There were two women who were picking through the rubble left by the bombs and they came over and spoke to me. One of the women said that she'd been at the market when the bomb fell on the top of her house. Her house has been turned into a huge bomb crater. Her husband and three children were all killed. Her oldest son was 25 years old, her next oldest son had been 22, and her youngest son was 18. Three families in this area were entirely destroyed by the bombs.

As I walked through the streets, beautiful Vietnamese girls looked at me through the doors and returned my smile. Their eyes seemed to be questioning: How is it that the Americans can do this to our city? We have done nothing to them.

I saw a secondary school where 600 students from 5th to 7th grade had been in class. The school had been hit by two bombs. I saw the center of a Chinese residential district, bombed — three places— houses razed to the ground.

The number 1 hospital of the city which had had 200 beds and it treated people from all over the city, large parts of it had been completely destroyed, particularly the pediat — pediatrics department and the supply dep — er — department where the medicines had been kept.

The large factory, the textile factories of Nam Dinh, in charred ruins. No one isn't [as heard] allowed to go in there because there are delayed reaction bombs.

I went to the dike, the dike system of the city of Nam Dinh. Just this morning at 4 o'clock it was bombed again, and I was told that an hour after we left the city, planes came back and rebombed Nam Dinh. The dike in many places has been cut in half and there are huge fissures running across the top of it.

Again, I am talking about these things and I am describing to you what I am seeing on the ground because I think that you must not understand that the destruction is being caused to civilian populations and residential areas, to cultural centers. I saw the pagodas bombed in Nam Dinh. The area in which there are theaters where people come to rest, the recreation centers were all destroyed in Nam Dinh.

What are your commanders telling you? How are they justifying this to you? Have you any idea what your bombs are doing when you pull the levers and push the buttons?

Some day we're going to have to answer to our children for this war. Some day we are going to have to explain to the rest of the world how it is that we caused this type of suffering and death and destruction to a people who — who have done us no harm. Perhaps we should start to do it now before it is, too late.

Perhaps, however, the most important thing that has to be said about Vietnam is that despite all that Nixon is doing here and that Johnson has done before him, despite all the bombs, the people are more determined than ever to fight.

7651

Take Nam Dinh for example. There are people who are still living in Nam Dinh. The factories have been dispersed and they are still working. There is still electricity. People are going about their business.

Perhaps the most important thing that can be said about Vietnam at this time is that in spite of, or perhaps because of, the bombs and the destruction that has been caused by the Nixon administration and was caused by the Johnson administration before him (?to) Vietnam, the resistance and the determination to resist has spread to every district, to every village, to every hamlet, to every house and to every Vietnamese heart.

This is very important to understand. Every man, woman and child in this country has a determination like a bright flame, burying them, strengthening their determination to go forward, to fight for freedom and independence.

And what interests me so much is that as an American, is that this is so much like the essence of the American people. The one unifying quality I believe about the American people, the common denominator that we all share, is the love for freedom and democracy. The problem is that the definition of, of freedom and democracy has been distorted for us and we have to redefine what that means. But the Vietnamese who have been fighting for 4,000 years know very well.

And as in Nam Dinh for example, all the rubble and all of the destruction has not stopped them. It is fascinating to see. There are people still living there, there is still electricity in the city. The factories have been dispersed, but it is still working. The textiles are still being produced. Families are still producing food for a (?certainty). They are still going to the markets, and they are still ready to pick up a gun if necessary and defend their homes and their land. [recording ends]

That was Jane Fonda's address to American servicemen involved in the Vietnam war after visiting U. S. bombed city of Nam Dinh.

Fonda on Quang Tri Liberation

Hanoi Domestic Service in Vietnamese [XX]

[Statement by actress *Jane Fonda*: first few words in English, fading into Vietnamese translation — recorded]

[Text] I am Jane Fonda. I am in Hanoi. All of us know that you, Vietnamese friends, are fighting for the just cause and the truth. Therefore, you do not have to bomb or imprison the people.

You friends might wonder why after waging the special war of [words indistinct] after the *United States introduced a million U. S. infantry troops into Vietnam* and after carrying out the Vietnamization program, all these strategies have failed. These strategies might be changed, but they have only been aimed at supporting the policy of turning South Vietnam into a U. S. neocolony. Why is Nixon, while speaking of peace and ending the war, sending many more U. S. aircraft to Vietnam and bombing on a scale unprecedentedly massive in the history of war? Because Nixon is trying to check the people's war of the Vietnamese people, 90 percent of whom are peasants who are intent on regaining power, determining their own destiny, acquiring land and plowing and transplanting for themselves.

7652

The situation in Quang Tri is very interesting. When the liberation troops entered Quang Tri and, in coordination with the peasants, liberated this province, all the people in the province arose like birds breaking out of their cages, as pointed out by a journalist back from Quang Tri. Why did the people arise? Why were they capable of defeating all the army units Thieu sent to Quang Tri? Why can they continue to fight despite the bombs and shells falling on their heads? Because they are free. Because they are fighting for freedom and are protecting their 4,000-year history and their future. They are protecting the sacrifices and the blood shed by their ancestors as well as their parents, children, brothers and sisters.

They have set up an administration. It is very interesting to note that some former members of the puppet army are participating in this administration. Many former members of the puppet administration in Quang Tri Province have now been elected by the people to the newly formed people's committees. Why is that? Because the people know that these persons did not betray them and did little harm to them. These persons previously were coerced or bribed by the Saigon administration.

Therefore, we find here an inspiring practical example of concord, a model of the tolerance of the Vietnamese people and a concrete example proving that one of the seven points set forth by the PRGRSV has been realized, whereby the revolutionary forces, various political and religious tendencies, neutralists and members of the present Saigon administration can cooperate with one another as Vietnamese patriots standing for their country's independence, freedom and democracy.

We Americans can also appreciate this because one of the revolutionary slogans adopted by patriot Patrick Henry was "liberty or death." This slogan is not very different from President Ho Chi Minh's "Nothing is more valuable than independence and freedom" slogan.

Press Conference

Hanoi Domestic Service in Vietnamese [XX]

[Recorded reportage]

[Text] On the evening of [XX] artist *Jane Fonda*, a well-known American pacifist visiting the northern part of our country, held a press conference at the Hanoi International Club. Attending were many domestic and foreign journalists.

In her opening statement Jane Fonda pointed out the following reasons for her current visit to our country: To discover the truth about the bombing the Nixon administration is trying to deny before the U. S. public and to discover facts about our country's overall situation that is being slanderously distorted by many American newspapers.

She gave a detailed account of what she had seen and heard while visiting hospitals, schools, factories, dikes and dams, cities and villages which were destroyed by U. S. bombs and shells and where definitely no military targets were found. She recalled the very emotional contacts she had with many of our people of various strata.

Recalling her visit to seven U. S. aggressor pilots detained in the north, she said all of them were healthy and repentant and hoped that the Vietnam war would soon end.

Artist Jane Fonda laid special emphasis on the undeniable crimes of the Nixon administration which bombed and strafed dikes and dams.

7653

Sister Fonda indignantly said: [first two sentences in English, fading into Vietnamese translation — recording] Melvin Laird the other day said that bombing of dikes may be taking place, but it is accidental and it only happens if there is a military target on top of the dike. Does he really take the Vietnamese to be foolish enough to put a military installation on top of a dike? Why did Mr Laird say that the United States might have accidentally bombed Vietnamese dikes, dams and sluices while the Pentagon was ballyhooing the "accuracy" and "smartness" of U.S. bombs?

She stressed the need to condemn the Nixon administration's bombing of dikes and dams because it is fraught with the danger of causing losses which may last for decades for the Vietnamese people.

She continued: [first few words in English, fading into Vietnamese translation — recorded] I believe that vicious Nixon knows what he is doing. By bombing the dikes and dams that have been built and protected for thousands of years Nixon has struck at the foundation of the Vietnamese nation. Nixon is trying to defend himself, but he has no right to bomb the DRV. He has violated the 1954 Geneva agreements and the commitment made in 1968 to stop bombing the north.

After analytically pointing out that Nixon's present war escalation originated in his setbacks in South Vietnam, sister Fonda said: [first few words in English, fading into Vietnamese translation — recording] The Vietnamese people have a 4,000-year history. These 4,000 years have readied the Vietnamese people to handle any action taken by Nixon. I have the impression that the Vietnamese people are struggling for their fallen heroes and heroines, for their 4,000-year history and for their future generations. What I have learned here and which I will never forget is that Vietnam is one nation, one country.

Refuting many of Nixon's fallacious allegations about the Vietnam problem, especially the claim that the north is aggressing against the south, sister Fonda stressed: [first few words in English, fading into Vietnamese translation — recording] Nixon cannot end the war if he insistently demands that the political issue be separated from the military issue. There is only one way to end the war: to seriously respond to the PRGRSV's seven-point proposal, which is the most fair, sensible, reasonable and humanitarian proposal. The United States must set a deadline for withdrawing all its military forces from South Vietnam and must cease its support for the Nguyen Van Thieu regime.

Jane Fonda answered many questions by domestic and foreign journalists. Answering a foreign journalist's question on the significance of the Democratic Party's nomination of Senator McGovern as the Democratic presidential candidate, sister Fonda said: The American people are fed up with the Vietnam war, which is radically dividing the United States. Senator McGovern is a symbol of change, of a way out. Many rapid changes have taken place in the United States.

In answer to a question about the fact that some American warlike elements are threatening to take legal action against her for treason, sister Fonda said: I think we must see the traitor. I want to publicly accuse Nixon here of being a new-type Hitler whose crimes are being unveiled. I want to publicly charge that while waging the war of aggression in Vietnam he has betrayed everything the American people have at heart. The tragedy is for the United States and not for the Vietnamese people because the Vietnamese people will soon regain their independence and freedom.

But I am afraid that it will take the American people years to wipe out the crimes that Nixon is committing in the name of the United States.

Asked about the most profound impression she had during her Vietnam visit, Jane Fonda answered with a sincere, emotional tone: [1 minute in English, fading into Vietnamese translation — recording] I have many profound impressions, but I will only speak of this morning. This morning while I was sitting in the shadow of the temple of literature in Hanoi the alert sounded. But I was watching the second act of a play by American playwright Arthur Miller. The performers had just come back from the front. This alone proves that the Vietnamese people will win.

7654

Message to U. S. Pilots

Hanoi in English to Southeast Asia [XX]

[Text] Now here is a recorded message from actress *Jane Fonda* to U.S. pilots involved in the Vietnam war: [follows recorded female voice with American accent]

This is Jane Fonda. I have come to North Vietnam to bear witness to the damage being done to the Vietnamese land and to Vietnamese lives.

Just like the Thieu regime in Saigon which is sending its ARVN soldiers recklessly into dangerous positions for fear that it will be replaced by the U.S. Government if it fails to score some strategic military gains, so Nixon is continuing to risk your lives and the lives of the American prisoners of war under the bomb in a last desperate gamble to keep his office come November. How does it feel to be used as pawns? You may be shot down, you may perhaps even be killed, but for what, and for whom?

Eighty percent of the American people, according to a recent poll, have stopped believing in the war and think we should get out, think we should bring all of you home. *The people back home are crying for you. We are afraid of what, what must be happening to you as human beings. For it isn't possible to destroy, to receive salary for pushing buttons and pulling levers that are dropping illegal bombs on innocent people, without having that damage your own souls.*

Tonight when you are alone ask yourselves: What are you doing? Accept no ready answers fed to you by rote from basic training on up, but as men, as human beings, can you justify what you are doing? Do you know why you are flying these missions, collecting extra combat pay on Sunday?

The people beneath your planes have done us no harm. They want to live in peace; they want to rebuild their country. They cannot understand what kind of people could fly over their heads and drop bombs on them. *Did you know that the antipersonnel bombs that are thrown from some of your planes were outlawed by the Hague Convention of 1907, of which the United States was a signatory? I think that if you knew what these bombs were doing you would get very angry at the men who invented them.* They cannot destroy bridges or factories. They cannot pierce steel or cement. Their only target is unprotected human flesh. The pellet bombs now contain rough-edged plastic pellets and your bosses, whose minds think in terms of statistics not human lives, are proud of this new perfection. The plastic pellets don't show up on X-rays and cannot be removed. *The hospitals here are filled with babies and women and old people who will live for the rest of their lives in agony with these pellets* embedded in *them.*

Can we fight this kind of war and continue to call ourselves Americans? Are these people so different from our own children, our mothers, or grandmothers? I don't think so, except that perhaps they have a surer sense of why they are living and for what they are willing to die.

I know that if you saw and if you knew the Vietnamese under peaceful conditions, you would hate the men who are sending you on bombing missions. I believe that in this age of remote-controlled push-button war, we must all try very, very hard to remain human beings. [recording ends]

Additional Message to Pilots

Hanoi in English to American Servicemen Involved in the Indochina War [XX]

72 B

[Text] And here is movie actress *Jane Fonda* addressing U.S. flyers and airmen [follows recorded female voice With American accent]

7655

This is Jane Fonda in Hanoi. I'm speaking to the men in the cockpits of the Phantoms, in the B-52's, in the F-4's; those of you who are still here fighting the war, in the air, on the ground; the guys in the Anglico Corps, on the 7th Fleet, the Constellation, the Coral Sea, the Hancock, Ticonderoga, the Kitty Hawk, the Enterprise.

You know the war isn't winding down. You know this because you're fighting it. You know this because you are to bomb (?and you call them in). You direct your artillery. You pull the levers to release the bombs. You know the tonnage and the damage. You can see the hospitals and churches in residential areas in smoke and ruin.

So you know that when Nixon says the war is winding down that he's lying; that he has simply changed his tactics. He thinks that he can get away with it, because he believes that we have no conscience; that if he reduces the American casualties but kills more Vietnamese people that we the American people won't care.

But I think he has a very low opinion of the American people. *And I think it's a shame that the United States of America is being governed by a person who thinks this way about us. He defies our flag and all that it stands for in the eyes of the entire world.*

All of you in your (?heart of hearts) know the lies. You know the cheating on the body counts, the falsified battle reports, and the number of planes that are shot down and what your targets really are. *Knowing who was doing the lying, should you then allow these same people and same liars to define for you who your enemy is.* Shouldn't we then, shouldn't we all examine the reasons that have been given to us to justify the murder that you are being paid to commit?

If they told you the truth, you wouldn't fight, you wouldn't kill. You were not born and brought up by your mothers to be killers. So you have been — you have been told lies so that it would be possible for you to kill. [recording ends]

That was Jane Fonda speaking to U. S. pilots and airmen.

Talk on Geneva Accords

Hanoi in English to American Servicemen Involved in the Indochina War [XX]

[Text] Now listen to the movie actress, *Jane Fonda*, addressing the GI's on the occasion of the 18th anniversary of the signing of the Geneva accords: [follows recorded female voice with American accent]

This is Jane Fonda speaking from Hanoi on the occasion of the 18th anniversary of the signing of the Geneva accords. And one again I'm addressing myself to the U.S. men who are — who have been sent here to fight, as well, as well as to myself, because I think that we, we have to remind ourselves a little bit about the history of the U.S. involvement in the war. It's, it's, umm, something that's been kept from us, and it's really important that we understand, uhh, what our history here has been.

During the French Indochina war, during the time when Roosevelt was president of the United States, he, Roosevelt, hadn't made up his mind what the approach of the United States was going to be to the French involvement in Indochina. But after Roosevelt came Harry Truman, and Truman decided that he was going to take the side of the French, support the French against the Vietnamese people. And Eisenhower, who became president after Truman, followed a policy that Truman had already started. Only he went a little bit further, and by 1953, under the Eisenhower administration, the United States was financing 85 percent of the French war against the Vietnamese people.

7656

Think of what that means in terms of taxes that our parents were paying in the United States, quite unbeknownst to them — the taxes that our parents were having to pay in order to finance, to buy weapons for the French to kill the Vietnamese people.

In 1954, the liberation forces of Vietnam defeated the French colonial army at Dien Bien Phu in an historical battle. Following this victory, there was the Geneva conference and the accords were drawn up, the Geneva Accords. The two principal points of the accords called for a temporary division of Vietnam into two military regroupment zones, two regroupment zones, separating Vietnam into, temporarily into, a northern part and a southern part. Two years after the Geneva Accords, that is to say in 1956, there was to be a general election. It was to be a general election held in which the people of Vietnam, from the north and the south, would elect their president and reunify their country.

However, in 1956 Eisenhower noted publicly that if the elections were held, Ho Chi Minh would have been elected president of Vietnam by 80 percent of the votes, by 80 percent of the people in Vietnam. And this was something that the United States didn't want. And so, a man by the name of Ngo Dinh Diem was installed as president of South Vietnam. Now, this act, which has been very thoroughly documented in the Pentagon papers—and I think we should all read those papers, at least the conden—condensed version of them, very attentively—it clearly shows that this was an act caused by the United States.

A quote from the Pentagon papers says: South Vietnam is essentially the creation of the United States. And that's a very important thing to keep in mind when our government tells us that there is an invasion from the north. We must remember, that there wouldn't be a north if it were not for the fact that, that the U.S. Government had violated the Geneva accords, that Vietnam is in fact one country, with one language, with one history of struggle, with one culture. There are no words in the Vietnamese language for North Vietnam or South Vietnam in fact.

President Kennedy once again violated the Geneva Accords when he set up the Military Assistance Advisory Group, or better known as MAAG, which supplied the Diem regime in Saigon with arms and military advisers. One of the stipulations in the Geneva accord was that there were to be no military personnel or advisers or arms sent into Vietnam.

There came a time in the beginning of the 60's when (?it) became very apparent that the people of Vietnam hated the Diem regime. The Buddhists began to uprise, umm, and uhh, at that time it became impossible to hide the fact that Diem was, uhh, was in fact installed by the United States, that he did not represent the people of Vietnam — no more than, than Thieu does today — and it be came necessary to replace him.

And once again if we turn to the — to the Pentagon papers, that is to say the documents that come from the United States Government, written by our leaders of that time, we see that there was a military coup, uhh, with CIA complicity, which removed Diem, uhh, from office.

And then we come to President Johnson, and once again we have to turn to the Pentagon papers, uhh, and it's very interesting when you read about the so-called Tonkin Gulf incident. You will find that it is a slight fabrication. This, this incident, which was used to justify our bombing of the Democratic Republic of North Vietnam, this was the point of course at which the United States sent, uhh, U.S. forces openly and in unit strength to Vietnam.

7657

Now, as Americans we should, we should appreciate, deeply appreciate, and understand the struggle (?that the) Vietnamese people are, are fighting because we live in a country, we come from a country of, uhh, which has fought a war of, of independence, and we shed much blood and there was much sorrow over the losses from our war of, uhh, our, our revolution, the American revolution, which we fought against the British, and we won despite the fact that our, our soldiers were, were less professional, had le — had less weapons. We won because we knew why we were fighting, because we were fighting for freedom and independence. And in that kind of a fight, there can be no compromise.

Now that is what the Vietnamese are fi— are fighting; they're fighting for freedom. That is all they're asking for.

There is an invasion taking place. It's taking place from the 7th Fleet, from the aircraft carriers, from Thailand, from Guam, but essentially from the Pentagon and from the White House.

You men, it is not your fault. It is in fact tragic to think how you are being so cynically used because the time is coming very soon, it is already half-way there, when people are admitting openly that this is one of the most horrible crimes ever committed by one nation against another.

(?Earlier) there was a time when Russia was, was the big monster. That was the excuse that we used uhh, in the United States to build up, uhh in, during the cold war to build up, umm, our military strength and, and develop nuclear weapons and terrible, uhh, arsenal of, of, of death.

But what is the situation today? Today we have business men from the United States going to Russia and doing business. We have uhh, uhh, you know our, our government leaders going to Russia. We have the, uhh, you know a peaceful coa—coalition, coexistence with Russia.

Then (?it was) China which became the big, uhh, the big threat; that China was going to suddenly come across the Pacific Ocean and attack us. Uhh, and what is the situation today? We have diplomats going to China. We have trade going on with China. Every day in the United States there are articles talking about, about the, uhh, the beneficial effects of the Cultural Revolution in China—when all these [words indistinct] of the United States—how the peasants are living better, how famine's been wiped out, how illiteracy and prostitution has been wiped out.

(?And then) Vietnam, this tiny little country—*but you see what is happening in the United States is that even the men who at one time were planning and plotting the war are admitting openly to the American public that this is a crime.*

Former Secretary of Defense under the Johnson administration Clark Clifford, just the other day, in the—in the, uhh, in the United States condemned the war in Vietnam. The former negotiater in Paris, Averell Harriman, recently admitted in a—in an interview with the *Washington Post* that Nixon is sabotaging the Paris peace talks, that a solution to the war does exist which would bring all of you home and release the prisoners of war. *This solution is the seven-point solution for peace put forward by the Provisional Revolutionary Government in Paris.*

Now, I'm saying this because I think it would be very sad for any of you to be killed for a war that very soon even, even the diehards in America are going to have to admit is, ahh, is, ahh, is, is, is, is truly criminal. I think that it would be very sad to go on killing innocent civilians—women, old people, and children—for a war that, ah, that is, is, uhh, that is being criticized all around the world. [recording ends]

7658

That was Jane Fonda speaking to GI's in South Vietnam. More messages of her will come to you soon.

Meets Nguyen Duy Trinh, Departs

Hanoi VNA International Services in English [XX] 22 Jul 72 [XX]

[Text] Hanoi VNA July 22 — American actress Jane Fonda yesterday paid a visit to Vice Premier Nguyen Duy Trinh who had a cordial talk with her and inquired about her health and her family.

Jane Fonda told the vice premier of her impressions during her visit to Vietnam. She said she had witnessed U. S. crimes in Hanoi capital, Hai Hung, Ha Tay and Nam Ha provinces and was deeply impressed by the Vietnamese people's solidarity and mutual sympathy and their determination to materialize President Ho Chi Minh's testament and bring the anti-U. S. aggression for national salvation to complete victory.

Jane Fonda voiced her heartfelt thanks to the hospitable Vietnamese people who, she said, have made a clear distinction between the U. S. imperialists who are the aggressors and the American people who are friends of the Vietnamese people in the struggle for peace and democracy. She expressed her admiration for the age-old history and culture of the Vietnamese people and their creativeness and tenacity. She said she was convinced that under the wise leadership of the Vietnam Workers Party and the DRV Government the Vietnamese people will certainly win brilliant victory.

The American actress left for home today.

Seeing her off at the airport were members of the Vietnam Committee of Solidarity with the American People and the Vietnam Film Artistes Association.

7659

Hanoi in English to American Servicemen Involved in the Indochina War [XX] 24 Jul 72 [XX]

[Text] Now let's listen to *Jane Fonda speaking* to U.S. pilots and airmen: [follows recorded female voice with American accent]

This is Jane Fonda in Hanoi. Yesterday, [XX], I'm told that the record for B-52 bombing raids in Vietnam, [was set] and on July 14th, UPI, United Press International, reported that in "Operation Linebacker" against North Vietnam in the first 99 days of the renewed air war in North Vietnam, U.S. bombers flew more than 20,300 raids. In each of these raids, an average of 2 tons of bombs were dropped on the country.

Now we know that B-52's are strategic bombers. These are planes that were built, invented to — in the event that a large country with its own air force and heavy arsenal of military weapons like Russia, uhh, would, uhh, need to be attacked. To use B-52's against the civilian population is like trying to kill a butterfly with a machinegun. It's barbaric.

I am assuming that because you are so far away from the land here, because you are on the ships, or because you are in Thailand, or because you are so high up in the sky that you can hardly see what it is you're bombing, that you don't really realize what the effect of these bombs is.

And I think, I — I think that — well, the other day, for example, someone told me that one of the pilots that was recent — recently shot down, uhh, near Hanoi, as he was, uhh, driven across the river, uhh, uhh, he was, he was, uhh, being being rescued by, uhh, the people and he was shown a bridge and the people said, uhh, that bridge was, uhh, bombed, uhh, recently. And he said: Well, my parents are rich. Uhh, we can buy you a new bridge, we can afford to build you a new bridge after the war. And the people said to him in Vietnamese and it was then translated by the interpreter, they said, but can your parents replace our, our children, our mothers, our wives who have been killed by your bombs? *And the soldier hung his head and he said: I didn't think of that.*

I've heard this from several of the, uhh pilots—I didn't think of that. I think we have to start thinking about it. I think we have to start thinking about the incend—incendiary bombs that are being dropped. These bombs asphyxiate people to death, people who are in the shelters. Now, who goes into shelters? The women, the old people, and the children—they're suffocating to death. They're being burned in ways that is beyond the imagination, and I think we have to think about that.

What are you being told by your commanders? Are you being told that you're bombing to help the people? To save the country for democracy? What kind of democracy? Fifty thousand American lives have been lost here for a one-man election. Is that a democracy? What kind of democracy when just after the last one-man election, the Thieu regime in the south passed new economic reforms which were planned and set up by the United States.

7660

And what in fact do these reforms do? They benefit the U.S. businessman. They give him tax-exempt go-ahead to make the most incredible kind of profits in South Vietnam. He will not have to pay taxes, the rich men in America. They will not have to pay taxes on the fortunes that they are making, off the riches in South Vietnam.

And this country is a rich country—the soil is rich, the growth is rich, the tin, the tungsten, the rubber, the lumber. Eisenhower knew it well, that why he said it was necessary for us to finance 85 percent of the French, the French-Indochina war against the Vietnamese people. The people in the Pentagon knew it. The Mekong Delta is called one of the richest pieces of real estate in Asia.

But what does this have to do with you? What does this have to do with the masses of people in America? It is not to our interest. In fact, it is quite the contrary. You know that there is rising unemployment in the United States. There is for the first time since 1893 a trade deficit, an imbalance of payments, inflation.

In fact, the war is falling on the backs of the working people of America. What are our corporate bosses doing? They are going into countries like Vietnam or trying to—they're going into the Philippines, into Brazil, into Okinawa, into other, what we call underdeveloped countries around the world, and they're setting up factories, factories which make component parts. One part will be made in the Philippines, another part will be made in Vietnam, another part will be made in—in Brazi. They would be assembled in Mexico and they'll be sold on the American market at American prices. But the American worker will not be given a job, and why are the bosses going elsewhere and why are they trying to go to Vietnam? Because the workers are paid from 40 to 90 percent less than the workers in the United States?

When you're on the ground in South Vietnam and you see the ESSO signs and the Shell signs and the Coca-Cola signs and the Hondas and the TV sets. And it is after all for that that you're fighting.

Is that worth risking your life for? Is that worth killing innocent people for? I think not. And in fact, what is the war doing? The war is only making the people of Vietnam understand who their enemy really is.

There was a time perhaps when a certain amount of the peasants were unclear. I don't really know because I have never spent enough time in Vietnam to really know that. But I do know now because I've talked to many, many, many people of all kinds in the er—the northern part of Vietnam. And I have spoken to many of the Vietnamese students in the United States. And I know that they say that because of the incredible killing and slaughter and the number of bombs that are falling on the people of Vietnam, they now know very clearly who their enemy is.

And their enemy is not — are not people from another part of their own country who are coming down to help them fight. The enemy to them are the people who are sending the planes to drop bombs on them. These people are — are, as I'm sure you know, their [as heard] 80, 80 percent of the people in Vietnam are peasants.

They live in their land. It is part of them and their land is being destroyed and so they will fight, and they will fight to the end. And this is not — these are not easy, empty words. When it comes to national freedom and independence, you can make no compromise. Like in — like in loving, if you love a woman, you don't compromise, you either love her or don't love her.

7661

For the United States of America, if our country was attacked, we wouldn't compromise, we would fight to the end.

Well, the Vietnamese people will fight to the end, and their determination is something incredibly beautiful to see. Despite all of the suffering, despite the tears that have been shed, there is much determination. They are continuing, as I'm sure you know, in the battlefields of the south, they are winning.

The Thieu regime has not taken back one inch of liberated territory despite all his promises. He has sent his two el — elements of his two best divisions into the Quang Tri area, and they are being decimated — the paratroopers and the marines— they are scared. Nixon and Thieu are scared. And that's why they are sending some of the — of their — of their ARVN soldiers into incredibly dangerous situations.

So I think that — that maybe American people have to begin to see clearly who is fighting who and for what, and should we be fighting on the side of the people who are, who are murdering innocent people, should we be trying to defend a government in Saigon which is putting in jail tens of thousands of people into the tiger cages, beating them, torturing them — I have met some of these victims and it is a horrible thing to see.

And I don't think as Americans, we who come from a country which was founded on freedom, independence, and democracy, that we should be risking our lives or fighting to defend that kind of government. [recording ends]

You have just listened to Jane Fonda's address to American pilots and airmen.

7662

HANOI BROADCAST [XX]

Talk to U.S. Pilots

Hanoi in English to American Servicemen Involved in the Indochina War [XX] 25 Jul 72 B

[Text] Now listen to Jane Fonda's recorded talk to U.S. pilots and airmen during her recent visit to Hanoi. [follows recorded female voice with American accent]

Perhaps it would be a good thing if all of us knew something about the country that we are fighting against and the country that you are dropping your bombs on. Vietnam is a very old country — 3,000 years before Christ was born the Vietnamese people fought against the Chinese feudal lords who had taken the land away from the peasants. In 40 AD the first insurrection occurred among the Vietnamese people to get the Chinese lords out of their land and win back freedom and independence. This insurrection was lead by two sisters, Trung Hi and Trung Trac.

The Vietnamese people have — have fought against many outside aggressors. For example, the Mongolian Army, lead by Ghenghis Khan, 500,000 profess— professional trained soldiers who had swept through Europe and Asia, who had conquered half of the world, arrived in Vietnam and were stopped by the Vietnamese peasants. After the — after the Vietnamese people defeated the Mongolian Army, they gave them the ships — Vietnam-Vietnamese ships, to take the Mongolian Army back to where they came from. The Vietnamese people have fought against the Chinese, have fought against the Japanese, and have fought against the French.

They defeated the French colonial army at the battle of Dien Bien Phu in 1954, and it was after that battle that the Geneva Accords were signed. These accords said that Vietnam would be temporarily divided into two parts — into two regroupment zones, but that this division was only to be a temporary one, and that Vietnam was to be reunited in 1956, by general elections. Dwight D. Eisenhower was president of the United States at that time, and he admitted that if elections had been held as they were supposed to be according to the Geneva accords, President Ho Chi Minh would have been elected president of the reunited Vietnam by 80 percent of the votes.

The United States did not want Ho Chi Minh to be president of Vietnam although this is what 80 percent of the Vietnamese people wanted, and so, as has been proven by the Pentagon papers, the CIA organized a military coup which overthrew [pause] which prevented elections, and installed a puppet government under Ngo Dinh Diem.

The Diem regime was no different than the Thieu regime of today. It is a regime which is kept in power because of American money and American technology against the wishes of the Vietnamese people. You are told many other things, perhaps, by the United States Government, but anyone who has been here and talked to the people, knows that the Vietnamese people do not like Thieu, they do not — not like the fact that he is arresting tens of thousands of people, like yourselves, young people in the streets of South Vietnam who are speaking out against the war and demanding peace.

7663

These people are being put into prison, they are being beaten, they are being tortured. The economy of their country is being ruined by the corrupt government in the south and by the presence of the U.S. military.

You must understand that the people of Vietnam are peasants. They live with the land — the land is a part of their lives, as it has been for thousands of years. Every time you drop your bombs on the heads of these peasants it becomes clearer to them — to them who the enemy is. How could they possibly by asking for help from a country which is destroying their land, their crops, killing their people, mutilating their babies. How can we continue to rain this kind of terror on these people who want nothing more than to live in peace and freedom and indepence.

All American people who consider themselves patriotic must begin to ask themselves some serious questions about what we are doing in Vietnam. We must stop thinking that we have to follow orders like robots. Let us stop being robots. [recording ends]

Talk with Saigon Students

Hanoi in English to American Servicemen Involved in the Indochina War [XX]

[Text] Now listen to *Jane Fonda's recorded talk with* Saigon students: [follows recorded female voice with American accent]

This is Jane Fonda in Hanoi. I am very honored to be a guest in your country, and I loudly condemn the crimes that have been committed by the U.S. Government in the name of the American people against your country.

A growing number of people in the United States not only demand an end to the war, an end to the bombing, a withdrawal of all — all U.S. troops and an end to the support of the Thieu clique, but we indentify with the struggle of your people. *We have understood that we have a common enemy — U.S. imperialism.* We have understood that we have a common struggle and that your victory will be the victory of the American people and all peace-loving people around the world. Your struggle and your courage in the face of the most unbelievable hardships has inspired all of us in the deepest part of our hearts. We follow very closely the crimes that are being committed against you by the Thieu regime; the people, the brave people who are speaking out for peace and independence, who are being put away into prisons, in the — in the tiger cages.

We have come to know something about your country because in the United States there are students from the southern part of Vietnam, from Saigon, from Hue, from Da Nang. They have taken a very active stand against the war, and they are speaking out loudly to the American people and explaining to us that Vietnam is one country with one culture and one historic struggle and one language.

As a result of their protest against the war, the repression of the U.S. Government and the Saigon clique is coming down on their heads as well. For example, in the first week of June, four of the students received letters from the U.S. State Department saying that their AID scholarships had been terminated as of June 1, and that tickets were waiting for them to take them back to Saigon on orders of the Thieu regime. Among these four students was Nguyen Thai Binh.

We condemn the murder of Ngueyn Thai Binh who wanted to do nothing more then to return to his people and fight for freedom and inde — independence for his country. We are investigating this murder and we will do everything we can so that the people responsible for it will be brought to justice.

The Vietnamese students in the United States are very homesick.

7664

They call themselves the orphans of Vietnam and they are longing for the day when they can return to — to Vietnam and live in a little house in the countryside and raise chickens. This is what they've told us. For the time being, however, they feel that their duty is to remain in the United States and do their political work among the American people.

As an American woman I would like to tell you that the forces that you are fighting against go far beyond the bombs and the technology. *In our country people are very unhappy. People have no reason for living. They are very alienated from their work, from each other and from history and culture.* We have discovered, especially the young people in the United States, that a society of luxury and wealth is not the answer to peace and happiness.

Your leading poet To Huu described the cancer of cons— of the consumer society as the poisoning of people's souls. We have followed closely the encroachment of the American cancer in the southern part of your country, especially around Saigon. And we hope very soon that, working together, we can remove this cancer from your country so that the misery and unhappiness that has come to the American people very deep in their souls will not happen to the Vietnamese people. And we thank you for your brave and courageous and heroic fight.

Recently in the United States we've been doing a lot of political propaganda work among the students and the soldiers with your Vietnamese comrades. And they taught me a song that they tell me was written by students in the prisons who have been imprisoned by the Thieu regime in the south and I'd like to sing the song for you, and I — I — I ask your forgiveness for my accent. I—I hope that I'm not going to make any mistakes and say anything obscene. [short laugh, then singing in Vietnamese]

7665

HANOI BROADCASTS ADDITIONAL ALLEGED JANE FONDA PROGRAMS

[XX]

Hanoi in English to Southeast Asia 1000 GMT 29 Jul 72 B

[Text] We now bring you a recorded speech to Saigonese troops by American actress Jane Fonda: [follows a recorded female voice with American accent]

This is Jane Fonda from Hanoi. I'm addressing myself to the ARVN soldiers.

Many people in the United States deplore what is being done to you. We understand that Nixon's aggression against Vietnam is a rascist aggression, that the American war in Vietnam is a rascist war, a white man's war—(?which) was very clearly indicated when Ambassador to Saigon Elsworth Bunker described the Vietnamization program as changing the color of the corpses.

We deplore that you are being used as cannonfodder for U.S. imperialism. We've seen photographs of American bombs and antipersonnel weapons being dropped, wantonly, accidentally perhaps, on your heads, on the heads of your comrades. And we note with interest that (?these) kind of accidents don't happen, at least not with as much frequency, to American soldiers, and we think this is an indication of the lack of concern that is being taken for your lives by the white American officers, both in Vietnam and in the Pentagon and in the White House—not to mention the officers in Saigon who have been bought off by the ruling class of the United States.

We've seen photographs of many of you clinging to the helicopters trying to escape from what you knew was a suicide mission. We understand that you have been pressganged, many of you, into the army because your land has been destroyed by American bombs, because there are no other jobs to be had in Saigon, perhaps because you have to support your family, because you will be the—you will be put in jail and beaten if you tried to avoid the draft.

We well understand the kind of situation that you are put in because American soldiers are in the same kind of situation, and we feel that—that you have much in common. You are being sent to fight a war that is not in your interests but is the interest of the small handful of people who have gotten rich and hope to get richer off this war and off the turning of your country into a neocolony of the United States.

We read with interest about the growing mumbers of you who are understanding the truth and joining with your fellow countrymen to fight for freedom and independence and democracy. We note with interest, for example, that as in the case of the 56th Regiment of the 3d Division of the Saigon army, ARVN soldiers are taken into the ranks of the National Liberation Front, including officers who may retain their rank.

7666

We think that this is an example of the fact that the democratic, peace-loving, patriotic Vietnamese people want to embrace all Vietnamese people in forgiveness, open their arms to all people who are willing to fight against the foreign invader.

We know what U.S. imperialism has done to our country in the United States, how it is affecting the working people of the United States and particularly the people of (?courage). And so we know what lies in store for any third world country that could have the misfortune of falling into the hands of a country such as the United States and becoming a colony. [pause]

We all are striving very hard, the peace-loving people of the United States, to end this war as soon as possible so that you can all return to your families in the condition of freedom and independence. We understand that the only way to end the war is for the United States to withdraw all its troops, all its airplanes, its bombs, its generals, its CIA advisers and to stop the support of the Thieu regime in Saigon, this man who has defiled not only his own country but the United States. The support of such a criminal is a blight on the American (?society which will take a long time to erase). [recording ends]

You've just listened to a Jane Fonda recorded speech to Saigonese troops.

[XX]

Hanoi in English to Europe, Africa and the Middle East 2000 GMT 28 Jul 72 B

[Text] We now bring you a recorded message by American actress Jane Fonda to U.S. servicemen in South Vietnam. [follows recorded female voice with American accent]

This is Jane Fonda speaking from Hanoi. I read in the paper yesterday that Melvin Laird has admitted that it is possible that the dikes in North Vietnam have been hit by American bombs. He goes on to say that — that this can happen when there are military installations on top of the dikes, military convoys or material on or near the dike.

As someone who has spent now 2 weeks in North Vietnam, who has travelled in the countryside, who has seen the dikes, I find this laughable. Does anyone really believe that the Vietnamese people would be foolish enough to drag military material, antiaircraft guns, through the rice fields where there are no roads, where it's difficult to even walk, and place them on top of the dikes, which are made of earth, thus attracting the bombs of the American planes? If you stand on top of any of the dikes in the Red River Delta, you can see around you for miles. It is flat land. It is rice land. It is very visible, very clear to anyone that there are no military installations whatsoever. There are no trucks. There are no convoys. There are no antiaircraft guns.

I have seen the dikes bombed. I have seen them cut in half. For miles around you can the rice paddies spread out, and suddenly right around the most strategic and vulnerable point of the dike system, the bomb craters begin — huge bomb craters, sometimes 10 meters across and 8 meters deep.

There are many kinds of bombs being dropped. Some of them are bombs that explode and cut the dikes in half. Some of them, however, pierce the earth laterally. They are delayed explosion bombs which lie dormant underneath the dikes to explode later. Some of them are causing earthquakes which make deep fissures into the dike system, so that later when the heavy rains come, the dikes will break and the area will be flooded.

7667

I make an urgent appeal for all people around the world. This is a very grave and a very serious situation. The season of heavy rains is soon to begin. The people of Vietnam have spent many thousands of years building their dike system. Since the Middle Ages the Red River Delta has been struggled against, just as the Vietnamese people have fought against foreign invading armies. They have struggled against nature and they have won back the Red River Delta. They have conquered the Red River. They have claimed the land as their own.

These dikes are made of earth. There is no way to convey the labor, the hundreds of people, whose labor goes into building these dikes. It takes many years to construct them, moving the earth, packing it in — packing it into place.

The dikes that are destroyed this year will take many years to be rebuilt because the earth has to become solidified in order to hold back the heavy waters during the — the heavy rain seasons. So the damage that is done this year by Nixon's strategic bombing of the dike system will endanger not only the lives and their crops of the people this year, but for many years to come. It may cause famine. It may cause epidemics.

There is only on way to stop Richard Nixon from committing mass genocide in the Democratic Republic of Vietnam, and that is for a mass protest all around the world of all peace-loving people to expose his crimes, to prevent him from following the people of the world into thinking that if there are floods this year it would be a natural disaster.

It is a very clever scheme that he is attempting to carry out. [words indistinct] in Vietnam to justify the floods if they happen. But since the revolution of 1945, when this country was mobilized and organized in such a way so that the dikes could be reparied and rebuilt and reinforced every year, there have been no disastrous floods. They have been minimized [words indistinct] fortified to such a degree that the terrible damages that were done in 1945 and 1946 have been prevented.

And I can tell you if someone who has witnessed this [words indistinct] that if this year this land is flooded the finger can be pointed at Richard Nixon. And I think — I think (?it's cited) by Professor Yves Lacoste of the University of Paris — who is a geographer and he has studied very carefully the situation here — the damage would be worse than if he had ordered the dropping of atmoic bombs.

Just to give you one example of the kind of incredible lies that are being told by the spokesmen of the White House, on July 18, at least a dozen foreign correspondents went to the district of Nam Sach to witness the bombing that had taken place to the dike system on July 9. While they were there, U.S. planes dropped 28 bombs on the most strategic and vulnerable point on the dike system. The 12 correspondents were almost killed by these — by these bombs. And several days later word came from the White House that the bombing had never ta — taken place. [recording ends]

That was American actress Jane Fonda speaking to U.S. servicemen in South Vietnam.

7668

ADDRESS TO GI'S IN SOUTH VIETNAM ATTRIBUTED TO JANE FONDA

Hanoi in English to Europe, Africa and the Middle East 2000 GMT [XX]

[Text] We now bring you American Actress *Jane Fonda's address to American GI's* in South Vietnam [follows recorded female voice with American accent]:

This is Jane Fonda speaking from Hanoi. A phenomenon has been taking place in the United States called the GI movement.

In 1968 the situation in the American army was qualitatively changed. Prior to 1968, many of the soldiers — the grunts, the [word indistinct], the ground troops in South Vietnam — had believed what their officers and their generals had told them: that they were there to help the Vietnamese people, that large areas of Vietnam had been pacified, that the war was about to be won.

If you recall, at the end of 1967 General Westmoreland announced: We can now see the light at the end of the tunnel. And 2 months later the Tet offensive occurred. And the soldiers were forced to face certain facts. They realized that in order for the offensive to have taken place, it meant that the very people that they were told had been pacified were in fact part and parcel of the liberation fighters. Is was these people who were helping the soldiers bring weapons into town, hidden into the laundry baskets and the — and the bunches of flowers. It was these people who were part of the struggle.

The men were attacked for the first time on their own American bases and they had to start asking themselves questions. And they began to realize that they had been lied to. And since these young men are no longer (?John Waynes) — they're not like their fathers in the Second World War — they began to say no: We no longer want to die for someone else's lies. We will no longer be wounded for a war that we do not understand and do not believe in.

In 1969–1970 the desertions in the American army tripled. The desertions of the U. S. soldiers almost equalled the desertions from the ARVN army, and in the United States we laughingly said it was the Vietnamization of the American army.

The new recruits sent to South Vietnam were separated from the guys who had been there for a while behind barbed wire so they wouldn't find out what had been going on. The men had to turn in their arms at night. Why? Because there were so many U. S. officers being killed. Fragging — the word fragging entered the English language. What it meant was that the soldiers would prefer to roll a fragmentation grenade under the tent flap of their officer, if he was a gung-ho officer who was going to send them out on a suicide mission, rather than go out and shoot people that they — that they did not feel were their enemy.

In America we do not condone the killing of American officers — we do not condone the killing of anyone — but *we do support the soldiers who are beginning to think for themselves. I've spent 2 years working with the antiwar soldiers in the United States, in the Philippines, in Okinawa, and in Japan.* I've seen the movement grow from a movement of individuals taking courageous action as individuals to thousands of soldiers taking collective action to voice their protest against the war — marching, demonstrating in uniform and holding up their ID cards, risking to — going to jail if necessary, jumping ship, the petition campaigns which started on the Constellation in San Diego and spread to the Coral Sea, the Ticonderoga, the Enterprise, the Hancock, the Kitty Hawk.

7669

And word about the resistance within the American military has spread throughout the United States. There was a time when people in the peace movement thought that anyone in uniform, anyone who was coming over here to support the Thieu regime, must be the enemy. But we have realized that most of these young men were not fortunate enough to get draft deferments, were not privileged enough to have good lawyers or doctors [words indistinct]. These are the sons of the American working class. They're the sons of the hardhats. They're guys who came because they thought it was the thing to do, or because it was the only way they could get an education, or because it was the only way that they could learn a skill. They believed in the army, *but when they were here, when they discovered that their officers were incompetent, usually drunk, when they discovered that the Vietnamese people* had a fight that they believed in, that the Vietnamese people were fighting for much the same reason that we fought in the beginning of our own country, they began to ask themselves questions.

And one of the biggest things (?they began to think) about the U.S. Government and about the U.S. military in particular is that it doesn't allow people to think for themselves. It tries to turn us into robots. And the young people of America, and particularly the soldiers, are beginning to say: We don't want to be robots anymore; we will define for ourselves who our enemy is.

Perhaps the soldiers who have been the first to recognize the nature of the war in Vietnam are those soldiers who have suffered the most in the United States — the black soldiers, the brown soldiers, and the red and Asian soldiers.

Recently on a tour of the U.S. bases on the Pacific rim — in Okinawa, Japan and the Philippines — I had the chance to talk to a great many of these guys and they all expressed their recognition of the fact that this is a white man's war, a white businessman's war, that they don't feel it's their place to kill other people of color when at home they themselves are oppressed and prevented from determining their own lives.

Women in the military — those who are so often forgotten — have their own way of identifying with the Vietnamese struggle. *I heard horrifying stories about the treatment of women in the U.S. military. So many women said to me that one of the first things that happens to them when they enter the service is that they are taken to see the company psychiatrist and they are given a little lecture which is made very clear to them that they are there to service the men. They are given birth control pills. This is a big shock to these girls who come into the service with all kinds of high ideals about what the army will do for them, and the kind of training that they will get.*

This very powerful grassroots movement — the GI movement — is forging probably the most important link in the United States — the link between the white middle class peace movement and the working class. These men who are coming back from Vietnam, their lives in fragments, are putting the pieces back together in a new kind of way with a new kind of understanding. And in doing so, as they go into the factories — those who are lucky enough to get jobs — or as they stand in — in the unemployment lines, they are beginning to change the political complection of the American working class.

In California particularly — at least I can talk about California because that's where I'm from — the rank and file insurgency among the working class has augmented in the last 6 to 7 months (?steadily), and this is particularly due to speed up of mandatory overtime, peculiarly true in the major industries such as steel and auto. The young workers, particularly with the new consciousness, have become aware of the fact that they've been sold out by the national labor leadership and they're indicating that a new alliance may need to be formed between workers and students.

Like the soldiers on active duty, the thing that the young workers resent the most is the fact that — that their lives are being destroyed that they are alienated from their work, that they're treated like robots.

I think it's important that people in Vietnam as well as other parts of the world know this — that while America preaches prosperity, the workers of America are suffering more than ever before. The suicide rate among workers has risen more than ever before. They are beginning to realize that Nixon's economic reform is in fact falling on their back. [recording ends]

You have just listened to American Actress Jane Fonda's address to American GI's in South Vietnam.

7670

ALLEGED JANE FONDA IMPRESSIONS OF TALK WITH U.S. POW'S

Hanoi in English to American Servicemen Involved in the Indochina War 1300 GMT 15 Aug 72 B

[Text] Here is Jane Fonda telling her impressions after meeting captured U. S. pilots in the Democratic Republic of Vietnam: [follows recorded female voice with American accent]

This is Jane Fonda speaking from Hanoi. Yesterday evening, July 19, I had the opportunity of meeting seven U.S. pilots. Some of them were shot down as long ago as 1968 and some of them had been shot down very recently. They are all in good health. We had a very long talk, a very open and casual talk. We exchanged ideas freely. They asked me to bring back to the American people their sense of disgust of the war and their shame for what they have been asked to do.

They told me that the pilots believe they are bombing military targets. They told me that the pilots are told that they are bombing to free their buddies down below, but, of course, we all know that every bomb that falls on North Vietnam endangers the lives of the American prisoners.

They asked me: What can you do? They asked me to bring messages back home to their loved ones and friends, telling them to please be as actively involved in the peace movement as possible, to renew their efforts to end the war.

One of the men who has been in the service for many, many years has written a book about Vietnamese history, and I thought this was very moving, that during the time he's been here, and the time that he has had to reflect on what he has been through and what he has done to this country, he has— his thought has turned to this country, its history of struggle and the people that live here.

They all assured me that they have been well cared for. They— they listen to the radio. They receive letters. They are in good health. They asked about news from home.

I think we all shared during the time that I spent with them a sense of— of deep sadness that a situation like this has to exist, and I certainly felt from them a very sincere desire to explain to the American people that this war is a terrible crime and that it must be stopped, and that Richard Nixon is doing nothing except escalating it while preaching peace, endangering their lives while saying he cares about the prisoners.

And I think one of the things that touched me the most was that one of the pilots said to me that he was reading a book called "The Draft," a book written by the American Friends Service Committee, and that in reading this book, he had understood a lot about what had happened to him as a human being in his 16 years of military service. He said that during those 16 years, he had stopped relating to civilian life, he had forgotten that there was anything else besides the military and he said in realizing what had happened to him, he was very afraid that this was happening to many other people.

I was very encouraged by my meeting with the pilots (?because) I feel that the studying and the reading that they have been doing during their time here has taught them a great deal in putting the pieces of their lives back together again in a better way, hopefully, and I am sure that when— when they go home, they will go home better citizens than when they left.

7671

HANOI RADIO ATTRIBUTES TALK ON DRV VISIT TO JANE FONDA

Hanoi in English to [XX] Involved in the Indochina War 1300 GMT 22 Aug 72 B

[Text] Here's Jane Fonda telling her impressions at the end of her visit to the Democratic Republic of Vietnam: [Follows recorded female voice with American accent]

This is Jane Fonda. During my 2-week visit in the Democratic Republic of Vietnam, I've had the opportunity to visit a great many places and speak to a large number of people from all walks of life— workers, peasants, students, artists and dancers, historians, journalists, film actresses, soldiers, militia girls, members of the women's union, writers.

I visited the (Dam Xuac) agricultural Co-op, (?in Ha Tay Province), where the silkworms are also raised and thread is made. I visited a textile factory, a kindergarten in Hanoi. The beautiful temple of literature was where I saw traditional dances and heard songs of resistance. I also saw an unforgettable ballet about the guerrillas training bees in the south to attack enemy soldiers. The bees were danced by women, and they did their job well.

In the shadow of the temple of literature I saw Vietnamese actors and actresses perform the second act of Arthur Miller's play "All My Sons," and this was very moving to me — the fact that artists here are translating and performing American plays while the U.S. imperialists are bombing their country.

I cherish the memory of the blushing militia girls on the roof of their factory, encouraging one of their sisters as she sang a song praising the blue sky of Vietnam — these women, who are so gentle and poetic, whose voices are so beautiful, but who, when American planes are bombing their city, become such good fighters.

I cherish the way a farmer evacuated from Hanoi, without hesitation, offered me, an American, their best individual bomb shelter while U.S. bombs fell near by. The daughter and I, in fact, shared the shelter wrapped in each others arms, cheek against cheek. It was on the road back from Nam Dinh, where I had witnessed the systematic destruction of civilian targets — schools, hospitals, pagodas, the factories, houses and the dike system.

As I left the United States 2 weeks ago, Nixon was again telling the American people that he was winding down the war, but in the rubble-strewn streets of Nam Dinh, his words echoed with the sinister [words indistinct] of a true killer. And like the young Vietnamese woman I held in my arms clinging to me tightly — and I pressed my cheek against hers — I thought, this is a war aginst Vietnam perhaps, but the tragedy is America's.

One thing that I have learned beyond the shadow of a doubt since I've been in this country is that Nixon will never be able to break the spirit of these people; he'll never be able to turn Vietnam, north or south, into a neocolony of the United States by bombing, by invading, by attacking in any way. One has only to go into the countryside and listen to the peasants describe the lives they led before the revolution to understand why every bomb that is dropped only strengthens their determination to resist.

I've spoken to many peasants who talked about the days when they and their parents had to sell themselves out to landlords as virtually slaves, when there were very few schools and much illiteracy, inadequate medical care, when they were not masters of their own lives.

But now, despite the bombs, despite the crimes being created — being committed against them by Richard Nixon, these pepple own their own land, build their own schools — the children are learning, literacy — illiteracy is being wiped out, there is no more prostitution as there was during the time when this was a French colony. In other words, the people lave taken power into their own hands, and they are controlling their own lives.

And after 4,000 years of struggling against nature and foreign invaders — and the last 25 years, prior to the revolution, of struggling against French colonialism — I don't think that the people of Vietnam are about to compromise in nay way, shape or form about the freedom and independence of their country, and I think Richard Nixon would do well to read Vietnamese history, particularly their poetry, and particularly the poetry written by Ho Chi Minh. [recording ends]

BIBLIOGRAPHY

There is a sizeable literature on Jane Fonda and her family. To the extent that the literature contains material germane to the subject of this book — Fonda's activities in wartime North Vietnam — it is cited below.

The literature on America's involvement in Vietnam is vast, and we have drawn on it only to the extent necessary to address our subject. Since central to that subject is the condition of American prisoners in Vietnam and their exposure and reaction to Fonda's activities there, we have drawn substantially on personal memoirs, some of which are cited below along with other books addressing the same point.

The subject of treason in American legal literature has not been addressed nearly as much as it should have been. Because most of what exists on the subject is found in the eight reported judicial decisions discussed in Part III above, we have not provided a treason bibliography here.

The only Congressional material on Jane Fonda's July 1972 trip to North Vietnam consists of the Hearing Report of the House of Representatives Internal Security Committee, September 19, 1972, cited below.

Adams, John Quincy. *Works of John Adams.* 1856.

Alvarez, Everett, Jr., with Anthony S. Pitch. *Chained Eagle.* New York: Donald I. Fine, 1989.

Andersen, Christopher. *Citizen Jane: The Turbulent Life of Jane Fonda.* New York: Henry Holt and Company, 1990.

Anton, Frank, with Tommy Denton. *Why Didn't You Get Me Out?* Arlington, TX: Summit Publishing Group, 1997.

Bailey, Lawrence R., Jr., with Ron Martz. *Solitary Survivor: The First American POW in Southeast Asia.* Washington: Brassey's, 1995.

Blakey, Scott. *Prisoner at War: The Survival of Commander Richard A. Stratton.* New York: Doubleday, 1978.

Brace, Ernest C. *A Code to Keep: The True Story of America's Longest-Held Civilian Prisoner of War in Vietnam.* New York: St. Martin's Press, 1988.

Chesley, Larry. *Seven Years in Hanoi.* Salt Lake City: Bookcraft, Inc., 1973.

Coffee, Gerald. *Beyond Survival: Building on the Hard Times — A POW's Inspiring Story.* New York: Putnam, 1990.

Collier, Peter. *The Fondas: A Hollywood Dynasty.* New York: G.P. Putnam's Sons, 1991.

Collier, Peter, and Horowitz, David. *Destructive Generation.* New York: Summit Books, 1989.

Daly, James A., and Lee Bergman. *A Hero's Welcome.* Indianapolis: Bobbs-Merrill, 1975.

Davis, Vernon. *The Long Road Home: U.S. Prisoner of War Policy and Planning in Southeast Asia.* Washington, D.C. Historical Office, Office of the Secretary of Defense.

Day, George E. *Return with Honor.* Mesa, Arizona: Champlin Museum Press, 1989.

Dengler, Dieter. *Escape from Laos.* San Rafael, CA: Presidio Press, 1979.

Denton, Jeremiah A., with Ed Brandt. *When Hell Was in Session*. New York: Reader's Digest Press, 1976.

Doyle, Robert C. *Voices from Captivity*. Lawrence, KS: University of Kansas Press, 1994.

Dramesi, John A. *Code of Honor*. New York: Norton, 1975.

Farrand. *The Records of the Federal Convention of 1787* 2 (1911) 144, 168.

Farrand. *The Records of the Federal Convention of 1787* 2 (rev. ed. 1937) 45.

Fehrenbach, T.R. *This Kind of War: The Classic Korean War History*. Washington: Brassey's, 1998.

Fonda, Henry. *Fonda: My Life*. As told to Howard Teichmann. New York: New American Library, 1981.

Gaither, Ralph, as told to Steve Henry. *With God in a P.O.W. Camp*. Nashville: Broadman Press, 1973.

Gragg, Rod. *Bobby Bagley, POW*. Van Nuys, CA: Bible Voice, 1978.

Grant, Zalin. *Survivors*. New York: Norton, 1975.

Guarino, Larry. *A P.O.W.'s Story: 2801 Days in Hanoi*. New York: Ivy Books, 1990.

Hayden, Tom. *Reunion, a Memoir*. New York: Collier Books, Macmillan Publishing Co., 1989.

Hearings Before the Committee on Internal Security, House of Representatives, Ninety-Second Congress, Second Session, 7679 et seq.

Hefley, James, and Hefley, Marti. *No Time for Tombstones: Life and Death in the Vietnamese Jungle*. Harrisburg PA: Christians Publications, 1974.

Herman, Gary, and Downing, David. *Jane Fonda, All American Anti-Heroine*. New York: Quick Fox, 1980.

Howes, Craig. *Voices of the Vietnam POWs: Witnesses to Their Fight*. New York: Oxford, 1993.

Hubbell, John G. *P.O.W.: A Definitive History of the American Prisoner-of-War Experience in Vietnam, 1964–1973*. New York: Readers Digest Press, 1976.

Jensen, Jay R. *Six Years in Hell: A Returned POW Views Captivity, Country and the Nation's Future*. Bountiful, UT: Horizon, 1978.

Johnson, Sam, and Jan Winebrenner. *Captive Warriors*. College Station TX: Texas A & M University Press, 1992.

Journals of the Continental Congress 5 (1906) 475; 6 Force, *American Archives*, 4th ser. (1846) 1720.

Journals of the Continental Congress 31 (1934) 497.

McConnell, Malcolm. *Into the Mouth of the Cat: The Story of Lance Sijan, Hero of Vietnam*. Bridgewater, NJ: Replica Books, 1997. Originally published NY: Norton, 1985.

McDaniel, Eugene B., with James L. Johnson. *Before Honor*. Philadelphia: A.J. Holman, 1975.

McDaniel, Eugene B., with James L. Johnson. *Scars and Stripes*. Philadelphia: A.J. Holman, 1975.

McDaniel, Norman A. *Yet Another Voice*. New York: Hawthorn Books, 1975.

McGrath, John M. *Prisoner of War: Six Years in Hanoi*. Annapolis: Naval Institute Press, 1975.

Morrison, Samuel Eliot. *The Oxford History of the American People*. New York: Oxford University Press, 1965.

Nasmyth, Spike. *2355 Days: A POW's Story*. New York: Orion Books, 1991.

Plumb, Charlie. *I'm No Hero*. Independence, MO: Independence Press, 1973.

Risner, Robinson. *The Passing of the Night: My Seven Years as a Prisoner of the North Vietnamese*. New York: Random House, 1973.

Rochester, Stuart I., and Frederick Kiley. *Honor Bound*. Annapolis: Naval Institute Press, 1999.

Rowan, Stephen A. *They Wouldn't Let Us Die: The Prisoners of War Tell Their Story*. Middle Village NY: Jonathan David, 1973.

Rowe, James N. *Five Years to Freedom*. Boston: Little, Brown, 1971.

Rutledge, Howard, and Rutledge, Phyllis. *In the Presence of Mine Enemies, 1965–1973: A Prisoner of War*. Old Tappan NJ: Fleming H. Revell, 1973.

Sides, Hampton. *Ghost Soldiers*. New York: Doubleday, 2001.

Smith, George. *P.O.W.: Two Years with the Vietcong*. Berkeley: Ramparts Press, 1971.

Stern, Lewis M. *Imprisoned or Missing in Vietnam: Policies of the Vietnamese Government Toward Captured and Detained United States Soldiers, 1969–1994*. Jefferson, NC: McFarland, 1995.

Stockdale, James B., and Sybil. *In Love and War: The Story of a Family's Ordeal and Sacrifice During the Vietnam Years*. New York: Harper & Row, 1984.

Vadim, Roger. *Bardot Deneuve Fonda.* New York: Simon and Schuster, 1986.

Webster's New American Dictionary of the American Language. New York: World Publishing Company, 1970.

Wolfkill, Grant. *Reported to Be Alive.* New York: Simon and Schuster, 1965.

INDEX